Eastern Africa Series

NAIROBI
IN THE MAKING

Nairobi in the Making

Landscapes of time and urban belonging

CONSTANCE SMITH

TWAWEZA
COMMUNICATIONS
Working Towards a Better World

JC JAMES CURREY

James Currey
is an imprint of
Boydell & Brewer Ltd
PO Box 9, Woodbridge
Suffolk IP12 3DF (GB)
www.jamescurrey.com
and of
Boydell & Brewer Inc.
668 Mt Hope Avenue, Rochester,
NY 14620-2731 (US)
www.boydellandbrewer.com

First published in paperback in Kenya, Uganda, Tanzania, Rwanda 2019 by
Twaweza Communications Ltd
Parklands Road, Mpesi Lane
Box 66872–00800 Nairobi, Kenya
www.twawezacommunications.org

Published in association with the British Institute in Eastern Africa

British Library Cataloguing in Publication Data
A catalogue record for this book is available from the British Library

ISBN 978-1-84701-233-3 (James Currey hardback)
ISBN 978-1-84701-326-2 (James Currey paperback)
ISBN 978-9966-028-97-6 (Twaweza Communications Ltd paperback)

Typeset in 10 on 12pt Cordale with Gill Sans MT display
by Avocet Typeset, Somerton, Somerset TA11 6RT

Contents

List of Illustrations

Acknowledgements

Research for this book was funded by an Emslie Horniman award from the Royal Anthropological Institute, the British Institute in Eastern Africa and a Hallsworth Fellowship at the University of Manchester. I am grateful to each of these institutions for their support and confidence in the project. In Nairobi, the Office of the President of Kenya gave me permission to carry out research. The Department of Architecture at Jomo Kenyatta University of Agriculture and Technology generously accepted me as an affiliate student. I am indebted to the BIEA for the extensive practical and intellectual support I received, from staff and fellow researchers as well as the guidance of the Directors at the time of my fieldwork, first Ambreena Manji and then Joost Fontein. Staff at the Kenya National Archives – in particular, the legendary Richard Ambani – made the archival work possible. Professor Crispino Ochieng' kindly accepted to be my affiliate supervisor. He not only provided advice and mentorship, but enthusiastically introduced me to Kaloleni. Without him my fieldwork might never have got going.

I am grateful to the many friends, colleagues and advisors who have provided support and help along the way. At UCL, where this project began, Chris Pinney's patient guidance and lateral thinking consistently challenged me and influenced the shape of this project from the outset. I was lucky to join a fantastic graduate cohort whose energy, humour and intelligent conversation enriched my time at UCL immeasurably. Special thanks to Emily Brennan, Ryan O'Byrne, Jill Reese, Kelly Robinson and Camilla Sundwall. At Manchester I am fortunate to be part of a generous and collegiate department, and I thank the many colleagues who read chapter drafts and whose insights improved the manuscript considerably. Particular thanks to Penny Harvey who has not only helped me to think about infrastructure differently but has been an unstinting mentor. Over many years, I have had the privilege to work for and with Henrietta Moore. From her I have learned more about how to do anthropology and how to think about Kenya than can ever be acknowledged in citations and for which I remain beyond grateful.

In Nairobi, Cat and Faraaz Charania, Sheila Kamunyori, Neo Musangi and Louise Skilling all helped to make fieldwork more enjoyable and more productive. Especial thanks to Laura Beckwith and Karimi Gitonga for taking me in and providing home comforts and hospitality. Joost Fontein has far exceeded his obligations as examiner and has continued to push my thinking further. His astute comments have greatly strengthened this book. Saffron Woodcraft has read and re-read many parts of the text, as well as providing a wealth of other support, and the book is all the richer for her insights. Hannah Elliott has generously dissected and discussed so much of this project along the way that it is impossible to imagine how it would have turned out without her enthusiasm, constructive criticism and recommendations for further reading.

Earlier versions of Chapters 2, 5 and 6 have been previously published and I am grateful to the publishers of *Etnofoor*, *Urban Planning* and *Social Dynamics* for permission to include parts of them here. I extend thanks to two anonymous reviewers for their helpful suggestions. My sincere thanks to Jaqueline Mitchell, Lynn Taylor and all at James Currey for their belief in the book and painstaking care in bringing it publication.

My greatest debt is to the residents of Kaloleni, past and present. Your openness, knowledge and patience made this book what it is, and I hope I have done justice to your trust in me. Its shortcomings remain my own. For their support and generosity, special thanks to Kaloleni Estate Residents' Association, Samuel and Eva Omondi, Kevin Ateku, Fidelis Bula and all the members at 'Vera Cruz' and 'Junta' bases. My debt to the extended Nyanya family is one not easily repaid. Sincere thanks to Judith and Dominic Nyanya for hosting the upcountry portion of fieldwork; Eunice and Tom Nyanya, Thatcha, Quivers, Randy, Barrack, Natasha and Brandon for welcoming me wholeheartedly into their Kaloleni home, letting me join in and helping me out in ways too many to mention.

This book could not have been written without two people. Tom Nyanya, whose boundless energy, sharp insights and kindness have provided impetus and laughter even in tough times during fieldwork. And above all, Dominic Williams, whose unflagging encouragement and willingness to join in make everything seem possible.

Introduction

One blazing hot day in early 2014, I was walking through Kaloleni, a rundown housing estate in the Eastlands area of Nairobi, Kenya's bustling capital city. Kaloleni was designed in the 1940s by British colonial authorities. It was planned as a model urban neighbourhood for African families but is now notable more for its dilapidation and decaying infrastructure than for its promise of a new kind of urban future. Terracotta tiled roofs are patched with tarpaulin, roads are more pothole than asphalt, and rubbish is piled up on the verges. Rounding a corner behind a row of ramshackle stone bungalows, I came across two men hard at work, sawing and hammering. A gleaming stack of new corrugated iron glinted in the sunlight, its silvered brightness contrasting sharply with the shabby textures of the houses. A square frame of wooden poles had already been assembled, and they were engaged in attaching the frame to the side of one of the houses. I recognised one of the men and stopped to chat. I asked what they were up to, expecting them to say they were building a storeroom or an ad hoc extension to the old house. Daniel[1] stopped hammering and stood up. Squinting in the sunlight, he grinned broadly. 'This? What you see here, this is Vision 2030!' he said. We have waited so long for investment in this place, he continued, but still it has not come. He explained how his house is overcrowded and his children have to sleep on the floor. That is why there is so much building work happening in Kaloleni: 'Now us people here cannot wait any longer. We are making our own urban renewal'.

Nairobi is seemingly on the cusp of dramatic urban change. As in many other countries across Africa, the Kenyan government has launched a series of infrastructure-led megaprojects under the umbrella of 'Vision 2030', a development blueprint for the future of the country. Nested within this larger vision is 'Nairobi Metro 2030', an urban plan that promises to reinvent Nairobi as a 'world class African metropolis'; a spectacular new node in a network of global

---

[1] In the interests of confidentiality, some names have been changed.

cities (Government of Kenya 2008). It is hardly surprising then, that Nairobi is awash with rumours of 'urban renewal', demolition and redevelopment. Yet, as a city born of British colonialism, many in Nairobi – including Daniel – also live among the dilapidated vestiges of imperial urban planning, in spaces designed to regulate colonial subjects. Though still a public housing estate, decades of mismanagement by city authorities have left Kaloleni rundown and decayed, and residents must manage their neighbourhood as best they can. Vision 2030 now promises long-awaited urban investment, but in the ten years since it was launched, very little has materialised on the ground.

Many ordinary Nairobians remain ambivalent about what Vision 2030 might mean: on the one hand urban renewal might offer a brighter future if it means increasing employment and raising living standards, but many are anxious that it will happen at their expense. Futuristic visualisations circulate in the press, online and on billboards around the city, presenting dramatic, glossy visions of skyscrapers, parkland and shopping malls, promising exclusive urban living in gated enclaves. Such panoramas position Nairobi towards an imagined global elite, seeking to capture flows of global capital, technology and expertise (Watson 2013; Myers 2014). Thus, while Vision 2030 promises urban investment, it does not seem intended for residents of places like Kaloleni. For them, these sleek yet speculative visions may be enticing, but also provoke anxieties of exclusion; the scenes do not seem to portray a future to which they will belong.

Unsurprisingly, as residents try to continue their day-to-day lives amid this climate of uncertainty, rumour and speculation flourish. As Boniface, one of Daniel's neighbours, explained: 'There's been stories. There's a time [I heard] they'd secured contractors to come down and build these structures, but it was only politics. It fades away, some other stories come. So nobody knows. Nobody knows for sure.' But reactions to Vision 2030 are not limited to words and debate alone. The spectacle of official planning has set in motion many kinds of anticipatory actions in response to the uncertain future hovering over the present. As Daniel's attempts to do his own urban renewal project suggest, the gap between the fantasy of the plan and its realisation is full of action: new ways of being and doing, of trying to make the future knowable in diverse ways (Abram and Weszkalnys 2013). Daniel and many others like him are no longer prepared to wait for a promised future to be delivered but instead seek to make it for themselves.

Daniel's DIY project also suggests that it is not easy to tease apart past, present and future in Nairobi. In a decaying housing estate, the material traces of the past and visions of the future are simultaneously remixed in the present. Since its beginnings as a depot on the colonial railway from the East African coast to Lake Victoria, Nairobi has transformed to become the largest and most powerful urban centre in the region. Nevertheless, the afterlives of colonial architecture continue to inflect the way that lives are made in the city, becoming incorporated into the politics of the present and fears of exclusion from the future. Such non-linear temporal engagements are also constitutive, remaking the time and place of the city across different material and discursive registers (Nielsen 2014).

This book explores what it means to make a life in such a city today, caught up between the remains of empire and global city fantasies. Surrounded by collapsing urban infrastructures and amid fantastical promises of hypermodern, globalised futures, how do ordinary Nairobians try to ensure a place for themselves in the city's future? Rather than viewing the city as a singular whole through the lens of planning or of state-led urban policy, it explores the fragmented and incomplete projects of people like Daniel, showing how it is through residents' everyday lives – in the mundane, incremental work of home maintenance, in the accumulation of stories about the past, in ordinary people's aspirations for the future – that the city is imaginatively, materially and unpredictably made. By examining the afterlives of colonial architecture – or 'imperial debris' (Stoler 2013) – it explores how such themes play out over time. However, rather than taking a conventional chronological approach, it highlights how the remains of the past are encountered from the present.

To think of a city as a landscape made over time is to think about processes of accretion and subtraction, making and unmaking, construction and destruction, in which even the rejected, demolished and discarded become churned into the fabric of the city. These remains – whether houses or gardens, piles of rubbish or broken infrastructure – are not simply encountered as obstacles or hindrances to be managed but as substances that continue to influence the form and dynamics of contemporary Nairobi. This shows how the relationship between people and substance is generative, how it can shape ideas about the past, about ideal selves and about how the future city should be.

* * * * *

The year 2013, when fieldwork for this project began, marked fifty years of independence in Kenya, making it a particularly fitting moment to reflect on the contemporary lives of Nairobians and their relationship to the colonial past and the city's future. As discussions around Vision 2030 gained momentum, they began to illuminate how the particular relationship between urban materiality, temporality and uncertainty in Nairobi might have consequence for the ways that people negotiated their inclusion in the future city. The research centred on Kaloleni, one of several City Council-owned housing estates in the Eastlands area of Nairobi. Kaloleni was built in the 1940s by the colonial Nairobi Municipal Council to help meet a huge shortfall in housing for Africans in the city (Hake 1977; Anderson 2001). Today these neighbourhoods are run down and overcrowded, but still vibrant: they are home to hundreds of thousands of Nairobians. Their formal architecture has been supplemented with self-constructed additions, such as Daniel's extension, accommodating many more people than they were originally designed to house. This is a process in which materials and plans but also socialities and intentionalities are reconfigured, cumulatively reshaping the urban landscape of the city.

Now, these estates have been slated for regeneration as part of the Vision 2030 Eastlands urban renewal strategy which intends to combat 'urban decay' in the city. As with so many housing schemes all over the world that get labelled as 'dangerous' or 'decayed' and earmarked for regeneration, Kaloleni was once a model estate intended by its designers to generate a new kind of future for its residents. Based on garden city ideals of urban design, it was one of the first estates in Nairobi aimed at African families. It marked a period of British colonial urban planning in Africa that moved away from functional 'bed spaces' for migrant labourers towards a more ideological model that would refashion domestic life and build the exemplary colonial subjects of the future.

Contemporary residents of Kaloleni thus inhabit an estate where the past is very much present, in the form of an architecture designed to implement colonial ideologies of class, race and domesticity, and where the future looms large, in the form of multiple, and often conflicting, urban planning strategies. Exactly what urban renewal will mean in practice, however, is hard to tell: there have been a number of conflicting announcements and exactly what will be demolished, what will be built and if residents will be evicted or rehoused remains unclear. Living in the shadow of Vision 2030, residents anticipate a future in which time is both compressed and stretched out. They do not know if or when their houses will be demolished: it could happen next week, in five years' time – or perhaps never. This uncertainty generates an experience of the future that is simultaneously frighteningly immediate and always just over the horizon.

Through extensive ethnographic fieldwork as well as archival research, this book explores the character of Kaloleni estate as a dense but shifting accumulation of infrastructures, materials, documents, remains, people, histories and ideas. This assemblage is contingent, subject to various reworkings, disputes and forms of claim-making, in which the physical estate – as well as its imagined place in the world – is generated over time. In this sense, though in some ways an endurance of colonial urban planning, the place of Kaloleni is still emerging, taking shape and acquiring new substance through its entanglements in larger flows and frictions. Kaloleni's material history continues to influence the lives of its residents, generating a particular sense of place and time, even as Vision 2030 tells them they should be focusing on a glossy, digital future, a vision of Nairobi as a 'global city' (Sassen 1991). Starting from individuals' lived experiences at home, I seek to understand not only how processes of self-making are generated by people's entanglement in material worlds, but the way in which their contemporary lives are inflected by a temporal recursivity, where material legacies of the past and visions of the future are simultaneously reworked in the present.

A major theme running through this project has been how the temporalities and materialities of urban change are shaped by the dynamic negotiations between the aspirations of ordinary citizens and the unpredictable trajectories of official, yet opaque, urban planning. These negotiations traverse spaces, forms and actions that might conventionally be described as 'formal' and 'informal', blurring any distinction between them. This suggests that the categories of 'formal' and 'informal' urban development in Africa, which still tend to dominate much of the literature on African urbanisation, need to be reappraised. Not only are the 'formal' and 'informal' not binary opposites but linked and often mutually constitutive, the terms themselves have become so expanded as to no longer be meaningful ways of demarcating areas of urban life (Perlman 2005; Hart 2010; James 2014). I propose instead that focusing on 'making' as both a conceptual category and an ethnographic process may enable a better grasp on how Nairobians work between different spatial, political and temporal scales and registers. By exploring the incremental processes of making time and making place in Nairobi, it becomes possible to trace the capacity of material forms to generate experiences of time and ways of relating to the past and future. It shows how landscapes of decay – crumbling houses, collapsing infrastructures, accumulating detritus – inflect the way that local people produce the city, generating practices of historymaking, ideas about urban belonging and attempts to refashion the future envisaged in Vision 2030 into something more meaningful and inclusive to ordinary Nairobians.

Making future selves

'If you don't have a good plan, you will be nowhere', said Calvin, a young third-generation Kalolenian. 'In this Nairobi, you need a hustle, you need to make your own luck'. It is no good waiting around for something to come up, he explained to me early in 2014, having your own tactics is essential. In Nairobi, hustling refers to everyday strategies of getting by in the popular economy. Calvin intends to set up a small *hoteli* (café) in Kaloleni, selling *chai* and simple foods on the side of the road, but in the meantime, he is selling second-hand clothes from his bedroom, working in another café and helping his uncle with occasional whole-sale deliveries. Hustling demands flexibility, remaining alert to every slim prospect, and the capacity to keep multiple plates spinning at the same time. For young people in Kaloleni, many of whom pursue their lives outside of formal training or employment, the 'hustle economy' has become the standard modus operandi of making a life in the city, an experimental yet vital way to deal with everyday uncertainty (Thieme 2017). It evokes the simultaneous sense of impossibility and potenti-ality that pervades Nairobi, a place where anything and nothing are equally likely to happen. In this way, hustling reflects how feelings of precarity and futility can be enmeshed with the fierce desire to create an alternative future. The hustle economy is one aspect of a more wide-spread temporality of uncertainty in contemporary urban Africa, one where 'particular senses and experiences of time, of potentiality and emergence, along with feelings of incapacity or impossibility, come together to make certain futures actualizable, inhabitable – and others not at all' (Goldstone and Obarrio 2017: 2).

This book tracks such apparent contradictions, following people in Kaloleni as they see possibility and room for manoeuvre even in the face of exclusionary urban planning and global envisioning. As many have observed, Nairobi is a city of contradiction, impasse, secrecy and perplexity and yet of resourcefulness and tactical strength (Charton-Bigot and Rodriguez-Torres 2010). It is a place constantly refig-ured by the struggle to endure in the face of provisionality and precarity, where seemingly straightforward trajectories are diverted by desire, speculation and assorted rearrangements of materials and resources (Simone 2016). As such, this book does not seek to overcome Nairo-bi's contradictions but to write from within them. Following Mbembe and Nuttall's lead, it explores what it might mean to 'write the world from an African metropolis' (2004); to see Nairobi's inconsistencies and startling juxtapositions not simply as paradoxes or indicators of failure or crisis, but as a site of emergence from which the city takes shape. The apparently simple opposites of urban exclusion and inclusion, presence and absence, present impossibility and future potentiality here emerge not as binary categories, but as historically contingent and temporally connected.

People in Nairobi find themselves simultaneously in times of rapid change and inexorable stasis. The future feels both near at hand and always just over the horizon. This is in part about how chronic uncer-tainty affects the management of everyday life: Nairobians now find themselves caught up in a time of perpetual uncertainty. Since the 1980s, the demands of structural adjustment have reorganised the state in Kenya, bringing shifting economic priorities, the privatisa-tion of state industries, burgeoning unemployment and a booming informal economy (Murunga 2007). These economic instruments were founded in a conviction of temporal payoff: short-term struggle for long-term gain; austerity now but a promise of future triumph. But this golden future has never materialised, and instead informality and provisionality have become entrenched aspects of life in Kenya, as elsewhere in Africa. Urban Africans have 'become accustomed to living in these circumstances – to anticipating and planning for grand, far-off futures while navigating perpetual uncertainty in the present' (Melly 2017: 17). This is an example of what Gracia Clark has described as a state of 'permanent transition': there is no defined rupture or distinct crisis, only the 'routinisation and rationalisation of uncertainty', hardship and impasse (2005: 45). Life in such a city is full of action and fluctuation, though often with apparently little to show for it. Residents of places like Kaloleni struggle to plan and anticipate; to make the future known and to bring it into being. But such uncertainty can itself constitute an urban resource (Simone 2016). While vexing and tiresome, it can also enable new constellations of thought and action, for people to see possibilities and mobilise resources in ways that might seem to offer marginal returns but nevertheless offer a flicker of opportunity.

In this context, Vision 2030 presents another version of a golden future. While in the present tense it appears highly exclusionary, prioritising globalised flows of connectivity and consumption, it also holds within it radical promises of future belonging and urban presence – in the world as much as in Nairobi. This deferred future is an iteration of what several scholars have described as life in the 'meantime'; in which urbanites are left hanging between a promise of modernity or development and a present of breakdown and fragmentation (Jansen 2015; Melly 2017). Stef Jansen has described the meantime in Bosnia-Herzegovina as characterised by 'yearnings' for 'normal lives' (2015). For residents of a Sarajevo housing estate, the meantime is experienced as a form of spatiotemporal entrapment, in which, people felt themselves stuck in place and in time and unable to move forward along the 'road to Europe' (2015: 19). Jansen observed that they yearned not for identitarian-based past or future selves, but for spatiotemporally located selves; no longer on the periphery, and no longer in temporal limbo (2015: 21).

This sense of obstruction, of being trapped in the meantime, has characterised much African ethnography in recent decades that has sought to describe experiences of, and engagements with, development, modernity and the future (Ferguson 1999; J. Smith 2008; Weiss 2017). Grievances about being 'stuck', needing to 'catch up' or 'going backwards' have become ways of framing the challenges of living during times of permanent transition, expressing a sense of temporal marginalisation and exclusion from developmental time. But though these expressions evoke the linear time of progress and modernisation, as critiques of political and governmental mechanisms they are also rooted in local ideas about social value and moral understandings of growth and potential (Weiss 2017: 210). Modes of critiquing dominant temporal trajectories, or seeking alternative pathways around spati-otemporal obstruction, are ways of acting on time and on the future. This is what James Howard Smith has called 'tempopolitics': the efforts to manage the flow of historical time to create alternative futures (2008: 247).

In Kaloleni, struggles over the meaning and value of the past, how to manage its material afterlives, and its relation to a highly uncer-tain future are often framed in terms of flow and blockage. While pathways of connection are always emerging, so too is a concern with getting stuck. Over the seventy years since Kaloleni was constructed, it is not surprising that families have come to feel rooted in the estate, yet this sense of belonging is not always comfortable. Later gener-ations did not move into the estate with the hope and aspiration of their parents, they were born in Kaloleni and now feel themselves left behind, unable to keep pace with a fast-changing Nairobi, and concerned about their capacity to find a place for themselves in the future. They feel themselves stuck in place and in time, unable to flow forward in their lives. This sense of being out of time, stuck in a recur-sive loop, is explored further in Chapter 6, but as my Kaloleni host and friend Tom put it: 'Others were lucky, they got their chances. Us, we're sticking in the mud, you see? Sitting and talking, but nothing is happening'. Daniel's and Boniface's remarks above reveal their suspicions that waiting for modernity to be delivered to them is a pipe dream, suggesting that exclusionary and clientelist state politics, as well as structuring global conditions, mean that such futures are forever bottlenecked (See Melly 2017).

But that doesn't mean that *nothing* is happening. Vision 2030 – even if it remains immaterial – has created new 'economies of anticipa-tion' where people live towards the future and try to ensure they will have a place within it (Elliott 2016; see also Cross 2014). The question facing residents of places like Kaloleni is how to make potential futures happen? How to do, make and act in the meantime so as to make certain futures more feasible for people like themselves? Melly has described the meantime in Dakar as 'a space and moment where residents worked to bridge the realities of a stalled and oppressive present with distant expectations of mobile futures' (2017: 72). This DIY approach, in which ordinary people seek their own techniques to bring the future into being, resonates with the projects of self-making I observed in Nairobi. Daniel's self-constructed extension, like Calvin's hustling, is a tempopolitical engagement; an attempt to overcome a stalled present and to craft a place for oneself in the future.

Making a home amid urban decay

The first time I visited Kaloleni, in the dusky 6pm light after a long day exploring the Eastlands area of Nairobi, I saw a man clipping the hedge in front of his house. The hedge was so neat and crisp and right-angular it seemed to have more affinity with suburban England or a continental formal garden than with the crowded assemblages of people, vehicles and constructions that are more usually associated with poor areas of eastern Nairobi. First impressions of Kaloleni are of a rather ramshackle neighbourhood of worn, leaky bungalows interspersed with rusting corrugated iron shacks. Accretions of plastic and food waste pile up in the street, broken street lights lean across the paths, and ancient items from cars to old sacks litter the estate. But I hadn't spent much time in the estate before I was noting down all kinds of ways that residents had taken it upon themselves to keep this deterioration at bay. Apart from planting and maintaining hedges, DIY modifications have been added, some houses have been painted externally; bright picket fences would emerge like mushrooms seemingly overnight; several residents cultivate small plant nurseries and do good business selling seed-lings to their neighbours (see Figure 1). Interiors similarly are often well-maintained: residents with a little disposable income have covered old floors with tiles and painted walls in bright colours, and those who have not often spoke wistfully of their dreams of home improvement.

Such forms of homemaking have not always been possible in Nairobi. Its history as a segregated, colonial city means that any sense of urban belonging cannot be assumed. As will be explored further in Chapter 1, the capacity to dwell in the colonial city was subject to gendered and racialised ordering as well strict regulation (White 1990; Harris 2008; C. Smith 2015). For the waves of African migrants who sought new opportunities in the burgeoning city, any association with Nairobi as 'home' was fundamentally contested, and sometimes subject to forceful prevention, through demolitions of settlements or the much-hated *'kipande'* pass laws that regulated African movement through the city (Lonsdale 2001).[2] Only slowly, over the course of the twentieth century, could certain spaces be remade into places of urban dwelling and belonging.

Before the Second World War, formal housing schemes had provided limited dormitory-style accommodation for single men, whose pres-ence in the city was allowed only as pass-holding migrant labourers (Lonsdale 2001). Such official restrictions did not, however, succeed in quelling the movement of people into Nairobi, but simply meant that

---

[2] Instituted in 1920, the *kipande* was an identity document that also acted as a record of employment and pass system for African men of working age. It could be checked at any time, and a valid *kipande* was necessary to enter certain areas of areas of Nairobi.

Figure I House fronts – various DIY additions to Kaloleni's original houses, January 2014 (Photo: Author)

they sought shelter in the outskirts and interstices of the city, constructing ad hoc settlements where they could (Lonsdale 2001; Myers 2003). Gradually, municipal authorities recognised that restricting African residency was a losing battle, a stance that was reinforced by growing concern that the squalid conditions of the African 'villages' were jeopardising not only public health but urban order (Cooper 1983; Achola 2001). Kaloleni was planned as part of a larger colonial shift towards a welfarist agenda that intended to reform, rather than restrict, African residence in the city (Harris and Hay 2007). As a model urban community, it would create a new kind of urban neighbourhood for Africans, aimed at promoting stable family life rather than transitory labour migration (Ogilvie 1946). By directly intervening into the design of domestic life, the municipal council hoped to produce African subjects compliant to colonial hierarchies; the model residents of the future colonial city.

Though this modernising imperative did produce higher quality housing than previous schemes and it became possible to build a life in Nairobi, legacies of earlier regimes of movement endured, and rural-urban connections have remained crucial to notions of belonging and identification (see Chapter 4, also Geschiere and Gugler 1998). Furthermore, while Kaloleni was regarded as desirable by many, colonial-era tenants were subject to intrusive scrutiny and strict regulations that prevented them from turning these new houses into homes (see Chapter 1). The elaborate home improvements of pruning hedges, painting houses and tiling bathrooms described above – not to mention the accretion of dirt and rubbish – show how today such regulations are no longer enforced and the estate is not so stringently managed. Though Kaloleni remains a public housing estate, it is in a state of considerable infrastructural collapse. Since the 1980s, there has been a retraction of municipal services and the City Council[3] no longer fulfils its duty of care towards these neighbourhoods, in what has been described as a 'sheer abdication of responsibilities' (Olima 2013: 295).

The ruination of Kaloleni is much lamented by its inhabitants, particularly older residents such as Dolly, who has lived in Kaloleni all her life. She described how the infrastructure of Kaloleni has decayed:

> It has really changed. We used to have water; [now] there's no water. The roads – you see how they are. We used to have footpaths, they are no longer there. This government...! the garbage now we are paying

[3] In 2013, the enactment of Kenya's new constitution devolved regional authority to the newly formed County Governments. Nairobi is now administered by the Nairobi County Government, replacing the City Council administration. However, at the time of my fieldwork (2013–14) this change was still very new and many Nairobians continued to refer to the city authorities as the City Council. To avoid confusion, I have preserved their terminology throughout.

[for collection]. City Council used to come and collect but these days we pay for these youths to take it ... Even planting this fence, it's for your own self. We did it. They never do anything.

Dolly's words also show how the withdrawal of services has caused the relationship between council and tenant to shift. Today, residents increasingly take on obligations that were once the remit of municipal authorities. They organise rubbish collection and water deliveries, and shoulder the responsibilities of home maintenance, creating vibrant homes for themselves amid the dirt and decay. Such DIY practices have rooted residents within the fabric of the estate, their reworkings and reconfigurations blurring distinctions between tenant and owner, ruin and renewal.

Though Kaloleni is much decayed, it is not derelict or abandoned. As the ongoing projects of its residents imply, it is a place oriented towards the future rather than a site of historical ruins. Whereas the category of 'ruin' abstracts the past, separating it from the present and fixing it in both time and space, in Kaloleni we see how the residual architecture of the past – in all its decomposition and reanimation – is persistently entangled in contemporary apprehensions and aspirations. It is not possible to neatly separate new houses from the old, the improved from the original or the ruined from the repaired. This is not because the estate is materially homogenous but because of the way that the old has been reimagined anew, the improved understood as original and the decrepit integrated into recent renovations. As Gastón Gordillo noted in his work on the remainders of Spanish colonialism in the Chaco region of Argentina, architectural traces are rarely fixable in time, but are sites redolent with other histories and other uses (2014). He found buildings reclaimed and reimagined by generations of indigenous and *criollo* people; bricks and stones recycled into cattle kraals, collapsed churches that had become central to local fiestas. The moment of disintegration was also not limited to a specific timeframe: sites were destroyed anew through the violence of agribusiness, the debris ploughed into vast soybean plantations expanding across the Chaco. 'It was the alleged pastness of these objects that began crumbling', he observed, 'as well as the boundedness I inadvertently projected on to their materiality' (Gordillo 2014: 2).

What Gordillo calls the 'ruptured multiplicity' – both temporal and material – of these sites led him to think in terms not of ruins but of rubble. But to describe such sites as rubble is not to demean or denigrate them. Rather, he tries to 'do away with the mainstream downgrading of rubble as shapeless, worthless debris, and instead to explore rubble as textured, affectively charged matter that is intrinsic to all living places' (Gordillo 2014: 5). As rubble, these sites form constellations with the rubble of the present, rich afterlives that affect bodies and places in diverse ways. Though it is also crumbling and disintegrating, Kaloleni does not comfortably fit within Gordillo's concept of rubble. It is too full of life, too crowded, too extant, to be described as rubble alone. Nevertheless, his sense of the temporal and material multiplicity of collapsed architecture resonates strongly. While tracing Kaloleni's architectural history, it quickly became apparent that to classify discrete housing morphologies and identify them with particular time periods would be not only inadequate but also artificial. What was needed was a different way of engaging with the remains of the past as we encounter them in the present, not as detached artefacts but as constitutive of a contemporary place, entangled in ongoing apprehensions and aspirations.

In this way, though Kaloleni is a place of considerable decay and disintegration, it is not simply a place of ruination or collapse. Recent literature on the ruination of modernity, industrialisation and colonialism has tended to emphasise an association with loss, fragmentation or absence (Edensor 2005; Navaro-Yashin 2009; Yarrow 2017). In Kaloleni, however, the loss usually associated with ruination is quickly tempered by something else: accumulation. The estate is conspicuously marked by a build-up of traces from multiple eras. As houses are repaired with ad hoc materials, as infrastructures break down and debris accumulates, as makeshift arrangements for extending decrepit water and drainage systems emerge, and as generations of residents leave traces of family life within the estate, we are left more, not less: accretions of sociality, materiality and history that generate a richly textured landscape.

Here we see how decay may be better understood as processes of accumulation rather than as loss or absence. This is explicitly examined in Chapter 2, which argues that ruination and decay, words often used interchangeably in the literature on architectural remains, should be uncoupled as synonyms. The accretion of vestiges, rubbish and dirt can effect and constrain certain atmospheres, attitudes and politics. By exploring how residents think about and manage the dirt and decay of their neighbourhood, the multiple substances and processes of decay emerge as a form of material history. What we see in Kaloleni is an excess of matter, rather than a lack; an excess generated by lives lived and things that have happened. To move away from the arguments of ruination as a process with the 'power to disintegrate the positivity of the given', as Gordillo puts it, and instead to see decay as accumulation, is not an argument for redeeming positivism. Rather, it attempts to account for the incremental build-up of the past. Though such substances are far from enchanting – in fact, they are often revolting – nevertheless this historicised matter reveals a landscape inscribed with multiple ordinary histories that continue to amass. In Nairobi, Vision 2030 promises to clean up such accretions, replacing dirt and grime with gleaming surfaces. In some ways, this would be welcome, though residents are anxious that such renewal might also result in their eviction and the end of Kaloleni as they know it. In this way, I propose, the loss usually associated with ruination may in fact emanate not so much from decay as from its elimination.

Urban landscapes, accumulated histories

Processes of accumulation also shape the character of this book more broadly. A city is a landscape of accumulation, an assemblage gradually deposited over time through processes of making and discarding, construction and destruction. The iterative texture of city-making illuminates how the traces of the past are not inert, but can constellate with, or become implicated in, projects in the present. This kind of thinking is well-established in environmental history and landscape anthropology, which have shown how, across the world, landscapes emerge across the *longue durée*. Certain features such as burial mounds or ancient stone circles remain vital across time, providing routes into the past that also animate present-day concerns and politics. As Chris Tilley has shown, being 'in place' is not an innate or *a priori* state, it is a historically particular production. Landscape is never just the background to human action; people are as much 'in place' as they are 'in culture' (Tilley 1994: 18). Agentive, vital landscapes, bearing accumulated traces, remains and narratives of the past can help to shape geographies, authority and moral claims in diverse ways (see for example Basso 1970; Cohen and Odhiambo 1989; Küchler 1993; Fontein 2015; Cormack 2016). 'The engagement with landscape and time is historically particular, imbricated in social relations and deeply political', Barbara Bender has proposed; landscape and time can never be 'out there', they are actively engaged with by those who live with and among them (2002: 104).

What happens when we bring such ideas about ancient landscapes into the terrain of the city? This book explores how the traces of the urban past – including those of relatively recent origin – accumulate, their powerful afterlives informing the development of an emplaced sense of belonging or identity. This approach enables us to go beyond thinking of the city as simply a container for human life, a spatial unit to which urban migrants must accommodate themselves, as the earlier 'situational analysis' of urbanisation in Africa implied (see J.C. Mitchell 1987: 98–105). Rather, this book starts from the idea that individuals and material forms are cumulatively generative *of* place, whether home or city. The asymmetric lifespans of humans and the landscapes we inhabit have always meant that we form connections with the remains of past cultures and societies, and that these connections continue to influence the way we seek to know the future.

From here we can begin to think in terms of how urban accumulations are churned, asymmetrically and unequally, over time (Brenner and Schmid 2017: 53). The making of urban landscapes is deeply influenced by geographies of social interaction, settlement, circulation and authority, but that does not mean that agency resides only with the human. Landscape is neither inert nor passive; enduring substances and forms remain active and affective. This is what Lindsay Bremner has called 'geoarchitecture': the excavation, mobilisation, reshuffling and reconstitution of materials and processes that make architecture a geological actor (2012). These materials are vital contributors to city-making, influencing the foundations – literal and metaphorical – of the city and shaping the design of life within it. In this way, attending to the dynamics of accumulation enables a perspective on the urban across the *longue durée*, in which densities of human, environmental and material processes unravel at different paces but are nevertheless mutually constitutive.

Thus, rather than an archaeological 'excavation' of a sedimented urban history, this book is concerned with the manifestation of the material past as we encounter it in the present. This highlights the co-presence of multi-temporalities, where 'the time of material culture is in fact a multi-temporal time, formed from accumulating durations, superimposed one upon the other' (Olivier 2002: 140). In his famous 'Theses on the Philosophy of History', Walter Benjamin described history as the piling up of wreckage, fragment on top of fragment (2007: 257). He argued we should not allow ourselves to be propelled blindly into the future, through 'homogenous empty time' where historical events unfurl in neat succession, unimpeded by temporal recursivity (2007: 261). Instead he advocated a materialist history, one that enables an experience *with* the past, *with* the wreckage that surrounds us. The materialist historian 'grasps the constellation which his own era has formed with a definite earlier one' (Benjamin 2007: 263). From this perspective, Nairobi's residents, as anywhere, live literally within such a history, experiencing the ongoing ruination and rejuvenation of its material forms (Navaro-Yashin 2009: 5). Contemporary Nairobi homes are in this sense also future deposits of the historical wreckage, material substances that will continue to unfold in the world through processes of decay and devastation, their geoarchitecture interacting with previous and future residues laid down over time.

Thinking about the city as an ongoing process of accumulation thus provides a different purchase on the relationship between materiality and time. Histories of household maintenance in Kaloleni show how, rather than discrete eras, various pasts and futures are interpolated into the present, fostering new practices of historymaking. As Chapter 3 examines, though Kaloleni residents were not responsible for the initial design or construction of their houses, they have been engaged in elaborate forms of home maintenance, extension and modification for many years. As city authorities gradually abandoned their management obligations, so residents have increasingly performed the responsibilities of ownership. Processes of maintaining and building houses across generations have interwoven temporal elements into the fabric of the house; materials and histories have become enmeshed (see also Morton 2007). This shifting materiality has not only reconfigured the landscape of the estate but residents' engagement with the colonial past more fundamentally, animating new historical narratives. Tempo-politics in Kaloleni thus has a material character: from asserting alternative histories of independence and disputing government records of public property, to declaring the ongoing legitimacy of colonial treaties, new histories of Nairobi are emerging from, and are nourished by, the place of Kaloleni itself.

These efforts to manage and act on historical time are not interested in the past for its own sake but seek to influence the politics of the present. The forms of historymaking at work in Kaloleni do not assume the chronological or linear unfurling of past, present and future but directly address the multiple ways in which the past interrupts, but can also address, present-day anxieties (Makris 1996; Masquelier 2002; Argenti 2008). Vision 2030 has awoken newly historical sensibilities among many Nairobians, where the pasts of their homes and neighbourhoods have begun to acquire new salience in the face of highly uncertain futures. By actively engaging with Kaloleni's accumulated histories, residents seek to bring their understanding of the past to bear on their hopes and anxieties and to make a place for themselves in a future which, for many, seems largely beyond their grasp. This is in contrast to other studies of historical production in Africa, which have tended to assume that oral tradition is the main avenue through which the past is processed and new histories are constructed (e.g. Peel 1984; Tonkin 1995). This can often imply that processes of historymaking emerge from a reimagined 'indigenous' or 'traditional' past, as in the debates about Mau Mau that have dominated the historical ethnography of Kenya (e.g. Odhiambo and Lonsdale 2003). What we see in Nairobi, however, is how historymaking is embedded in the persistent materialities of an urban landscape, even as it seeks to refashion potential futures of exclusion, uncertain yet hovering on the horizon.

This hints at other, more commercial, connotations of 'accumulation'. Vision 2030 also conceives of Nairobi as a site of accumulation; as a place from which value and profit can be accrued through globalised markets in land, property and services (C. Smith 2017). Launched in 2007 by the then President Mwai Kibaki, Vision 2030 mobilises now-familiar vocabularies of neoliberal development, emphasising competition, management, performance and accountability as it seeks to create a 'democratic political system that is issue-based, people-centered, result-oriented and accountable to the public' (Government of Kenya

2007: 22). To be financed by conglomerates of private capital and developed and managed through private partnerships, the large-scale infrastructure projects of Vision 2030 are an example of 'the spread of neo-liberal ideology that brings state and national governments into close collaboration with corporations' (Moser 2015: 31). It conforms to the spatial logics and aesthetics of a certain brand of global city master-planning where a seductive set of visions, policies and templates have duplicated the same spectacular skylines, neoliberal structuring and corporate management systems in multiple city plans across Asia and Africa (Bunnell and Das 2010: 278).

As Searle has astutely observed in India, such privately financed urban enclaves have become 'landscapes of accumulation', not in terms of places marked by the gradual accretion of history, but as sites of revenue generation (2016). Vision 2030 does not conceive of Nairobi as a distinctive, heterogeneous city, but as a place where land is mobilised as a global financial resource, and where real estate is financed, constructed and leased through international markets. How these two modes of accumulation – as historical substance churned over time, and as real estate that accrues value – might intersect forms the background to much of the ethnography of the book and is more closely examined in the final two chapters. The new horizons emerging in Nairobi are not limited to Vision 2030 alone but are shaped by much smaller-scale ways of conceiving and constructing the future.

Lines of desire and obstruction

Finding one's way in Kaloleni can be difficult. Unlike the systematic grids of many public housing projects, Kaloleni seems like a warren of winding paths. The original design followed garden city principles of urban planning, with neat concentric circles divided by radial roads to form a spider-like web design. Curving lines of bungalows were interspersed with large green spaces and planted with trees and shrubs. Though now in a state of decrepitude, with roofs falling in and roads disintegrating, very little has been deliberately demolished. Instead, the remains of the original buildings have been added to and extended, and the green spaces filled with corrugated iron structures like Daniel's (see Figure 2).

Moving through the estate, the juxtapositions can be surprising, evoking stereotypical scenes of both urban squalor and bucolic parkland. Walking down a muddy narrow passage strewn with rubbish, one can suddenly emerge into a grassy, sunlit area, framed by huge jacaranda trees, while elsewhere rusty corrugated iron shacks give way to clipped hedgerows. The making of Kaloleni has in this sense been additive; an incremental amassing of materials and constructions that

Figure 2 Constructing an extension, May 2014
(Photo: Author)

reconfigure spaces and adjust daily routines, reformulating the orderly flow embedded in the original design. New extensions, fences, gardens and other forms of enclosure have blocked off sightlines and severed many original paths, turning them into redundant dead ends. Other routes have faded from significance, and now trail off into the grass or mud. New pathways are emerging that follow no aerial plan. These desire lines meander in and out of the new structures, going around newly fenced front yards and forging new linkages across the estate.

Lines in African cities immediately conjure up racialised lines of spatial segregation, grid-like garrisons of housing and the formality of the planned city. Certainly, colonial and apartheid regimes of urban governance were committed to lines as dividers, barriers, categories and sightlines of surveillance (Bremner 2004). In Nairobi, British colonial urban policy used the planning and management of the city to spatialise order and control, partitioning the populace as well as space and resources (Werlin 1974; Slaughter 2004; Harris 2008; Otiso 2009). The line also evokes the techniques on which colonial rule relied: mapping and surveying, regulating flows of people and infrastructure, and methods of surveillance that prioritised rationality and order (T. Mitchell 1988; Joyce 2003; Myers 2003). The line as border and boundary was central to this process, a delineation of inside and outside, container and contained, at various spatial scales, facilitating legibility (T. Mitchell 1988: 33).

But the emergent lines of Kaloleni suggest a different process is at work. The reinscription of Kaloleni by alternative routes and pathways reveals not only how colonial regimes of orderliness have been remapped, but also how everyday life comes to be etched in the landscape, revealing histories of movement and connectivity. Urban desire lines undo the rigour of formal planning, patterning the city with routes made by expedience or deviation (de Certeau 1984). Paths both record and permit the embodied movements and everyday encounters through which people make the city their own. They introduce new dynamics to planned space, withdrawing it from the linear, unirhythmic time of the state, fracturing it into a multiplicity of rhythms that chart new temporalities and socialities (Lefebvre 2004: 96). Rather than a modernist sensibility of the line as static and controlled, fixing categories and dividing spaces, pathways are made iteratively, marking the accumulated traces of use and evoking movement and growth (Ingold 2016: 4).

These lines also extend beyond Kaloleni, linking it to the rest of Nairobi and beyond. This ethnography could have been territorially defined, delimited by the borders of a physical neighbourhood, but Kaloleni is by no means a bounded community. I have sought to avoid an island perspective and instead demonstrate the routes linking the estate and its residents to much larger imaginative and material worlds. Kaloleni is embedded in the wider history of Eastlands, once the 'African quarter' of colonial Nairobi and now a mix of old council housing estates, informal settlements and more recent poor-quality private developments. Spatial, temporal and imaginative networks that extend far beyond Nairobi continue to affect life in the estate. Kaloleni is connected by labour, kin, leisure, politics, ethnicity and education to the rest of Nairobi and beyond, and in particular retains deep links to rural western Kenya (Chapter 4). Residents also participate in wider conversations about the future of Nairobi and Kenya, in which their own aspirations and desires are entangled. All these flows into and out of the estate are not just of academic interest but are valorised by residents themselves. Their regard for mobility and flow manifests in various ways, from fear of 'getting stuck' in Kaloleni to aspirational dreams of living a 'digital' life (Chapter 6). It is not just people who move along lines of connection but materials too. Houses move across a landscape in a particular manner (see Chapter 4) and water flows through a drain (see Chapter 2).

It should be clear then, that this attentiveness to the lines, tracks and pathways of Kaloleni does not indicate a focus on linearity. My preoccupation is not with the straight lines of the grid, of chronological timelines or the cartographic gaze, but with lines that connect (Were 2010). Lines that join dots into complex patterns and networks across time and across space. In this sense, the line has a rhizomatic quality, it is what constitutes people and things into lateral networks and assemblages, and here its genealogy can be traced to influential recent scholarship in anthropology, science and technology studies and critical theory (Deleuze and Guattari 1988; Latour 2007; Farías and Bender 2012). This work seeks to re-engage with an active and efficacious nonhuman world, undoing distinctions between lively subject and dull object. It finds instead networks of 'actants' (incorporating humans and non-humans) or assemblages of 'vibrant matter' (Latour 1993; Bennett 2009). The lines of Kaloleni are recursive and accumulate; they weave together time and place, biography and economy, belief and pleasure. They link day-to-day manoeuvres with geopolitical wranglings. They mark the entanglement of humans and things, and the unfolding, relational way in which their networks and assemblages take shape – provisional alignments that are always subject to change.

The accumulated materialities of Kaloleni also reveal how blockage and obstruction, as much as lines of flow and motion, characterise the landscape of the estate. While learning my way around Kaloleni in the early part of my fieldwork, I asked several residents to show me the childhood routes they used to take from home to the bus stop, to school and to the shops. In many cases, this was now impossible; we would set off only to be brought up short as we encountered a corrugated iron wall or thorny hedge bisecting the path. In some ways, such blockages are part of a desired effect: the enclosure of Kaloleni's houses with fences and hedges seeks to sever the surveillance sightlines embedded in the colonial plan, which sought to ensure security through visibility. Today, in the absence of formal estate management, break-ins, crime and insecurity have become very real concerns and residents have taken it upon themselves to build new architectures of security out of what materials they can afford. In a city of gated communities and privatised enclaves, there is also a certain prestige and desirability to living behind a high fence (see Chapter 5). But the collapse of Kaloleni's infrastructure, including failed sewerage pipes and blocked drainage ditches, has induced more repellent substances of obstruction. The leakages and residues of waste are producing new forms of excess, seeping into the ground and producing new topographies of contamination (see Chapter 2). The future potency of such toxic accumulations is uncertain, but they reveal how the accumulation of decay is unforeclosed, an ongoing process of accretion implicated in the future as well as the past.

The reinscription of Kaloleni through emergent pathways of desire and connection, as well as its excess materialities of obstruction, suggest the imbrication of mobility and matter, flow and accumulation. As Kalolenians live with decay, repairing and modifying their estate in ways that disrupt a design intended to produce compliant subjects, they intervene in a landscape of accretion. The tangibility of these interventions resists a recent discourse on urban Africa that has tended to disregard substance and matter in favour of language, representation and the invisible. In Kinshasa, a city of seismic infrastructural collapse, De Boeck has argued that it is the spectral, shadow world of rumour, speculation and magic that has the upper hand over the haptic, physical city (De Boeck and Plissart 2004: 57). 'Spoken form regularly seems to dominate the built form', he writes (2004: 30). Amid such breakdown, reality itself seems to collapse under an excess of semiotic interpretation; 'there is no reality that is strong enough to resist language' (2004: 59). In urban Nigeria, Jane Guyer has stressed how it is the invisible pathways of the popular economy that structure and organise the city, shaping forms of urban growth (2004). AbdouMaliq Simone has argued that it is city dwellers themselves who constitute urban infrastructure, and it is they, not the stuff of the city, that make urban Africa 'work' (Simone 2004b). His analysis of changing life in four African cities is divided into sections on the informal, the invisible, the spectral and patterns of movement (Simone 2004a).

Unquestionably, the call to recognise the creative sociality of African cities is important. Simone's work, along with many others, has responded to a previous academic generation's emphasis on urban structures, planning and modernisation – or, more accurately, the crisis afflicting them in postcolonial, late twentieth-century Africa (see Nuttall and Mbembe 2008: Introduction). This emphasis tended to describe the informalisation of African cities and economies in terms of political, economic and structural failure. From the 1990s onwards, the trope of 'Africa in crisis' pervaded academic and public debate, particularly around cities and governance, and the simplistic cliché of Africa as a continent of failed states still casts a long shadow (see Roitman 2017). Simone's appeal that we focus on 'something else besides decay'; on the social infrastructures, improvisatory economies, on the collaboration and tenacity that makes African cities is therefore significant and timely (Simone 2004b: 407). But it is also not the whole story.

This book can be read in part as an attempt to put materiality back in the picture. It responds directly to Simone's call to recognise the humanity of urban Africa, foregrounding the everyday challenges of life in Nairobi. But it does so not by overlooking material fragmentation and infrastructural decline, but by examining how it is that material, structural and social assemblages together produce 'cityness' across time. Life in Nairobi *is* provisional, it *does* rely on strategy, creativity and having many plates spinning at the same time. Speculation, rumour and promise *are* powerful forces in the midst of fragmentation and infrastructural decline. But, I suggest, the existence of all of these does not signify that the city is somehow insubstantial. As Daniel's remixing of colonial architecture with makeshift DIY suggests, the material world of Kaloleni exposes important dynamics of place and belonging.

Likewise, just because a roof is collapsed or the council has abandoned garbage collection does not mean the broken roof or the piled-up rubbish is less affective – in fact, it is often in their very breakdown that their materiality asserts itself in everyday life (Bennett 2005; Larkin 2008). The remains of the past and the stuff of the present are entangled in contemporary Nairobi. The textures, colours and materials of the city – in all their messy decay and rejuvenation – are necessarily interpolated with the social, economic and shadowy dynamics of the less easily seen. Without assuming any neat separation between them, this book attends to the distinctive politics of the human *and* the material, as well as their mutual imbrication.

Urban planning and everyday life

Attention to the lines of connection Kalolenians make across different scales and temporalities presents a challenge to the conventional distinction between the 'informal' and 'formal' city that frames so much of the study of urban Africa. By imaginatively connecting his ad hoc extension to the futurescapes of Vision 2030, Daniel's assertion that his extension 'is' Vision 2030 suggests that the practices and desires of an apparently local, makeshift urbanism cannot be straightforwardly categorised as 'informal' as though beyond the reach of formal networks of urban planning. In certain contexts, regimes of legibility, visibility and regulation can seem to offer opportunity, while in others they might leave one's interests exposed. Though they sometimes preferred to keep out of sight of official scrutiny, I saw how Kalolenians often tried to involve themselves in the machinations of City Hall, seeking to make formal planning more knowable even when official logics could seem exclusionary and opaque. The lengths to which residents go to grapple with the procedures of urban planning in Nairobi were highlighted by one particular occasion during my fieldwork.

In May 2014, I was invited to a gathering of the Kaloleni Estate Residents' Association (KERA). We met under a tree in the centre of the estate, and as we chatted they showed me a tender notice in that day's *Nation* newspaper. It invited proposals for a consultancy to undertake a feasibility study and spatial plan for an upgrading project in the Eastlands area of Nairobi. As this was under the remit of Vision 2030, and would encompass Kaloleni, KERA were understandably anxious. The notice had no details; to see the full brief meant purchasing the tender documents from City Hall at a cost of 1,000 KES (GB £8 or US $10) – not a lot of money, but more than anyone had going spare. Intrigued, I offered to pay, and the next afternoon we went through the documents. The forms were written in highly technical language and it was not entirely clear what the scope of the project would be. But it announced that all the bids would be opened publicly at City Hall the following Friday, and 'those with an interest' were requested to attend. We were not certain who 'those with an interest' included, but consensus was that, as residents, it should definitely mean them, 'and anyway it says it's public'. I was asked to go too; 'they cannot refuse you', I was told.

When three of us arrived at City Hall the next week, the gates to the offices on the first floor were locked shut. There was some confusion over who was allowed to witness the opening, and it seemed it was meant to be only those who had submitted a bid. James, muttering about the need for public transparency to anyone who might hear him, pushed me forward. 'She is a researcher on urban projects', he told the guard, who finally agreed to unlock the grille. Smiling uncertainly and not seeming to know what to do with us, members of the 'opening committee' introduced themselves and kept talking about how important it was that we were there to 'participate'. Each of the bids was opened with much ceremony. The Technical Proposal for each was held aloft, and then the confirmation of a bond from the applicants' bank was read aloud and the details marked down in a huge ledger. We got the sense that this performance of bureaucracy was for our benefit; the chairman of the committee kept glancing at us and telling his juniors to make sure everything was recorded properly. We were asked if we had any questions, and Paul queried the lack of map among the tender documents. 'We need a map, or how can we know who is affected?' he said, before quickly adding: 'You know, the map is needed for research purposes'.

We eventually made our way outside, laughing: the event had been slightly ridiculous but also revealing. 'This transparency is just joking', James said. It was only by making our presence felt – and by KERA using my presence as form of leverage – that City Hall had accepted to give us access to what had already been promised would take place in public. 'They see us coming from Eastlands and they will just refuse us', James added. Even after our visit, and despite the new Kenyan language of 'public participation' and 'transparency', the planned trajectory for the renewal project, the intended focus and the affected neighbourhoods still remained obscure.

This incident highlighted how, rather than operating in a different sphere, the circulating plans, globalised vocabularies and imagined futures of Vision 2030 provoke new entanglements. Despite this, much of the literature on urbanism in Africa still tends to assume that the dynamics of the informal sector and state-led processes of urban planning are discrete phenomena. The story of Nairobi is often presented as a dual one: the history of the formal, planned city and that of informal settlements at the margins and interstices – representing a parallel 'self-help city', which already by 1971 housed a third of Nairobi's population (Hake 1977: 85). The 'informalisation' of Nairobi has been a significant focus of research by historians and social scientists, who have observed how, since the 1970s, economic stagnation, structural adjustment and rapid urbanisation dramatically undermined reliance on the formal sector for employment, goods and services and intensified the significance of social networks, makeshift neighbourhoods and entrepreneurial tactics for making life workable for Nairobi's urban majority (Hake 1977; King 1996; Robertson 1997; Charton-Bigot and Rodriguez-Torres 2010). In international development research and practice, Nairobi's informal sector, as well as its vast informal settlements (in particular the famous 'slum' of Kibera), have become classic case studies of informality (ILO 1972; Amis 1984; Livingstone 1991; Stren 1992; Syagga and Kiamba 1992).

Though diverse scholarship on the cross-cutting linkages between the formal and informal sectors in Kenya – for example, on political clientelism, land markets and entrepreneurship – certainly exists (see, for example, Smedt 2009; Lynch 2011; Boone 2012), this has not overridden a wider propensity to describe informality as somehow operating according to a different logic to a 'mainstream' system. But in fact, formality and informality are often two sides of the same coin, deeply enmeshed but highly asymmetrical. As early as the 1970s, Janice Perlman demonstrated through her work in Brazilian *favelas* that dwellers in informal settlements are not separate from or on the margins of the system but are tightly bound to it, albeit in a manner that often entrenches unequal relations (1979: 242–4). Far from being exiled from the world economy or flows of technology and expertise, as Mike Davis has argued (2006), the 'marginality' of the informal has long been a 'myth' (Perlman 1979).

It is also easy to overstate the capacity and foresight of formal planning. Studies of colonial urban Africa have tended to present planning and management as all-encompassing. Drawing heavily on Foucauldian ideas of surveillance and governance, this approach has highlighted the production of colonial subjects through the ordering of urban space, a form of governance at once material and ideological (T. Mitchell 1988; Myers 2003; Slaughter 2004; Otiso 2009). While such work represents a necessary interrogation of the way power is exerted not just through restriction and force but by acting from within to produce compliant subjects, it does not tell the whole story. Since the beginning of the city, Nairobi's population has grown more quickly than authorities could manage, and colonial attempts at town planning and housing provision for Africans were generally reactions to expanding unregulated settlement rather than ideological strategies conceived at the outset (Lonsdale 2001). Elsewhere, postcolonial scholars have demonstrated how, even when officially compliant to colonial policy, slippages and misreadings of colonial power could also be productive, subverting attempts to produce 'proper' imperial subjects (Chakrabarty 1998; Bhabha 2004).

Nairobians have long pursued alternative trajectories within formalised processes, in ways that undid official procedure and created room for manoeuvre (White 1990; Frederiksen 1992). Procedures of planning and development have sought to make informal neighbourhoods legible through land titling or regularisation projects, but so too have occupants of such settlements pursued formal legitimacy and security of tenure through legal and bureaucratic channels (Huchzermeyer 2008; Rigon 2014). The shape of the 'formal' neighbourhoods in the city has also long been influenced by ordinary Nairobians: the city's development is as much a story of land disputes, informal construction, citizen resistance, subverted policies and incremental processes of reconfiguration as it is of rational, strategic planning (Klopp 2011; Manji 2015a). Engagement (or not) with bureaucratic procedures such as planning is sometimes tactical, sometimes a force of circumstance, and often refutes the very legitimacy of any assumed classification as formal or informal. This is certainly apparent in Kaloleni, where residents' everyday lives have undone aspects of the estate's plan. From the proliferation of residents' living room kiosks that undermined the planned 'village centre' (see Chapter 1) to arguing that forms of supposedly illegal housing are rightful property (see Chapter 3), residents seek to destabilise easy categorisation in a multitude of ways.

The multi-temporal accumulations of Kaloleni, as well as the actions and strategies of groups like KERA, emphasise the problem of reifying a separation between state and citizen, a macro-formal scale and a micro scale of everyday life. During the fieldwork for this book, I was frequently brought up short when what seemed to me like the improbable fantasies of Vision 2030 were met with enthusiastic approval, even as residents recognised it as a future from which they might well be excluded (see Chapter 6). At other times, elderly residents declared their nostalgia for the colonial management of Kaloleni, which they remembered not as a time of intrusive surveillance but of order and cleanliness (see Chapter 2). Erik Harms has emphasised that anthropologists of urban spaces should be wary of reproducing a false binary between the ideals of planners and the everyday 'reality' of ordinary people (2011). People's actions are not simply in opposition to some higher level of authority – in fact they regularly deploy the idealised terms of governance to explain their own situations. 'These categories, in turn, structure many of their interactions with each other' (Harms 2011: 25). In this way, my observations of residents' appreciation for, as well as their criticisms of, state practices of planning should be seen as part of the larger way in which people take up certain ideas and images and seek to make them more knowable. For example, when a billboard depicting flawless highrise apartments appeared among the worn-out houses of Kaloleni (see Chapter 6), the endurances of earlier materialities became mingled with scenes of seductive futures. As Nairobians seek to live with the changing landscape of the city, so they must manage and make sense of startling juxtapositions and contradictions.

Nairobi made, Nairobi felt

Since it first emerged in the 1970s, when Keith Hart (1973) used it to describe income-generating activities in Accra, Ghana, that were widespread but unregulated, 'informality' has achieved wide popularity in academic and development circles. It is not just that, since structural adjustment and deregulation, reliance on the formal sector has been a receding possibility for many in Africa. As Hart himself has argued, the neoliberal commitment to free markets, outsourcing and labour casualisation means that, at a global level, the formal and informal have 'leaked into each other to the point of being indistinguishable' (2010: 151). Informalisation has been used to describe everything from housing to livelihoods to off-shore banking and online media. While urban planning, state structures and bureaucratic systems are of course still powerful mechanisms, disentangling their formal and informal characteristics is increasingly difficult and arbitrary. In this sense, then, we have reached a point where 'informality tells us too little about what is actually going on' (Hart 2010: 152). This is not to say that in Nairobi all areas of the city now look the same, far from it, but rather that the formal/informal pairing may not be the most salient lens through which to make sense of Nairobi's shifting character.

In light of this, rather than perpetuating awkward distinctions between informal and formal Nairobi, a realm of the state and a realm of the everyday, this book conceives the city as a composite, shifting assemblage, made up of constructive as well as destructive processes that make and remake place over time. In particular, it takes up the concept and practice of 'making', not as a specific instance of craft or technique but as a form of incremental intervention that works across different urban scales, connecting practices of home maintenance with large-scale urban planning, and enabling flow between different forms of making, from informal construction practices to the production of history. In so doing, I bring discourses on making into the more complex, dynamic terrain of the city, seeking to link the provisional, emergent humanity of recent work in African urbanism with scholarship that emphasises the affective and constitutive capacities of architecture, urban planning and infrastructure (Abram and Weszkalnys 2013; Buchli 2013; Harvey and Knox 2015).

A small but growing field within the anthropology of material culture and design has examined making as a transformative process that weaves together humans, nonhumans and materials to build landscapes, knowledge, art and sociality (Marchand 2011; Ingold

2013). Much work in material culture studies has focused on complete objects, examining their 'social lives' (Appadurai 1986), capacities for agency (Gell 1998) or constitutive role in generating social relations, memory-making or networks of exchange and collecting (Strathern 1988; Küchler 2002; Knappett and Malafouris 2008; Miller 2010). Research on makers and making, on the other hand, has tended to emphasise materials and process more than the finished product or object. Ethnographies of apprenticeship have examined how tactile, embodied engagement with materials facilitates forms of communication, a process through which technique is not simply replicated nor knowledge simply passed on, but both are remade anew (Marchand 2001, 2009). Studies of, with and by designers and makers explore not only the importance of technique and skill, but how these embodied actions enable improvisatory and open-ended ways of working, in which making is a mode of problem-solving rather than the mechanical reproduction of a preconceived object (O'Connor 2005; Bunn 2013). It is in this vein that researcher and furniture maker David Gates describes his own experimental, yet deeply skill-dependent, practice as 'perpetual prototyping' (Gates 2017: 118). A common thread connecting much of this work is the way that problems are solved, knowledge is made, and people are transformed in and by the flow of making, in a generative process. The place of craft, skill and tacit knowledge is undoubtedly important, but the creative interventions of makers and making draw on this accumulated experience in a forward momentum that gives rise to form, a perspective from which making has more in common with processes of growth than with extraction or excavation (Hallam and Ingold 2016).

What might such ideas about making bring to the study of cities? Cities are undoubtedly made, they do not simply pop up overnight. But the anthropology of making has tended to focus on specific instances of creation, usually in relation to a particular practice or type of material. Makers are generally identified as having a specialist skill or craft, experts who work in a particular material domain. Trevor Marchand's pioneering ethnographic apprenticeships with minaret builders in Yemen and masons in Djenné (Mali), though they explore the making of urban buildings, do so by focusing on a specific craft rather than the making of a city per se. Cities are materially diverse and structurally miscellaneous; their spaces, buildings and infrastructures accumulate over time, incrementally and sometimes haphazardly, entangled in complex histories of politics, planning, industrialisation, colonialism, migration and technology. They are certainly the work of experts, from architects and engineers to politicians and construction workers. But such experts do not necessarily engage with materials, nor do they work in concert. They may be distributed across time or actively seeking to unmake the work of others. Moreover, cities are not made by experts alone, but in the daily intricacies of urban living; in DIY projects and household labours; in leisure and work and in civic engagement. What can ideas about making offer the complex, dynamic terrain of the city?

This book examines the efforts of ordinary Nairobians to make a life in the city – to dwell and to thrive. It explores how it is through residents' everyday lives that the city is made, imaginatively, materially and unpredictably, across time. This approach draws on the generativity of making, of the way that problems are solved on the hoof, and how a place – as much as a thing – can take shape incrementally, through exploration and improvisation. It seeks to follow what Ingold has described as an 'art of enquiry', a way of feeling things out through doing, of working with materials in which grain, texture and possibility offer lines of enquiry to be followed. It is this, he argues, that is fundamental to the question of what it means to make things (2013).

Here making is not understood as a project, a fixed goal or image to which materials and resources are bent in order to realise a preconceived shape. Instead making is 'a process of growth' where the maker is from the outset 'a participant in amongst a world of active materials' (Ingold 2013: 21). A maker then is not someone who stands apart, imposing their designs on a world passively waiting to receive them, but is more humble, simply making an intervention in 'worldly processes that are already going on' (2013: 21). From this perspective, a city is never simply planned and constructed according to a preconceived vision. It takes shape iteratively and slowly, accumulating over the *longue durée* of urban time, with the destruction and disintegration of past architectural masterplans, the alternative uses to which urban spaces may be put and the unpredictable twists that undo and reconfigure the flows and tensions of the city.

As such, the generation of cities, like other material interventions, should be understood as a process in which 'form is ever emergent rather than given in advance' (Ingold 2013: 25). An approach that Brian Massumi has described as a way to assert 'the primacy of processes of becoming over the states of being through which they pass' (Massumi 2009: 37). To be sure, this is often a highly political and contested process, in which not all the actors have the same capacity to bring their lives and their city into the form they might wish. This political aspect is often side-lined in the anthropology of making, in which it sometimes appears that the process of making is constrained only by the properties of materials themselves, rather than by the frictions of the world in which they unfold. As we will see, Nairobi has certainly been subject to urban plans and overarching visions to construct very specific types of future, to which not only materials and landscapes but people were expected to conform. These have been the source of upheaval and anxiety, sometimes of violence, but, as anywhere, the realisation of such schemes has never been all-encompassing nor comprehensively put into practice. Seen across a longer duration, it is clear that Nairobi has always been worked out in the flow of its making, with spaces of resistance and room for manoeuvre carved out from within. As Jennifer Robinson has asked in relation to South African cities,

> Can we begin to shift our experiences and our visions to capture and understand the world of always moving spaces? What do the spaces of change and dynamism look like? In what sense was even the apartheid city – a city of division – a place of movement, of change, of crossings? (Robinson 1998: D7)

The art of enquiry offers an expansive perspective on how to think about the making of Nairobi: as a city in flux, as a place of accumulation. Its form is incomplete and open-ended. The city is a place in which lines of possibility, history and materials criss-cross and are constantly reworked, their points of interconnection giving rise to prospective futures in the making. This unfolding urban fabric is densely matted, its accumulated texture generated by points of interconnection and resistance. Cities are often depicted with metaphors of textile, their 'urban fabric' described as a 'weave' of interconnections and endeavours, infrastructures and socialities. Lines as threads and traces are woven together to produce surfaces, but also knowledge; the words text and textile come from the same origin, from *texere*, 'to weave' (Ingold 2016: 62).

The analogy of weaving, as an incremental practice of fabric making, to describe the density and complexity of urban worlds is beguiling. But it is not altogether apposite of life in Nairobi. Weaving entails the structured interaction of two sets of parallel threads set perpendicular from each other; the warp strung vertically on the loom and the weft threaded cross-wise, with each strand passed under and over the warp at regular intervals. The woven cloth that results is systematic and highly structured, the lines forming a grid-like relationship that does not seem to speak to the makeshift, opaque, contingent qualities of Nairobi. Instead, a more consonant textile might be felt. Felt is non-woven, made from densely matted, entangled wool fibres that are held together through friction. As an act of making, felting is vigorous and active. The lines of the fibres do not follow a regulated pattern, but are agitated and roughened, and then compressed, the fibres bonding together, gradually building up to make a new whole.

To speak of 'felted' urban space, rather than woven, is to emphasise entanglement and interconnection, not structured warp and weft: an emergent, improvisatory place which bears the reconfigured traces of the past in its materials and surfaces. A place in which lines cross in all directions, embedding themselves in each other. A place that is matted, accumulated, produced by friction. Friction can, but does not always, imply obstruction or conflict. As when the wheels of a car encounter the surface of the road, friction produces movement, action and effect (Tsing 2011: 6). Friction is what happens at points of intersection, when accumulated remains encounter plans and aspirations. Nairobi's felted texture takes shape through entanglement with interconnected scales; through the friction of worldly encounter. Felted space is also intimate and personal, the dual meaning of the word 'felt' conjuring a tactile, haptic place of feeling as much as of knowing. The urban is felt in the body: in the possibilities and constraints of movement, in the traces of the past marked on bodies and buildings, and in the mutual making of persons and places.

A note on structure

This ethnography was produced 'in place', in the streets of Kaloleni. It does not seek to present a bird's-eye view and as such this parti-ality may sit uneasily alongside observations of Nairobi as seen from elsewhere. I do not provide a chronological history of Kaloleni nor a cartographic overview of the estate as seen from the air. Typically, a study of this kind might start with an ethnographic map of Africa, gradually zooming into Kenya, then Nairobi, in ever decreasing circles of enquiry before finally hovering over Kaloleni itself. This has become a relatively normalised way of introducing the time and place of a fieldsite, but rarely reflects the modes of temporal and spatial engage-ment of the people that actually live there. Rather, it reproduces the ways of seeing that were, and often still are, central to state-led plan-ning and mapping techniques that sought to make legible, governable subjects (Scott 1998). Instead, rather than imposing a single concep-tual thread linking chapters across the book, I try to allow the material itself to evoke something of the inconsistent, messy lives of Kaloleni residents.

Kaloleni is taken as a crucible from which to explore six intersecting challenges facing Nairobi: making a home amid the remains of colo-nial urban planning; the management of urban decay and renewal; the politics of the past and the making of urban history; the genera-tive relationship of the urban to the rural; terror and the construc-tion of security; and building a future in the shadow of Vision 2030. Each chapter refracts a different sightline that crosscuts with that of another, but the sequence is not fixed. Here I have ordered the chapters in a way that gently suggests a scalar shift from the intricacies within Kaloleni outward to national and global networks. But the reader could approach the chapters differently if they so wish, creating new junc-tures and connections.

The book is divided into two sections. The first, 'Present pasts, uncer-tain futures' explores the making of belonging amid the afterlives of colonial architecture, and under the uncertain shadow of Vision 2030. Chapter 1 introduces Kaloleni through an exploration of the pathways and lifeways that crosscut the estate. It argues that grasping a sense of place is in part a matter of perspective. Colonial plans for Kaloleni to be a model urban neighbourhood are explored alongside the way that residents sought to rescript them, their arrivals and departures revealing how place is not just made from within but through wider relations with the city and further afield. Finally, the chapter introduces the Eastlands urban renewal strategy and Kaloleni's future uncertainty. Chapter 2 takes a more material and infrastructural focus by exploring the materiality of dirt and decay. The order of Kaloleni's origins is in stark contrast with contemporary infrastructural breakdown and municipal mismanagement, and the chapter highlights residents' ad hoc attempts to manage and repair their neighbourhood in the face of disintegration. Rather than seeing Kaloleni in terms of loss and ruination, it explores what a focus on accumulation might bring to the vitality of remains in the present. Chapter 3 continues the theme of a place produced over time by investigating the ways that residents' relationship with the past is deeply related to their material management of Kaloleni. As they take on the responsibilities of ownership, performing obligations that were once the remit of the City Council, so residents are increasingly challenging official narratives and histories of Kaloleni. The chapter takes up ideas about the production of historical knowledge to examine residents' practices of historymaking, and how these are another trace or accretion that constitute Kaloleni.

The second section, 'Making new horizons', moves beyond the confines of Kaloleni to consider how linkages with urban and rural elsewheres and elsewhens are reshaping the way that people live towards the future. Chapter 4 considers how Nairobians' ongoing urban-rural connections influence forms of belonging and dwelling as well as ideals about what constitutes a successful life. It explores how, for Kaloleni men, full achievement of urban masculinity relies on the conspicuous construction of a rural home. These homes are also important as places of burial – an upcountry burial being regarded as the culmination of an urban life well-lived. The chapter explores negotiations around funerals and burials, examining how planning for a 'good death' is an important part of self-making in Kaloleni.

Chapter 5 examines how security is remaking the city across all scales. By juxtaposing the 2013 Westgate Mall terror attack alongside 'everyday' incidents of insecurity in Kaloleni, it explores how in Nairobi security is always about exclusion: it is built into the city's architectures, from private malls to gated communities. In this way, security is not only about managing urban safety, but also indexes prestige, with the elite vistas of Vision 2030 promising securitised exclusivity on a grand scale. Chapter 6 considers the spectacle and temporality of

Vision 2030 and the way in which residents of Kaloleni seek to build a future in its shadow. But their anticipatory actions are not straightforward, and their attempts to live towards the future are characterised by temporal dissonance, where the future city is experienced as both near at hand and forever out of reach. Finally, in the Conclusion I return to the theme of making and its analytical purchase for uniting the spatial and temporal dynamics that shape cities in Africa. Making is crucial to the contested politics of Nairobi: belonging is not something already assured from the past, but rather an emergent future to be crafted.

Part One

PRESENT PASTS, UNCERTAIN FUTURES

I

Making a Place over Time

'Meet me at bomb blast'

If you ask for directions in Nairobi, the answer will usually be something along the lines of 'Come, I'll show you'. Instead of listing a set of
instructions, this helpful person will guide you to your destination. This
is not because people in Nairobi are nicer than elsewhere nor because
they don't have anything better to do, but rather it indicates a different
way of knowing the city. Lifelong Nairobians often do not know – or
do not need to know – the official names of the city's streets, beyond
the major thoroughfares. Instead of navigating by lefts and rights
along specific named streets, most will refer to landmarks and places
of memory. This is in part a matter of perspective. Most Kenyans have
not grown up using maps – indeed, before Google Maps began making
digital headway, road maps of Kenya were hard to get hold of – and so
they do not carry an objectified aerial view of the city in their minds.
Their view is from the street rather than from up above. They know a
route by experience: a familiar sequence of movements, sightlines and
memorable places. This knowledge, located as it is in experience, is hard
to translate into a verbal list of directions; it is easier to simply show
someone the way.

'Meet me at bomb blast' Fidelia said to me on the phone. We had
arranged to meet so I could help her shop for her cousin's wedding.
I had already reached the city centre and, wondering where to find
her, I called her mobile. But before I could query her startling choice
of meeting point, she hung up. Not wanting to appear ignorant, I was
reluctant to call her back. Instead I turned tentatively to a smart
young woman standing nearby. 'Do you know bomb blast?' I asked.
She nodded. 'Come, we go' she said, leading the way. Bomb blast, she
explained, is a common meeting place in Nairobi city centre, the site of
the 1998 al-Qaeda-linked bomb attack on the US Embassy. Constituting
a small garden of dusty shrubs, a couple of benches and a memorial to
the attack, the site is now a tiny oasis. Its dramatic name belies the
respite offered by this patch of green amid the concrete of downtown

Nairobi. Though I knew the location of the old embassy, and I knew the history of the attack, I failed to meaningfully bring the two together to navigate the city. Rather than saying, 'Let's meet at the old US Embassy' or at 'the junction of Moi Avenue and Haile Selassie Avenue', the phrase 'bomb blast' evokes a particularly painful event in the city's collective memory. To say 'meet me at bomb blast' is to invoke an urban landscape that is not simply a backdrop to contemporary human affairs, but redolent with past actions that continue to encroach on the present. These traces constitute a powerfully located sense of history and the past; an affective link that pulls together personal experience, a shared trauma and architectural iconoclasm into a potent site of memory. This is a mode of urban navigation that cannot be plotted on a map.

European forms of mapmaking, by contrast, have long been part of a colonising mission – and a colonising gaze. Timothy Mitchell notes that nineteenth-century European visitors to Egypt struggled with what he calls a lack of pictorial order, the lack of distance between 'oneself and the view' (1988: 22). Sightseers and later colonisers sought to enforce such order through various means: photographs, technical drawings, maps and plans. These forms of representation required a point of view; a spot that allowed one to separate oneself from the world, and so constitute it as a panorama. A large hill, a minaret, especially the Great Pyramid at Giza, all provided suitably elevated positions from which to panoptically survey the scene beneath (T. Mitchell 1988: 24). Not long after, the 'discovery' of central Africa by Europeans was recorded by charting rivers and surveying topographies, squeezing landscapes into a two-dimensional scientific mode of seeing (Fabian 2000). As well as a navigational tool, maps work as a form of surveillance, their totalising gaze implying comprehensive knowledge of the terrain below, the better to traverse or occupy it (Harley 1988; Wood and Fels 1992). Of course, the idea that elevation can give total vision is itself a fallacy: aerial perspective is necessarily flattening. Textures, temporalities – not to mention people – are lost. While the view from the street is also partial, it offers a different outlook. The embodied action of moving through the streets means that things come in and out of focus, and sounds, sights, smells and textures are more relevant than any supposed universals of north or south. There is a depth of field not possible from a bird's eye view, a sense of place that is experienced in the body.

It is this sense of being in place that this book tries to capture. Both colonial urban planning and the recent spectacular plans of Vision 2030 have sought to redefine Nairobi from an aerial, totalising gaze. But, at the time of my research, most residents in Kaloleni had never seen a map of their neighbourhood. When I managed to locate a plan in an old government publication it was the source of much interest, though it took most people quite a while to read it and understand its orientation, and I was frequently called upon to explain where their houses were on the plan (see Figure 3). This book aims to follow their perspective, to take the view from the street. This is not to say that Kalolenians are disconnected from modes of planning and organising the city – in fact, as we shall see, they often petition to be directly involved in such processes. Rather, I examine how views from 'above' – including the original design of Kaloleni, as well as schemes for its redevelopment – become entangled in the everyday generation of a textured, felted landscape, and how these entanglements contribute to different ways of making the city.

What for urban planners is a space on a map is for the residents of Kaloleni a place they have made their own. While colonial planners designed Kaloleni as a model neighbourhood, hoping that architectural intervention into domestic life would remake Africans according to European ideals of domesticity and subjectivity, I examine how the arrival of new residents and the unfolding of their everyday lives rescripted these colonial intentions. Over the past seventy years, the co-constitutive relationship between residents and their material world has enabled very particular forms of urban dwelling, but this dwelling is neither stable nor can it be taken for granted; it must be constantly crafted and renegotiated. In recent decades, this has been intensified by the City Council's inability or unwillingness to manage and maintain a public estate that was once a desirable – if highly regulated – place to live in mid-twentieth-century Nairobi (Olima 2013: 295). Kaloleni's declining standing as an urban neighbourhood and its exclusion from municipal services mean that now residents must manage for themselves. This has brought significant challenges, but also opportunities for residents to modify and reconfigure their homes. This chapter considers the politics and materialities of such changes, as residents' settlement of Kaloleni shifted it from a model urban neighbourhood to a jumbled, makeshift estate where decrepit infrastructure sits alongside a DIY approach to making a life in the city. It also considers departures and exits: the ways that people come to leave Kaloleni, the connections between the estate and elsewhere, and the possibility of a more fundamental exit in the form of urban regeneration schemes that threaten to demolish Kaloleni completely.

Making a neighbourhood

As one of Nairobi's older neighbourhoods, Kaloleni is close to the city centre. It comes just after the Industrial Area, squeezed in next to City Stadium, a shabby but well-used football field. Reaching Kaloleni from the centre of Nairobi is in theory not hard: take a *matatu* (shared minibus) or *tuk-tuk* from Tom Mboya Street in the centre of town, alight at Burma market and cross Jogoo Road to the entrance of the estate. In practice though, the journey can be somewhat tortuous. Although only a couple of miles, it can take thirty minutes or even more to navigate Nairobi's notoriously jammed streets, where vehicles refuse to recognise the authority of traffic lights or one-way streets. Wheezing and snarling, the *matatu* eventually reaches 'Burma', a hodgepodge market of food stalls, butcheries, second-hand clothes, fresh fruit and vegetables. It dates from the 1930s, founded as the market for the African quarter of Eastlands, and some of the colonial-era red-tiled stalls still remain, though the tidy rows have now been disordered by an infill of informal kiosks. The market has leaked out on to the side of Jogoo Road, filling the dusty bank of the bus stop.

From the hectic intensity of Burma, arriving in Kaloleni – via a footbridge over Jogoo Road – is a relief. Dusty and relatively green, Kaloleni can at first seem forgotten and sleepy. Small bungalows are set back from the main road, interspersed with swathes of corrugated iron structures that make it difficult to get any sense of the layout of the neighbourhood. There are no through roads, so the noise of *matatus* and markets remains at a distance, and people stroll unhurriedly along the worn-out paths. A few sheep may wander past, foraging amid the drifts of plastic detritus and household cast-offs that litter the estate. The bedraggled scene gives little impression that this was once a model estate planned to create a new type of urban African; one hoped to form the basis of the future colonial city.

In a discussion about his family's history, an elderly man named Eddy described a very different scene of arrival into the streets of Kaloleni:

> My father was among the first, can I say, tenants of Kaloleni, in 1946 ... First, he came to Nairobi from Siaya [western Kenya] in 1928, as a boy. Then he was eleven. He came to work with his uncle [who] was a dhobi, doing ironing and washing at Pumwani.[1] And then, after a while my father was recruited into the army, I think it was 1938 or 1939 ... And he stayed in the army for I think six years or seven years. That is 1946, he left, and then he came to Kaloleni. He came on foot! With only a handcart. They were army men and this place had discipline, that army discipline – if you didn't follow the rules then you were out.

Eddy's remarks draw connections between the movement of rural Kenyans to Nairobi and their continued passage into the Second World War. Many of Kaloleni's first residents were war veterans, having served in the Kings African Rifles. This military legacy followed them back to Nairobi and, in Eddy's telling, helped to shape their experience of a regulated post-war urban life. Though Eddy's family have an

---

[1] Pumwani was then one of the 'Native Villages' of Nairobi, outside of the formal centre but mostly tolerated by the colonial municipality (see White 1990).

unusually long history of residence in Nairobi going back to the 1920s, his account described a fairly common narrative of managed relocation among Kaloleni's first residents.

In the early colonial period, there were not many housing options available to Africans in Nairobi. Up until the Second World War, Nairobi had been regarded as the domain of European administration and of colonial settlement. The city was marked by decidedly ambiguous attitudes towards Africans' urban presence: while they provided essential labour, notably for the railways and in domestic service, in theory at least urban Africans were not meant to exist at all. Men were only tolerated in the city as temporary migrant labourers, and their wives and children were expected to remain on the rural reserves (Hake 1977). Formal housing – when it could be accessed – was in dormitory accommodation calculated in bed spaces; there was no provision for family housing. 'Until the 1950s, colonial pass laws and the very limited official provision for housing were designed to constrain single men to generally brief periods of work in towns, as distinct from living out their lives there' (Lonsdale 2001: 212). In reality however, there were many men as well as women permanently resident in the city, far too many to be housed in the meagre settlements that were then available (White 1990).

In the late 1930s, growing labour unrest and several general strikes rocked the colonial administrations in Nairobi and Mombasa (Stren 1978; Cooper 1983). The strikes provoked the worst urban insecurity the colonial government had seen and were in part stimulated by poor urban living conditions. This forced municipal authorities to acknowledge the sheer numbers of Africans living in urban areas, and a number of reports were ordered into the conditions of housing, welfare and employment of Africans in urban areas. Slowly, this awareness began to manifest into official concern that overcrowded and unplanned housing was not only unsanitary but breeding further urban unrest. In 1941, Dr Anderson, Chairman of the Municipal Public Health Committee, and Tom Askwith, Municipal Native Affairs Officer, both argued that urban Africans could no longer be ignored, and that settled, family housing would improve self-identity as well as security (see Anderson 2001: 145; Lewis 2000: 138–9). Reinforced by increasing complaints from employers about lack of accommodation for their 'native' employees, urban migration of educated Africans seeking employment in low-level white-collar roles, and fears of disease outbreaks, the government began to take action. In the mid-1940s, the Council began to imagine a new future for Nairobi, in which housing – identified as one of the causes – also became seen as one of the cures for urban disorder.

In Nairobi, as in other colonial cities, the management of dirt and disease, the enforcement of municipal order and racial segregation converged in new planning agendas that sought to remake the city

(Hake 1977; White 1990: Chapter 3; Achola 2001). The Council brought in a South African team to develop a new urban plan for the city, resulting in the *Master Plan for a Colonial Capital* (Thornton White et al. 1948). The drafters of the Master Plan saw spatial design as a civilising influence, linking the council's twin concerns of ensuring order and fostering modernity. Wide boulevards lined with trees, manicured parks and a boating lake would create a European-style 'City in the Sun', to be the envy of the empire. Rather than just increasing provision of rudimentary accommodation for Africans, administrative thought and practice began to shift towards a more welfarist agenda, one aspect of which was to develop communities through permanent housing provision (Lewis 2000). Building urban communities, with the stabilising presence of wives and children, became regarded as a better way to exert authority and develop the colonial capital for the future (Ogilvie 1946). An appropriately orderly neighbourhood plan meant that 'from early childhood the ways of modern, regular, timebound life can be instilled, and need not be acquired arduously in later life', enabling the production of model colonial subjects (Thornton White et al. 1948: 7).

This was the climate in which the plans for Kaloleni began to take shape. In July 1942, W. W. Ridout, the Acting Town Clerk, wrote to the Commissioner for Local Government regarding the question of housing for Africans in Nairobi. Ridout observed that 'the Municipal Council of Nairobi has for several years seen the need to develop its native villages on more progressive lines ... it is now accepted that much of the housing which already exists ... is in type and layout inadequate for the present standards of Native life'.[2]

Instead, the emphasis should be on social and recreational spaces that would foster stronger communities and uplift the wellbeing and morality of Africans in Nairobi. The Council 'wishes to build homes for the African in the town and not mere houses' Ridout continued. 'It wishes to develop semi-rural villages on garden suburb lines, to expend more on the laying out of open spaces and on social recreation'.[3] Kaloleni was to be modelled on a nostalgic ideal of an English village and intended to produce a new community of urban Africans. It was envisioned that appropriate material environments would inculcate aspirations of modernity and domesticity modelled on suburban Britain, while producing subjects obedient to colonial hierarchies of race and power. Residents of places like Kaloleni were intended to become role models of self-improvement, prototypes of the urban colonial subject of the future.

The necessary finance was raised from the Colonial Development and Welfare fund and construction of Kaloleni began in 1943. The first resi-

[2] Kenya National Archives (hereafter KNA), File JA/4/26: Native Affairs Department, Municipal Council Housing 1941–43, folio 54A
[3] KNA, JA/4/26, folio 54A

Figure 3 The original plan for Kaloleni estate, designed by A. J. S. Hutton. (From G. C. W. Ogilvie, *The Housing of Africans in Urban Areas of Kenya*. Nairobi: Kenya Information Office, 1946)

dents began to occupy the houses from 1946. Yet despite the new municipal housing agenda, Nairobi's housing supply never caught up with the ever-growing demand (Anderson 2001: 147). This meant that it was not long before getting a house in Kaloleni was difficult: despite the relatively high rent, as it was one of the most spacious and well-maintained neighbourhoods that were then accessible to Africans, there was competition for tenancies. By the 1950s, Kaloleni was home to a tiny but growing African middle class, including civil servants, teachers, accountants and clerks, as well as the first African mayor of Nairobi. As Eddy described it to me, 'this was the best estate for the Africans at that particular time … let me say the elites of the Africans lived here'.

Traces of past futures

Today, crumbling and in places dilapidated, Kaloleni's old atmosphere of prestige is no longer obvious. The planned future of the colonial past has become churned into a more makeshift landscape. But within this dirty and disrupted neighbourhood, the vestiges and influence of colonial planning are not hard to trace. The project's British architect, A. J. S. Hutton, designed the estate according to the planning principles of the garden city, as originally developed by Ebenezer Howard in late Victorian England (Howard 1902). This influence is clearly apparent in the concentric circle design of Kaloleni, with radial paths spanning out from a village centre like spokes on a wheel – a common feature in many garden city suburbs elsewhere in the world (Ward 1992, and see Figure 3). Along the pathways, sturdy, stone-block bungalows of one or two bedrooms were arranged in twenty-six subgroupings or courts, identified by letters from A to Z. Keen to avoid the repetitive grid of identical units and harsh right angles of previous housing schemes in Nairobi, Hutton proposed a more variegated and organic spatial plan:

> The layout of the houses themselves follows the pattern of a series of blocks comprising small cottages, either singly or in pairs, or as occasion demands, in a block of four dwellings with an access passage … by staggering the building line along roads and paths, monotony is avoided. Variety in design is further obtained by placing differing types of houses in such a manner that out of approximately a dozen type designs it will not be apparent that there are forty houses of the same type scattered throughout a scheme of four hundred and thirty-five houses.[4]

Today's residents refer to the groupings of bungalows as 'lines', as in *laini ya A* (line A), *laini ya B* (line B) and so on, though they are far

[4] KNA, JA/4/26, folio 176C: A. J. S. Hutton, Memorandum to the Local Government Housing Committee, 11 June 1943

from linear. Each line forms a rough loop or court, the houses facing outwards and backing on to a communal grassy area to the rear which formed the centre of each court. Many of these communal spaces are now inaccessible: they have been subdivided and fenced by residents of the main houses to create private backyards, which many have filled with self-built corrugated iron (*mabati*) structures (see Figures 4 and 5). The lines of the estate are arranged around a central circle of what was once grass – the so-called village green – around which are shops, a small welfare clinic (now standing empty), a post office and the large, though crumbling, social hall and library.

Hutton's orderly plan was accompanied by strict regulations. Many residents remember a stringent set of policies and behaviours to which all were expected to comply. Rules included compulsory house fumigation, no gardening or keeping of animals, no walking on the grass, mandatory registration of all overnight guests, the restriction of paint to a council-approved palette of three colours and absolutely no modification to the houses' structure. New tenants had to be approved by the Estate Officer – up until the late 1950s, a position occupied by a white official. Residents remained strictly tenants, subject to the inspections of the Estate Officer, and – as Eddy's remarks above indicate – there was an air of military discipline about the management of the estate. Saleh, an elderly man regarded as a fount of historical knowledge about Kaloleni, remembered a strict regime: 'The Estate Officer, he was going round and checking everything, that there is no paper, there is no mud anywhere. ... If he finds anything ... any dirt and whatever, you assemble to his office ... So it was – there was order, a lot of order'.

Like Saleh, many of the older residents today tend to describe the colonial period primarily in terms of its order and cleanliness – with neat lawns, playing fields and daily inspections – rather than as defined by intrusive scrutiny. Houses tended to be allocated to those who were considered relatively skilled and educated, with preference to those working for the City Council. In practice, this meant that many residents had already been exposed to certain colonial ways of being and doing, codified behaviours and practices that would, officials hoped, be further reinforced through the fabric of the estate. In this sense Kaloleni is one example of the myriad ways that, across the empire, British authorities tried to realise the 'domestication' and 'civilisation' of colonial subjects through the design of daily life (Hall 2002; see also Comaroff and Comaroff 1991). This was a project into which residents were themselves co-opted, becoming low-level teachers or assistants within the estate. In this sense it also offered possibilities for new ways of being, of forming new identities within the shifting terrain of a hierarchical colonial administration (see Cooper and Stoler 1997).

One woman who took advantage of this situation was Sarah, for whom life in Kaloleni was also an opportunity to craft a new sensibility.

In November 2013, when I first met her, she had been living in Kaloleni for fifty-three years. Her arrival into the estate in 1960 came during the last years of British rule; she was newly married to an accounts clerk in the City Council who had been allocated a Kaloleni house. She was 'fresh off the bus', having come direct from her rural home in Western Province: 'I didn't even know Kiswahili' she told me. Today she still lives in the same house, now with her youngest daughter. Her husband has passed away and her other children and grandchildren are far-flung: from Tanzania to California. Her house is near the centre of the estate, close to the central circle of shops within what the colonial planners referred to as 'the village green'. Her home is clean and bright, with pale blue crocheted doilies covering most of the surfaces. Though her two-bedroom home felt spacious compared to others, she assured me this was a new atmosphere, having until recently been home to ten people: herself, two children and an assortment of grandchildren. Her front room is dominated by a large dresser stuffed with crockery, knickknacks, family photographs and an array of thermos flasks. This conspicuous display of doilies and domesticity brought to mind 1950s suburban England. This, it turned out, had been a major influence on her early life thanks to colonial home economics classes that had been taught in Kaloleni.[5] Through the course of my fieldwork I visited her home regularly, where, seated on a plump sofa, she served me tea from a doily-covered teapot and regaled me with stories.

Though she was young and unused to city life, Sarah quickly became a fixture in the estate. She had had some vocational training in tailoring and sewing at a mission school near her rural home and, through her husband's connections in the council, she got work with *Maendeleo ya Wanawake* [Women's Development]. MYWO, as it is known, was run by the colonial municipal Welfare Office to instil appropriate forms of domesticity in African women. Under the watchful eye of a white British woman – 'her name? No, that's long gone my dear' – Sarah tutored other young African wives in knitting, sewing and crochet; they produced baby bonnets and cardigans from patterns sent over from Britain. Later, when she had herself acquired the skills, she also taught cookery: 'Those women only knew *ugali* [thick maize porridge] and *sukuma wiki* [stewed greens] – imagine! We taught them eggs, rice, even the cakes and biscuits'. These classes took place in Kaloleni Social Hall, a relatively grand building at the centre of the estate. It was intended for sanctioned leisure activities and to encourage new types of knowledge among residents: from adult literacy to ballroom dancing, home economics to table tennis. By intervening in the social as well as

[5] There is a large literature on the impact of colonial teaching about hygiene, domesticity and femininity (see for example Hunt 1990; Lindsay 1999; Lewis 2000; Thomas 2003).

the domestic sphere, Kaloleni's planners intended a new type of urban African community to take shape. As her disparaging comments about the skills of other wives suggest, Sarah remembers her early years in Kaloleni with fondness; she is quite nostalgic for a time she recalls as orderly and structured. 'There were rules – ah! So many! – but things were organised. It was not this mess you see now.'

But not all residents took the regulations of the municipal welfare agenda to heart in this way. From the outset, the way that Kaloleni was occupied started to undo certain aspects of its design, and archival research shows that Nairobi's housing schemes were not necessarily filled with the ideal, amenable urban subjects of the colonial imagination. Tensions frequently arose between the council and African residents seen to be flouting the rules of their tenancy. There were disputes over subletting rooms, some tenants opened up informal shops or *dukas* on the circulation roads, and unofficial milk vendors undercut the prices of the government supplies available in the shopping centre (Makachia 2013). Cumulatively, such small contraventions could undermine colonial intentions embedded in the plan. The centralised design of the estate, with shops and amenities placed at the heart of the radial streets, was intended to foster a village-like community, but this was in part neutralised by the opening up of informal commercial activity across the estate.

The social hall, intended as a place for the education of tenants and the cultivation of sanctioned leisure pursuits deemed appropriate for a new urban community, also began to be used for other types of activity (Frederiksen 1992). Already by the late 1940s, it was at the heart of emerging nationalist politics, becoming an important meeting place for activists, and known locally as the Houses of Parliament. In 1950, a formative meeting was held there, which agreed an African boycott of the civic celebrations marking Nairobi's royal charter and new city status (Frederiksen 2001: 229). In addition to these new urban political affiliations, Kaloleni residents also maintained strong ethnic associations as well as links to rural kin and clan. The majority of Kaloleni residents identify as Luos and Luhyas originally from western Kenya, and the hall became the meeting place for ethnic welfare associations that managed arrangements for upcountry funerals or made provision for rural kin (Cohen and Odhiambo 1989: 43 and see Chapter 4). In particular, it was the base of the Luo Union in Nairobi, a powerful diaspora organisation that featured prominent politicians and organised for the welfare of Luo people in the city. The new alliances and coalitions generated by the Union became increasingly significant in the run up to independence (Carotenuto and Luongo 2009: 201–2). Thus, despite the best intentions of the Estate Officer and municipal Welfare Office, life in Kaloleni was never firmly under their control. Residents' needs, aspirations and hopes for the future sought to reroute the form and practice of everyday life. Over time, these incremental shifts gradually accumulated into a vibrant urban landscape in which Africans began to dwell in the city on their own terms.

Tenants and residents

With Kenya's independence from Britain in 1963, this remapping of colonial orderliness was strongly intensified. At Nairobi's City Hall, the politics of the future began to look rather different, and the notion of Kaloleni as a model for the future of the capital was soon forgotten. For Kaloleni's residents, the opening up of previously proscribed areas of the city had a major impact on urban living and the demographics of the estate. As Eddy pointed out, Kaloleni had become home to many of the country's new political and economic elites, from the first African mayor of Nairobi and national government politicians to lawyers and business owners. Areas of Nairobi which had been designated as places of European residency were now accessible, and gradually these more successful residents began to leave Kaloleni for bigger and smarter homes elsewhere, in leafy areas such as Lavington and Muthaiga, while others bought plots of land and began to build their own urban homes (Cohen and Odhiambo 1992). Over time, this meant that the status of the public housing estates, previously the only option of formal housing available to Africans, gradually declined. But, though the aspiration for many residents was to move up and out of Kaloleni, often one sibling stayed behind, meaning the house remained occupied by the next generation of the same family. This 'inheritance' of tenancies has continued, and today many residents are the third or even fourth generation to inhabit what has become regarded as the 'family home'.

Over time, council regulations in the public housing estates were less strictly enforced. Structural adjustment policies from the late 1970s onwards brought the shrinking of the state and the privatisation of many state services. The kleptocratic era of President Moi in the 1980s and 1990s saw the hollowing out of public authority in Kenya at both municipal and national levels, leaving government systems fragmented and corruption rife (Branch and Cheeseman 2009; Mueller 2008). Combined with the privatisation of services, this has led to poor infrastructural investment (Adams et al. 2013). At the level of public housing, this brought a retraction of state oversight, a withdrawal of the council's maintenance of, and investment in, their public housing. For residents, the right to reside in Kaloleni was no longer decided by an Estate Officer, or even by the Housing department at City Hall, but was largely agreed informally, often through personal and familial connections. Houses were exchanged between residents, tenancy cards bought and sold, and houses sublet to less affluent kin. This increasingly unofficial process makes it unsurprising that families have come to feel the neighbourhood 'belongs' to them. However, this sense of belonging is not static, and residents constantly recraft their presence within the estate in various ways.

During my fieldwork in Kaloleni, I lived with Tom and Eunice Nyanya in house Y12. Located down the western side of the estate, perpendicular to Jogoo Road, Y12 previously belonged to the family of Tom's brother-in-law. Tom and his brothers and sisters were all brought up in Kaloleni, in house A20 on the other side of the estate, a house which his father Dominic Nyanya was allocated in the early 1970s. After Tom married Eunice, he negotiated with his elder sister's husband to take over the tenancy card for Y12, and they moved in in 1992. The house has one bedroom, a living room, a small kitchen, a store and a toilet and shower room. Eunice and Tom have three children, who during my fieldwork were aged eleven, seventeen and twenty. Also living with them was Eunice's sister and at least one or two other cousins, nephews or nieces, who variously stayed for extended periods. For 2013–14, the household also included me, meaning there was a minimum of eight people living in a one-bedroom house at any time. This is not an unusual situation in Kaloleni and nor is it new. Tom is one of six children and A20 is also a one-bedroomed design. He and his brothers used to put down mattresses at night to sleep on the floor in the living room while his sisters slept in the tiny kitchen.

With the gradual lapse in oversight by the City Council, these days residents have developed other ways of coping with the lack of space. Even though they are still paying the rent using the tenancy card of Tom's brother-in-law, Tom and Eunice have gradually – within their minimal financial resources – adapted the house to meet their needs. In the mid-1990s, Tom converted the indoor store, a small walk-in space about 1 metre by 2.5 metres, into a 'double decker': a bunk bed that occupied the full size of the store. By the late 1990s, council management had declined further, and some residents had begun to construct *mabati* (corrugated iron) lean-to extensions at the back of the houses to add more space. Due to lack of funds, Tom and Eunice built their extension slowly, gradually adding sections. What was the back door of the original house now opens into this space, which has been partitioned to make two small bedrooms and a storage area. One bedroom is shared by the women, and the other has two bunk beds for the boys. The 'double decker' then reverted to a store, until 2013 when I came along. Tom and I cleaned it out and, with the help of a couple of other residents, rigged it up for me; a tiny literal bedroom (there was no floorspace at all) in which I slept, my belongings stored on shelves above my head and under the bed.

These kinds of modifications are now fairly common across the estate, and most of the main houses have some kind of *mabati* extension that supplements the sleeping space of the original house. More recently, some residents have also added other types of structure. The communal spaces at the rear of the houses have been enclosed into backyards, and within these many residents of the main houses have built single-room structures, also of *mabati*, that they rent out to supplement their income. Although the word 'extension' (in English) is used for both, the lean-to structures are regarded as distinct from the extensions that are rented out to others. The lean-tos are primarily used for family members, whereas the rental extensions can be sublet by anyone; they are physically separate from the main house and usually have their own entranceway (see Figure 4). Other extensions have also sprung up along the pathways, and are used as kiosks, small hair salons, cafes and other informal businesses, including one or two who have managed to get a satellite TV connection and enterprisingly charge people to come and watch English Premier League football matches (see Figure 5).

The net result of all these incremental modifications and constructions is that there is no longer a clear line between formality and informality in Kaloleni. As highlighted in the Introduction, observers of Nairobi and other African cities have tended to distinguish between the formal city, where citizens are more-or-less subject to the governance of the state, and what Hake has described as a parallel 'self-help city' of informal settlements, where people live without access to state services and there is not even a pretence at official construction regulation (Hake 1977). Kaloleni – and the other 'formal' housing estates in Eastlands – demonstrate that the artificiality of this distinction. Residents pay rent to the City Council even as they act as unofficial landlords to others. They creatively manage their own residency rights, negotiating and occasionally selling tenancy cards among their own networks. They live in homes that resourcefully synthesise the features of the original 1940s construction with contemporary cheap materials. Making a life in Kaloleni is no longer – if it ever entirely was – demarcated by the strict regulations of the City Council and the estate manager, but relies on a much subtler series of negotiations.

Home improvements

In this way, while residents struggle with infrastructural failure and the retraction of council management, there are also new domestic freedoms to be found. The domestic consequences of lapsed municipal maintenance are countered by other materialities that reveal practices of comfort and care. Opening a front door can reveal the dramatic modification and vivid redecoration of a proud resident's home, while others have hedged and planted beautiful front gardens to create private outdoor space and keep the encroaching rubbish and mud at bay.

Figure 4 Corrugated iron (*mabati*) extensions behind one of the main houses, Line E, April 2014
(Photo: Author)

Figure 5 Many extensions are used as kiosks and cafés, January 2014
(Photo: Author)

Many residents invest considerable time and thought into making their homes inviting and cosy, painting them in bright colours, inside and out – a dramatic contrast from the strict colonial tenancy agreements that specified a restricted palette. Boniface, now in his forties, inherited his house from his father and immediately set about doing renovations: 'The house has changed a lot because what happened when my dad decided he's going to go back to the rural home upcountry, this house was unpainted. The City Council used [whitewash] ... and then the windows, the frames were not painted'.

Boniface's house now is colourful and spacious; he has removed several interior walls and reorganised the layout. What was the kitchen is now an extra bedroom, and the new kitchen is housed in lean-to at the rear. He has given considerable thought to his use of colour, explaining:

> That red over there, that was like, I didn't get the right colour, the right shade of the red. I wanted what we call ruby red, but this is what we can call crimson red but since the *fundi* [handyman] was here I was like let's just paint this and get this over with ... I like purple for the bedroom because to me it lightens ... it's a vibrant colour. It's a polite colour. Maybe it inclines more to the ladies, but I decided let me just do it, no problem with that. Then out here I did a blue and this blue was initially deep blue like this but I bought white paint so I just mixed it till it gave me that blue that I wanted. I call it milky blue, that's my name for it.

Helima's home is another that reveals a great deal of care and attention to detail. A Muslim woman of around sixty years, she now lives alone in the house in which she grew up. She has undertaken extensive renovations, modifying the interior and exterior in her desire to create a warm, cosy home. Her house is surrounded by a neat clipped hedge and a bright yellow, homemade picket fence. Inside she has added a varnished wood ceiling, tiled the floors and added a modern bathroom, even though – as in all the houses – there is rarely water running in the pipes. She has a selection of well-worn but carefully selected furniture, and crafted all the soft furnishings herself, using the skills she learned as a young woman when she studied upholstery. These are hand-sewn in coordinated shades of coffee, biscuit, ivory and dusky pink, balanced by splashes of turquoise, the colours and textures chosen with care to create the kind of ambience she desired. She was proud of being fastidious and exacting, and explicit about her desire to make the house feel more like a home. Like Boniface, Helima sees colour as very important to this process, as was clear from her description of how she chose her wall paint: 'He brought a chart and I said I am not satisfied with the chart ... I wanted a colour which is, you know, when you apply and you go to that house, you feel warm. You know, homely. He said ok fine and he mixed this one'.

For Helima, her attempts to create homeliness in Kaloleni were unequivocally about transmuting the colonial limitations on homemaking that she saw as restricting the kinds of persons residents were able to be. As she explained:

> When my mum and dad lived here it was all standard [i.e. across the estate] it was necessary that City Council come and paint for them. The colours were bad! … there were no ceilings … you were not free [to do what you want] … then I sat and said, 'now what kind of life was that?!' … I want to live in a beautiful house.

Thus, as well as being pragmatic responses to their abandonment by the council, such DIY projects of modification and reconfiguration take advantage of the decline of state presence in Kaloleni to 'possess' the houses more fully. For Helima, the process of making a home, of crafting and curating colours and textures, has been transformative not just of her material environment but of herself as well. Through material practices of homemaking, residents have upended restrictive colonial architectures designed to produce certain types of amenable bodies and express their new-found capacity to make decisions about their homes and exert a sense of proprietorship. Residents' engagements with the architectural fabric of Kaloleni not only intermingles the present with the traces of the colonial past but is also hoped to be generative of future selves, as they remake their homes for the future. Municipal misman-agement – though unwelcome – has enabled new ways of making a life, or at least thinking about potential ways to make such lives possible. In this way, the cumulative landscape of Kaloleni has allowed residents to make themselves at home, and to consider a future of urban presence.

Extensions

Not all residents feel themselves so rooted in the estate; the shifting terrain of management and tenancy has also generated more tempo-rary forms of habitation. Rhoda is a young woman in her twenties and a newcomer to Kaloleni. Previously she had lived with her partner and two small children in a rented flat in Kayole, a neighbourhood further out of the city. Now separated, she had come to Kaloleni with her chil-dren, looking for a cheap and convenient place to live. She chose Kalo-leni as she had some friends there, and it was through them that she was linked up with a resident of one of Kaloleni's 'main houses'. He had built a number of extensions in his backyard and agreed to rent her a room on a monthly basis. Rhoda is part of an expansion in Kaloleni's popu-lation as new residents have once again started to flow into the estate, primarily to occupy the extensions. Known as *watu wakukam*, literally 'people that come', these newcomers have contributed to a demographic spike that means Kaloleni's population is many times higher than its original intended capacity. In November 2014, I estimated that there were around six extensions per main house, though since then they have proliferated even further.

Rhoda's extension was adjacent to the house I lived in, and over time we got to know each other. When I first met her, she was 'tarmacking', an evocative Nairobi expression referring to the endless walking required when looking for a job. She chose Kaloleni partly because she could walk to town and save money while she was job-hunting. Her older sister was helping pay the rent and Rhoda was also trying to send her oldest child to nursery school, though she was constantly in trouble for not paying the fees. Her situation was hardly ideal, she acknowledged, especially for her children – 'this is not a good place – no proper bathroom, the water is expensive – but I'm trying'.

Although the extensions are the newest structures within the estate, in some ways they seem the most decayed. *Mabati* rusts quickly and the extensions have been cheaply constructed. They are not built with an eye to permanence, not just because the owners cannot afford quality materials but because extensions are officially illegal and their owners wish to minimise their losses in case the council demands their demolition. It is not just the materials of the extensions that are temporary, so too are their occupiers; their manner of being in place is very different to the more longstanding families and has not generated the same sense of belonging. Many, like Rhoda, have not arrived in Kaloleni with any notion of having reached home, but are looking for a temporary fix to their living situation. Some are students looking for a cheap room close to the city centre, others are young families starting out in life and some have lost their homes elsewhere. But despite this transience, life in the extensions also generates its own traces and residues. Not only does the design of the extensions alter the flow of the estate, blocking off former pathways and sightlines and introducing new points of connection, but the makeshift quality of the construction means it is the tenants of the extensions who often bear the brunt of failing infrastructures and the ad hoc practices of their landlords.

Rhoda's one-room *mabati* home was sparsely furnished. There was one bunk bed on which she slept on the top and the two children on the bottom, a faded maroon sofa, an ancient TV that hardly worked, a small kerosene stove and some utensils. One bare lightbulb hung in the middle, an informal power connection rigged up to the mains by the landlord. This connection often went out during storms or when her landlord failed to pay his electricity bill. Frequently we sat together chatting in the darkness, using only the light on our mobile phones. The latrine and shower room – also *mabati* – were shared between her landlord's six extensions. These had no running water and were poorly connected to Kaloleni's original sewerage system, meaning flooding was common, along with seepage of more noxious substances. Despite this rather depressing material environment, Rhoda was full of hope for the future. Her 'tarmacking' was also an attempt to tread a path out of the dirt and decrepitude. She saw Kaloleni as a stepping stone, a transient situation rather than a permanent home. Coming to Kaloleni had been a setback, a force of circumstance, she said, but 'I'm starting over. I'll be out of here soon'.

Departures and exits

It is not only the *watu wakukam* who are looking further afield, seeking new horizons beyond Kaloleni. Despite the longevity of many residents and their more recent ventures into home improvement, few see Kaloleni as the only place they will live during their lives. Older people tend to aspire to retire to a rural 'home', a place where many were born, where they retain extended kinship networks and may have invested energy and finances to build a house and compound. Many younger residents, meanwhile, no longer maintain these linguistic and geographic connections, and do not regard Kaloleni as desirable in the way it was to earlier generations. Their aspirations are more urban, and many seek to establish themselves by purchasing land and building a home in the emerging suburbs around Nairobi. In the meantime, some are also seeking employment opportunities further afield: I was frequently called on to help with applications for temporary work in the Middle East and Asia. As such, the story of Kaloleni is as much the story of departures as it is of arrivals, whether to old homelands or new environs.

Thus, residents' lifeways encompass Kaloleni – are often enriched by dwelling in it – but are hoped not to be delimited by it. From their perspective, my research encountered them in the 'Kaloleni phase' of their lives, and the stories that were shared with me often contained caveats along the lines of 'It is good you came this month, as by next I will be at home' or 'You are lucky to find me – I'm just waiting for my papers then I leave'. One man laughed when he returned from three months working on a Doha construction site to find me still in Kaloleni. 'Some of us are trying to leave but you're just staying! You must be enjoying. For me, no. What would I do?' he asked.

Of course, there is many a slip between people's dreams and what happens in practice, and mobility is not always easy to achieve. Blockages and obstacles that obstruct the flow of a desired lifecourse were recounted in many residents' biographical narratives. The extremely high levels of youth unemployment speak to this sense of stuckness, of an inability to flow out of the estate, to move on with one's life. Many young men, in particular, expressed their frustration at feeling their horizons reduced to the boundaries of Kaloleni. For some, departure from the estate does not come until after death, when even the poorest families will usually strive to send the body upcountry for burial (see Chapter 4).

There are not many elderly people resident in Kaloleni, as by that age both men and women tend to have to retired and 'gone home' to a house on inherited family land built with the proceeds of a lifetime's urban employment. During my fieldwork, I met several older individuals and couples who were preparing to make this move, and I was sufficiently intrigued by it to extend my fieldwork to include ex-Kalolenians in their rural homes (explored in Chapter 4). Stephen and Jemimah are a couple in their sixties, both from the Luo ethnic group, who trace their homeland to the region of south-western Kenya near to Lake Victoria. When I interviewed them in May 2014 they were laying plans for their departure. 'I'm thinking of home in the near future ... I've got my home, I have a piece of land', Stephen told me. Jemimah reinforced this sense of return saying: 'You know, after retirement that is when we can go back home and leave these houses with the children ... our children are going to remain here'. Stephen had a clear sense of passing things on to the next generation, that town life is for the young: 'I've been in town since 1967 ... and once somebody is tired of town, you can't admire it, you know?' He intends for his adult son, Calvin, to 'inherit' the Kaloleni house. It's time now, he said, 'to leave it to the young ones, because I've enjoyed enough'.

Calvin, whose commitment to hustling we encountered in the Intro-duction, has other ideas for his future. Echoing the sentiment of young people caught up in housing troubles the world over, he hates that he is in his twenties and still lives at his parents' home, along with his sisters. The house is small, only one bedroom. 'We are squeezed', he told me, 'we have to put down mattresses and sleep in the sitting room'. If his parents depart, he'll stay in Kaloleni 'for convenience ... we the chil-dren, we are going to remain here and it's going to cut costs. Probably it will cut costs more than if I decide to move out'. But in the longer term he dreams of something different. He explained to me that for his dad's generation Kaloleni was desirable, 'when it opened, people aspired to live here, it was an achievement'. Instead, he wants to 'hustle outside', that is, to go abroad and 'earn dollars'. With this capital he hopes to buy a plot of land in somewhere like Kitengela, one of the emerging suburbs on the edge of Nairobi that are extending the city out onto the eastern plains. 'I want to build my own house', he said. 'Imagine coming home to a house that is yours'.

Nevertheless, like many Kalolenians, Calvin still acknowledges a strong affinity with the estate, saying, 'this is where we come from. It's been influencing most of us. It made us the way you see me now'. Residents' plans for their futures come in many shapes and sizes, as the differences between Calvin and his dad imply. Whether or not these hopes include leaving the estate, many residents – past and present –

feel a deep connection to the place, a sense of belonging generated from its landscape. This sense of place and history, as well as questions of mobility and departure, frame the way that individuals and families plan ahead: how they negotiate unknown futures, how they try to turn aspirations into realities. But residents' capacity to drive the direction of their lives – and the future of Kaloleni itself – has recently been thrown into doubt by news of the potentially radical redevelopment of the whole neighbourhood. The looming potentiality of Vision 2030 is perceived as a threat to urban presence, generating anxieties of eviction and erasure.

Uncertain prospects

On 14 May 2014, an article appeared in the *Nairobi News* paper with the headline 'In Comes Chinese Money, Out Go Eastlands Estates'. The article describes a Memorandum of Understanding signed between Nairobi County government and two private Chinese companies to build 55,000 apartments on the site of current council housing, as part of the city's 'urban renewal' programme. Kaloleni was listed as one of the targeted estates. The article provoked deep anxiety among residents since it announced the new apartments are to be designed, constructed and then sold by the companies, in effect suggesting that this will be the end of public housing in this area of Nairobi. The article stimulated an outpouring of discussion and apprehensions, but it was only one of a range of overlapping and sometimes conflicting announcements of redevelopment projects that have emerged in recent years (explored further in Chapter 6).

These announcements come as part of the wider Vision 2030 initiative and the reinvention of Nairobi as a 'world class African metropolis' (Government of Kenya 2008). In 2013 the Nairobi County government completed the development of Nairobi Integrated Urban Plan, or NIUPLAN for short, a new technical masterplan for infrastructural development that was completed in conjunction with JICA, the Japanese development agency (Nairobi City County 2014). Nested rather deeper within the NIUPLAN is mention of an 'Eastlands Renewal Strategy' which plans to combat so-called urban decay in the city. Exactly what this strategy will mean in practice, however, is hard to tell: announcements and documentation are riddled with contradictions, and exactly what will be demolished, what will be built, and how residents will be affected remains unclear. For example, though the 2014 *Nairobi News* article suggests new housing will be for sale rather than rental, the government has also stated that residents will not be evicted, despite the fact that very few have the capital needed to purchase property. The project, titled the Nairobi Metropolitan Services Improvement

Project (NaMSIP), is partly facilitated by the World Bank in conjunction with both the Nairobi city authorities and the national Ministry of Nairobi Metropolitan Development. These different units all have different agendas and are also highly politicised, leading to considerable delays and hiatuses with the scheme. Their various tiers of intersecting and sometimes competing authority do not shed much clarity on the direction of the strategy (see Myers 2014). Documents relating to the tendering process complicate the position of council estate residents still further, with one stating that an output of the tendered consultation must be a 'framework to guide the re-settlement of sitting tenants' (NaMSIP 2013: 12).

As yet there have been no final official statements about what the future of Eastlands will look like, and no plans have been released. Residents remain ambivalent on what the future holds: on the one hand, urban renewal might offer a brighter future if it means increasing employment, raising living standards and reducing poverty, but many are anxious that it will happen at their expense. One professional Nairobi architect told me this scheme will be 'the biggest gentrification [project] in Africa', bringing the displacement of thousands of poorer households in favour of high net-worth renters and buyers. He and many others also pointed to the problems and scandals linked to other recent housing schemes in Nairobi, such as the 'upgrading' of part of the large slum Kibera (see also IFRA 2012). Substandard concrete highrises were quickly thrown up, many units of which were later revealed to have been allocated to wealthier Nairobi figures rather than residents of the slum, who then rented the apartments back to them (Rigon 2014).

The possibility of demolition and eviction loomed over this research and framed its course in various ways. The convoluted, shape-shifting, often secretive character of Kenyan politics means that getting a clear picture of administrative plans and proposals is never easy. This lack of clarity is often frustrating – for residents, as well as for researchers – but it is also a reminder of the partial ways in which news travels and the future is understood. The planners and technocrats of the World Bank, City Hall and national government carve up the Nairobi area on a map, often ignoring the peopled reality of the city, as they plot the courses of new highways, rail networks and technoparks. Meanwhile residents in Kaloleni grapple with the fallout of such visions, seizing on scraps of confused and confusing detail that they come across, incorporating them into the fabric of everyday life that continues to roll forward despite the gaze of planning. One resident, Hassan, put it like this:

> We are waiting to see. We are still wondering about that plan, but I don't know if they'll follow or they'll tell us to just go. So we don't know. If they upgrade it can be ok, but if it is 'Oh come with that sum, that deposit' to get allocation, then you will not migrate into that

house. How? You will fill their forms but then their own person will get. We hear a lot of stories. We are thinking what they could do to us.

These uncertain futures, just as much as Kaloleni's rich past, are a part of the generation of place, a sense of belonging, informing the flows and attachments that the estate provokes. Residents' stance on the street treads new desire lines through this uncertainty, ones that do not necessarily obey the route of the plan, but are founded in the environing material, social and temporal world of the estate. It is these pathways, in all their messy, improvised texture, that the rest of the book seeks to follow.

2

Dirt, Remains and Decay

In Nairobi, July is the 'cold' season, when the overnight rain is persistent and the mornings are foggy and drizzly before the sun is properly up.[1] Early on one such July morning in 2014 I carefully picked my way down a flooded, swampy path through Kaloleni. Slowly making my way to meet someone on the other side of the estate, I passed people sheltering in doorways, swathed in scarves against the cold. The waterlogged path forced my gaze to the ground as I attempted to avoid a slide into the greenish ooze. Stepping slowly and gingerly, my sightline reduced to the thick malodorous sludge at my feet, I contemplated how much more unpleasant Kaloleni is in wet weather than in dry. Rain brings mud and flooding (see Figure 6). The pace of movement alters drastically. Perspective narrows, life becomes slower, people stay at home more, the cold, damp evenings no longer conducive to sitting outside and chatting.

In many African contexts, rain has positive connotations. In Kenya, you will often hear people say *'mvua ni baraka'* – rain is blessings. In rural areas, rain is essential for successful cultivation and harvesting and so is often both fundamental to, and a metaphor for, fertility and reproduction (Sanders 2008). The power of rain and of those with the authority to command it means the politics of rain and rainmaking is an old theme in the scholarship of (especially, southern) Africa (see, for example, Dornan 1927; Schapera 1971). More recently, Fontein noted how in rural southern Zimbabwe rain has enabled hope for the future to be translated to optimism (2015: 16–19). Amid the violence and confusion of Zimbabwe's fast-track land reform, sky-high inflation and widespread hunger, one season of good rainfall and a plentiful harvest allowed people to be optimistic about the future. The tentative uncertainty of land reform during earlier years of drought was reconfigured into promises of abundance and fertility as the rain promised the fulfilment of local aspirations, centred on access to land (Fontein 2015: 20).

---

[1] An earlier version of this chapter was first published in 2018, in *Social Dynamics* 44(1), as 'Accumulating history: Dirt, remains and urban decay in Nairobi'. I am grateful for permission to include parts of it here.

Figure 6 Rain in Kaloleni brings mud and flooding, March 2014
(Photo: Author)

In Kaloleni, rain is not so optimistic, but it is efficacious. In this dilapidated public housing estate, rather than fruitfulness and plenty, rain materialises infrastructural failure: the consequences of the City Council's poor management and underinvestment. As Jane Bennett observed of the North American power blackout in 2003, it is sometimes only at times of breakdown that infrastructural assemblages make their presence felt (2005). When running smoothly they are invisible, quietly facilitating mundane processes of daily life. In dry weather, Kaloleni's infrastructural failings remain mostly covert, but during the rain the deterioration makes itself known, intruding on people's lives. Paths, which in the dry season can be quite pretty as they wend their way between tall unkempt grasses, in the rain rapidly deteriorate and become barely passable. The neighbourhood's central roads, their asphalt long gone, quickly become flooded. Children track mud through the front doors, bringing the muck outside into the houses. Frogs – considered dirty vermin akin to rats – chorus through the night, mosquitoes begin to breed in stagnant pools. A fierce trade in gumboots gets going around the fringes of the estate. The old *mitaaro* – open drainage ditches – choke up with rubbish that council workers no longer come to clear away. Swirling with rainwater, they sometimes overflow into stinking muddy pools. The much-decayed sewerage system, unmaintained for decades, is today groaning under the strain of more recent ad hoc connections. The rains stretch this system to breaking point, and the waste water seeps into already flooded paths. A kind of damp lethargy hangs over the estate; the simple acts of daily life become hard work.

This chapter considers what dirt and decay can reveal about urban life in Nairobi, and the way that nonhuman substances and materialities are also imbricated in the making of place. While Kaloleni remains vibrant and home to around eighteen thousand Nairobians, since the City Council's 'sheer abdication of responsibilities', it has become very rundown (Olima 2013: 295). Accumulations of broken-down infrastructure, along with the affective presence of mud, rubbish and decay, intrude on everyday life, constraining and producing certain atmospheres, attitudes and politics (see Figures 7 and 8). These substances are not regarded as a natural or intrinsic part of everyday life, but rather they reveal and make manifest particular histories and grievances. As such, they are situated: this is the dirt *of* Kaloleni, of a place, of a community. Its accretion then, while not usually welcomed, does tell particular narratives, enabling alternate insights.

This decaying materiality is both of the past, in the sense that it is an accretion built up over time, but it is also inherently future-oriented: many of the by-products of human activity will long outlive human lifespans. Contrary to much of the scholarship on the subject, therefore, I argue that decay should not be conflated with ruination, loss

Figure 7 Remains of broken streetlights from different eras, November 2013
(Photo: Author)

Figure 8 In the absence of municipal services, rubbish accumulates in the streets, May 2014
(Photo: Author)

or oblivion. In Kaloleni at least, decay is a process of accumulation: it produces *more*, not less. This excess, illuminating yet obdurate, constitutes a form of material history. As historical traces, this dirt does not become inert, but remains active, erupting into the present. The chapter also considers what might happen if and when such deposits are wiped away as part of proposed urban renewal projects. I draw a distinction between urban decay as a category of governance and control, in which certain communities are labelled as 'deteriorated' or 'failing', and urban decay as a material process. I suggest that part of the perceived threat of urban renewal is the obliteration of a landscape inscribed with residents' histories and stories. Community apprehension over Vision 2030 is in part an anxiety about censorship: the oblivion and loss usually associated with ruination in fact emanate not so much from decay as from its elimination.

Mud and filth

During my research in Kaloleni in 2013 and 2014, rain always led to mud, and so to dirty shoes, clothes and floors. However straightforward a sequence this might seem, for some residents it was regarded as an abomination. For older residents, the presence of mud in Kaloleni epitomised a regression from previous regimes of orderliness. During a conversation with Eddy, whose familial arrival in Kaloleni was described in Chapter 1, he bade me to imagine myself back in the Kaloleni of the past: 'You've been in Kaloleni, you can see the ruins. But … try to think exactly how it was. You can see that it was tarmacked up to the house directly, I never stepped on mud from nursery school! It was tarmacked right from the door. And then the litters, they were picked one by one, you see?' In Eddy's mind, mud is an interloper, a new, unwelcome, reality of life in the estate. He invoked the remains of old tarmacked roads as a means of conjuring the order that has been lost. He and many other residents stressed that dirt and mud are not inherent to Kaloleni; are not an unavoidable part of life but rather products of a particular history. In Kaloleni's early days, dirt was managed: various technical interventions from drains to tarmac prevented mud and waste from accumulating. Today, many Kalolenians describe their daily lives in terms of a battle to keep dirt at bay as they try to compensate for the council's dereliction of duty. They feel that their attempts to make a life are being thwarted by the withdrawal of state resources and the perceived failure of the state to fulfil its duties of care.

In conversation with a man named Kish, a third generation Kalolenian who now works mostly in Mombasa but returns to Kaloleni regularly to visit family, he began to complain about the degradation of the estate. Pointing at the roof of his family's home, he said:

You see these tiles, if it was broken, you had to go to the hall, you make a report and then it is replaced. It was quite organised. Any damage to the house, you have to report and it is replaced. That is ... as per colonial, that is how they organised. So people followed that rule up to 1970s, 80s, then things went the other way. Now they decided to neglect the houses so they could get damaged.

Kaloleni residents' sense of neglect at the hands of city authorities finds resonance with the experience of public housing occupants in many areas of the world. The material and social disintegration of post-war council housing in Britain, for example, is often regarded as a consequence of neoliberalism, a retraction of welfarist regimes of governance and a cloistering of the poor on badly neglected estates. In a study of social housing tenants in London, Daniel Miller suggested that over time, the welfarist ideologies manifest in the city's tower blocks undermined tenants' agency, leaving them alienated from and fatalistic about their material environments. The 'cities in the sky' of post-war London council housing were meant to 'liberate [their] inhabitants, who would themselves become modern in the mirror of their new environment' (Miller 2010: 81). Gradually however, the tower blocks were condemned as breeding grounds of crime and violence, convoluted bureaucracy restricted residents' capacity to report faults and get their homes repaired, while paternalistic care was increasingly replaced with a more punitive regime of surveillance which curtailed personal domestic freedoms. Under such conditions, these council tenants came to feel that the flats themselves were like the presence of the enemy, and their relationship with their homes 'reeked of alienation' (Miller 2010: 87).

But the material neglect and sense of abandonment I observed in Kaloleni do not seem to have resulted in what Miller terms alienation, so much as provoked transformative acts of making. As we've seen, from the early days of Kaloleni, residents have creatively reconfigured its spaces, reorienting their intention in a way that often left authorities on the back foot. In reference to council housing in south-east England, Insa Koch has suggested that to assume that the ordering regimes of state authorities simply result in alienation fails to account for tenants' everyday agency and actions (Koch 2014, 2015). Rather than withdrawing from authorities, she examines how residents often find ways of appropriating state roles and personnel into their everyday efforts to create moral boundaries and maintain homes. In an African context, meanwhile, Patience Mususa has observed how in the mining towns of the Zambian Copperbelt the withdrawal of company welfare provision did not lead to the assumption of state roles so much as a proliferation of DIY activity. The practices of making do within their old neighbourhoods was felt to withdraw their community from the category of 'town' and instead produced a material and social atmosphere more akin to village life (2012).

In Kaloleni, the politics of dirt were used to emphasise the contrast between the obligations placed on residents today and the work of the council in the past. As described in the previous chapter, Kaloleni's infrastructural breakdown is in part a legacy of the retraction of state presence and rapid fragmentation of municipal authority in Nairobi over the past few decades, with residents increasingly left to fend for themselves (Branch et al. 2010; Olima 2013). The subsequent encroachment of mud and dirt has become one way in which this is felt in everyday life. Georgio, a softly spoken man in his fifties, lives in a very neat house with freshly painted yellow shutters that look out on to one of Kaloleni's larger roads. He takes great pride in keeping the area around his house 'smart', regularly scything the grass and keeping the hedges trimmed. This is necessary, Georgio explained to me, because the council no longer cares about dirt. The council are

> not spending their money [i.e. the income from rent]. Where is the money going to? You do [it yourself] from inside up to outside. You do the cleaning, you clean your compound, you do the garbage, you do everything for yourself. You pay to upkeep because you can't live in a dirty house ... you know, this dirt is not good for me, is not good for my children, it's not good for the community so you take it off.

Other residents saw their attempts to keep dirt at bay as a part of claiming space in Kaloleni more fully, echoing Koch's observation that appropriations of the state's responsibilities can be ways that residents seek to maintain physical and moral boundaries. Pamela is a middle-aged woman who was born in Kaloleni and now shares her house with her two sisters and their children. Discussing the situation in Kiswahili, she told me how the City Council '*hawatengenezi* estate': they are not maintaining the estate. But nor, she observed, were all of her neighbours taking on their fair share of responsibility in this new era of self-management. Without the council's oversight, '*kila mtu anafanya vile anataka, ikawa ni chafu*': every person does whatever they want, so it becomes dirty. In order to counteract this, she and her sisters decided to enclose their outdoor space to keep the dirt out. '*Tujiweka* fence *yetu, ni* territory *yetu*' she said – we ourselves put up our fence, it is our territory – before adding, '*Hizi zote ni sisi tunaweka na pesa zetu*' – all these things we are doing with our own money. Pamela's use of the words 'fence' and 'territory' in English suggests a particular sense of space and proprietorship, conferred by their labour and investments. She and her sisters have carved out an area which they can take care of for themselves, a place under their control. Though their household is markedly poorer than some others in Kaloleni, nevertheless they have made several home improvements: the space inside their fence is neatly tended, with shrubs, flowers and a couple of small trees. They have also, on either side of the path to the front door, laid out two patches of

Figure 9
Homemade 'keep off the grass' sign, Pamela's house, June 2014
(Photo: Author)

lawn. Staked into the lawn is a handmade sign which reads 'Keep off the grass', as though to reinforce their statement of territory (see Figure 9).

But some residents did not link the intrusion of mud and dirt just to the decline in estate management but specifically to an influx of *watu wakukam* ('people that come', or outsiders) resident in the rental 'extensions'. One longstanding resident, Juliet, was adamant that Kaloleni's problems were rooted in the development of extensions, which were causing overcrowding and problems of hygiene and cleanliness:

> You see, my neighbour ... he has built I think eight or six [extensions]. They don't have drainage there ... these people who are staying there, when they clean dishes where does that water go? Also they want to go to the toilet. The toilet is one ... Imagine! Now how is that place going to be clean? It can't ... That is why Kaloleni it has changed. It is dirty. It is very dirty by the way.

Here the accumulation of dirt is understood as intimate and corporeal: an accretion of waste and detritus produced by bodily functions and everyday domestic life in an inadequate, makeshift lodging. Echoing older colonial ideas of dirt and hygiene, Juliet associated dirt not only with place – that is, as a consequence of lack of access to drainage and sanitation in the extensions – but with people themselves. She linked the unknown status of the incomers, that they are outsiders to the long-term community of Kaloleni, with their dirtiness: 'the people who are staying in those structures, we even don't know one another and they are even – let me say, they are dirty'. In an article on 'filth' in Calcutta, Kaviraj notes how colonial conventions governing everyday behaviour in public spaces were internalised by the city's Indian middle classes (1997: 84). The disciplinary effect of signs and prohibitions in places such as parks continued after independence, but their authority was gradually eroded by the influx of rural poor with no other space in which to settle. The *détournement* of public, recreational parks into squatter settlements – and the transition of lower class users from tentative interlopers to permanent dwellers – Kaviraj describes as creating a 'soiled conception of public space', a sentiment with which Juliet would probably have some sympathy (1997: 104).

Ruins and remains

As Eddy's entreaty that I look beyond the 'ruins' of Kaloleni suggests, many residents express a sadness and nostalgia about the decay of Kaloleni, a loss of pride in a place that was once desirable and orderly. Their preoccupation with declining infrastructures and architectural decay – the amassing of rubbish heaps, the problems of dirt, blockages and flooding – might suggest the ruination of Kaloleni, that it is a relic of a colonial dream now destined for oblivion. Such postcolonial melancholy is a thread running through much of the scholarship on the architectural remains of imperialism, which implies ruination, abandonment and desolation. In *Expectations of Modernity* (1999), James Ferguson describes the failed promises of modernisation and an atmosphere of pessimism on the Zambian Copperbelt in the 1980s. Where once the industrialising, urbanising landscape had stood for progress and aspiration, the collapse in copper prices and the decline of the mining industry now predicted regression and backward momentum. Ferguson describes this as 'modernisation through the looking glass' where the anticipated future seems to be moving ever further from, rather than towards, an idealised image of modernity (1999: 13). Yet, despite the sentiments of the residents cited above, I am wary of such wistfulness. Ann Laura Stoler has encouraged us to consider the political life of imperial debris, 'the material and social afterlife of structures, sensibilities and things' (2008: 194), and this afterlife is vibrant in Kaloleni. What I observed was not so much the failed dream of reaching 'modernity' as shifting ideas about how to make a home and a life in the city.

Whereas 'ruin' tends to evoke something from the past that is lost, decay is an unforeclosed process, rolling forward into the future. The transformation of Kaloleni from a controlled welfarist project to something much more makeshift was not just a consequence of state failure 'from above' but about residents seeking out new prospects in times of political and material hardship. It is these dynamic processes that suggest that ruin and decay are terms that should not be conflated. Residents do not turn away from the remains of the past, but rather incorporate them into contemporary concerns and make them meaningful in new ways. The intimacy I observed in Kaloleni between architectural decay and practices of self-imagining point to both a more human and a more productive engagement between decay and belonging than is usually found in scholarship on ruins. Rather than desolation, remains – though sometimes repellent and usually unwelcomed – have produced certain ways of being in place, acting as sites of memory as well as opportunities for new ways of living.

Though ruins have held a place in the European imagination for centuries – stretching back to the Renaissance fascination with the remains of ancient Greece and Rome – in recent years, ruins have received renewed attention from art history and anthropology, in what Shannon Lee Dawdy has termed an 'archaeological horizon' or 'ruin revival' (2010: 761, 762). This work has moved away from the 'ruin lust' that characterised earlier romantic and nostalgic preoccupations, particularly in art and literature (Macaulay 1953; Dillon 2011: 12; 2014). Recent scholarship has taken an approach that is more dynamic and temporally situated; a concern with 'ruination' as a process, rather than 'ruins' as a fixed object (Stoler 2013). Rather than being strati-graphically or processually oriented, this move 'indexes an emerging fixation on time itself', where the emphasis on recent, often urban, ruins demands an engagement with folded and churning temporalities (Dawdy 2010: 762; see also Olivier 2001).

But though many scholars highlight the vibrancy of intransigent remains, alerting us to their 'vital refiguration' (Stoler 2008: 194), nevertheless ruins are still commonly regarded as melancholic, even abject (Navaro-Yashin 2009). They also tend to be devoid of people. The quintessential image of ruins is one of loss, a monumental relic of a decaying past: a decrepit fort, an abandoned factory, a deserted village. Where people do figure, they are often represented as subject to a powerful determinism, passive casualties of the whims of disin-tegrating infrastructures. Even in accounts of recently ruined homes and cities, people lurk only in the margins. Even Dawdy, who draws on her ethnography in New Orleans to make a claim for the 'social life of ruins', couches such human engagement in terms of misdemeanour, noting that just because 'many of these activities in the ruins ... involve some kind of trespass does not mean they are not socially important' (2010: 776).

Though Kaloleni is undeniably materially decayed, it is far from abandoned. Thanks to the extensions, the population today is approx-imately triple that which it was originally designed to accommodate. Neither are its residents trespassers: even the occupants of the exten-sions – who might in an official, legal sense be regarded as squatters – have their situation informally legitimated by being the tenants of residents in the main houses. In any case, their presence is persistent. They live and even work within the estate; their status is not encom-passed by the transitory, ad hoc implications of the term 'trespasser'. Kaloleni's residents live literally *with* the decay, surrounded by the remains of the past as they pursue their lives. Just as earlier residents sought to rescript Kaloleni's design by occupying the estate in ways that diverged from the intentions of colonial planners, more recently Kalolenians have begun to reconfigure the architectural form and substance of their neighbourhood, taking advantage of decay to enable new modes of living.

Most recent incomers to Kaloleni reside in the extensions, but some have been integrated into the original fabric of the buildings. The estate's architect, A. J. S. Hutton, planned semi-detached or short blocks of bungalows arranged in a series of loops or courts, each backing on to a grassy communal area. This shared space was accessed via the back door of each unit, around the sides of the short blocks, and occasionally by arched passageways through the terraces. Known colloquially by residents as *otuchi*, a Luo word for tunnel, the passages added a rather grand element to the bungalows' simple design. But as households have taken advantage of decreased regulation, gradually fencing off the communal areas and filling them with extensions, the *otuchi* no longer provide passage to anywhere. For some enterprising residents, the *otuchi* suggested new residential possibilities: already roofed and with most of the walls already in place, if the arch was blocked in and a door and some flooring added then an *otuchi* could easily and cheaply be made habitable. Accordingly, in many instances they have been co-opted as living space, some as extra rooms for the house to the side, some as separate 'bed-sitters' to be rented out, with only the outline of their original purpose remaining (see Figure 10). In other places, the *otuchi* are still passable, but are much deteriorated. Many now lack roofs, as – given the absence of council maintenance – residents have 'borrowed' the expensive terracotta tiles to repair the roofs of their homes.

Though repurposed or decayed, this does not mean that *otuchi* have suffered a parallel loss of consequence. Their residual architecture in fact presences certain histories about people and place, and are thus implicated in important memory-work in Kaloleni (see DeSilvey 2006). Unprompted, *otuchi* would often intrude on conversations I had while walking around the neighbourhood, the remains of an *otuchi* becoming incorporated into a story as we passed by. Several people specifically remembered their conviviality when sheltering from the rain; one man knowingly recalled the half-darkness of the *otuchi* as an excellent place for meeting girlfriends, and many residents recollected playing under them as children. For the boys of 'HAB' (an informal crew of young men from the houses in rows H, A and B) in the early 1990s one *otuchi* acted as their base and lookout point. Now fathers in their 40s, their HAB days were recalled with fondness, and several of them showed me copies of the same photo of the crew at their *otuchi* base (see Figure 11). The material traces of the *otuchi* allow the presencing of certain narratives from the past, encroaching on the present and acting as sites of memory.

Figure 10 An archway, or *otuchi*, converted into living space, October 2013
(Photo: Author)

Figure 11 The boys of HAB at their *otuchi* base, c. 1990
(Photo: courtesy of Tom Nyanya)

The passageways of the *otuchi* are not the only routes to have been cut short. The paths in Kaloleni used to be smartly maintained – tarmacked or gravelled – with neat kerbstone edges. As official maintenance has declined, many residents have fenced-in yards around their houses to keep dirt and detritus at bay, abruptly cutting off old pathways with hedges and fences. Now that they lead only to dead ends, many of the stone edgings have been unearthed and repurposed elsewhere, such as for creating flowerbeds in the new private yards. What kerbstones still remain act as a reminder of old ways now abandoned. The residual lines of kerbstones leading to nowhere are like an echo – a faint trace on the contemporary terrain of previous paths, routines and habits that are no longer possible. Instead, new paths have emerged that twist between the fences and new structures. Unlike the formal routes laid out by colonial designers, which conformed to a more-or-less symmetrical aerial plan, the new ways are not planned. They are the inscriptions of a more recent habitus: 'desire lines' emerging organically, made by the repeated tramp of feet wearing out the grass (de Certeau 1984).

The intimacy I observed in Kaloleni between architectural decay and practices of self-imagining point to both a more human and a more productive engagement with processes of decay than is usually found in scholarship on ruins. The continuing consequence of the residual architectures of the *otuchi* and the kerbstones reveal how, rather than being victims of decay, Kaloleni residents are implicated within it. Their engagements with the materiality of timeworn architectures can be productive and formative. This points to a much more complex relationship between notions of ruin, decay, sociality and subjectivity. Decay and ruination are not only material processes of disintegration, they are embedded in assemblages of other human and nonhuman actants, some of which may resist, reconfigure or curtail not only the meanings of decay but the process itself.

Urban decay

Given the decades of council neglect and the labour that they have had to shoulder for themselves, there are many residents who would welcome some form of state-instigated investment within their estate. During 2013–14, with Vision 2030 looming on the horizon, the possibility of modernising their neighbourhood was superficially very attractive. What they feared, however, was that any new scheme would not be for their benefit. In a world of 'big man' politics, residents have little voice and minimal financial clout, and they know that officials will seek – formally or behind the scenes – maximum revenues from any project that goes ahead. Conflicting announcements in newspapers and on the news make it hard to tell how things will proceed: whether this will be a City Council or Ministry of Housing project; whether it will be for rental or for sale; if it will involve Chinese or Kenyan developers (see, for example, Waitatu 2013; Waithaka 2013).

Such uncertainty is understood by residents to reflect struggle between competing parties all eager to get their bite of the cherry. In the fray, it is those with no voice who are trampled underfoot. The founder of the Kaloleni residents' association explained this to me with a Swahili proverb: *Fahali wawili wakipigana, nyasi ndiyo huumia*: when two bulls fight, it is the grass that suffers. 'They are treating us like the grass' he clarified, 'it is us small people, the *waskini* [literally, poor people], who are suffering'. This sense of marginalisation, of not being able to participate in the renewal process, in part stems from resentment at the notion that it is not only Kaloleni the place that needs regenerating, but the community too. The association of dirt and decay with people as well as places was not just formative of colonial urban policy, as Kaviraj reminds us, but is central to much recent urban planning around the world, being implicit in the concept of urban decay. Understood as a 'result of the interaction between social, economic and physical changes', the 'blight' of urban decay encompasses social and architectural breakdown and disorder, the treatment for which is usually planning regeneration schemes (Andersen 2002: 154).

As a policy category imposed by the state, urban decay works as both a judgement and justification for certain actions. Yet in some ways, anthropologically speaking, the term is quite promising. By indicating the material, social, economic and even moral breakdown of an urban area, it manages to encapsulate many of the ideas that the recent scholarly attention to material culture has tried so hard to convey. It recognises the influence of architectural spaces on social lives, implicitly acknowledging the co-constitutive relationship between humans and their material worlds (Miller 2001, 2005; Buchli 2013). This is perhaps quite surprising for a policy-led term. As scholars, we are used to calling out such jargonistic phrases, yet this term seems to encapsulate a dynamic and uneasy set of relationships.

Despite this promising start, urban decay remains a problematic term. Who would self-identify as decaying? Is this decay an organic process, part of a natural cycle of death and regeneration? Or something produced by specific (political, economic) processes? Who gets to decide what gets included in this category? Despite its possibilities for highlighting material efficacy, urban decay remains an externally imposed classification, one which condemns both the place and those that live within it. Once branded as a site of urban decay, that place becomes dead-end, futureless. The terms which follow – decanting, demolition, regeneration – are equally ominous. It implies material and social failure and the condemnation of a whole community, while simultaneously veiling the culpability of those who were responsible for its management.

Given the energy and care that so many residents have invested in their homes, compounds and businesses, unsurprisingly many reject the connotations of urban decay. In the words of Onyi, an old man who spends his afternoons sitting under a tree at the back of Kaloleni's social hall, 'who is it that is decaying? Me, I'm not dead yet'. In particular, by refusing the label of urban decay, Kaloleni residents deeply object to the evasion of responsibility that such a classification implies, arguing that the disrepair of their neighbourhood is politically motivated. Many residents regard the material degradation of Kaloleni as a political act on the part of the city authorities. They feel that the council are deliberately running it into the ground so the estate can be condemned as decayed, its demolition and redevelopment justified, and the current residents evicted in the process.

One evening, I was sitting together with Onyi in the late sun. He pointed out the crumbling roofs of the houses nearby. 'This is what we call neglect', he said melancholically. 'You neglect something when you want to sell it. Our so-called custodians who are the trustees, the Council, they just neglected the place purposely, to fail it, so as to dispose it off … But that's how things are done here. Run down the place, totally run it down and then dispose.' This gives a very different gloss to the infrastructural failings described earlier. These are not neutral processes, the product of some natural cycle of decay, or the consequence of Kaloleni being simply 'forgotten' by city authorities. Household maintenance is a political issue for residents; their practices of management and repair inscribe the houses with their own personal histories. They are not simply repairing their homes for functionality and comfort, but in a small way trying to stem a much bigger tide of institutional neglect, making a statement about their right to reside in the estate.

Public rubbish

The creative interventions of residents such as Helima, Boniface, Pamela and others offer a counter to the defeatist, futureless associations of urban decay, as well as to the technological determinism to which an over-emphasis on infrastructure and architecture can be vulnerable. Yet their preoccupation with the dirt and mess of their neighbours nevertheless emphasises that waste and decay are materially affective in Kaloleni. The failure of facilities intended to aid the flow of waste *out* of Kaloleni – drains, sewers, pipes, rubbish collection – means they are now keeping that effluence *in*. The issue of what to do with household waste in the absence of any service for its collection is hard to resolve, particularly for poor households with no transport of their own. In Nairobi, almost everything comes wrapped or bagged in plastic. There is an enormous build-up not only of biodegradable waste such as food scraps, cardboard and paper but of plastic-based packaging. Kaloleni is covered with 'plastic papers' as they are usually called, which blow around in the wind and get caught in trees or trampled into the mud. Mounds of detritus accumulate in the interstices between buildings, heaped up by the wind or thrown there haphazardly. These heaps grow ever higher and increasingly putrid. Periodically they are burned, producing noxious fumes that trail across the estate. There are periodic attempts by local groups to organise collections or litter picking events, which are only partially successful – the scale of the task can sometimes seem insurmountable.

When I was sitting with Juliet in her living room, drinking tea and discussing her concerns regarding dirt and extensions described above, after some time we began to smell acrid smoke. It smelt strongly of burning plastic, but rather than coming from behind the house (and therefore indicating that her neighbours were burning their rubbish heaps) the smoke was seeping in through the windows at the front. Juliet's house looks on to the main entrance road into Kaloleni, a wide road with a central grassy area running down the middle. Originally this was formally laid out with flowerbeds and shrubs, but today only a few shaggy bougainvillea bushes remain. Dorothy, Juliet's adult daughter, opened the front door to see what was going on. A man had lit a small fire on the grassy central reservation, from which rose plumes of pungent black smoke. It turned out he was burning scavenged electric cables and wire to remove the plastic coating and get at the copper inside – a valuable scrap metal. An argument ensued; Dorothy told him he was being a nuisance and he shouldn't be doing this in front of the houses where the smoke was disturbing the residents. In response, the man gesticulated with his arms to indicate the street and said '*huku ndiyo* no-man's land': this place is no-man's land.

Here then is a more conceptual problem concerning waste and dirt in Kaloleni; it is not just a utilitarian question of services. Rather than the open land of the estate – that not occupied by formal or informal accommodation – being understood as public or community places, for some people at least they are regarded as 'no-man's land'; non-space or negative space in which anything goes. Instead of feeling any sense of civic duty or pressure to conform to particular behaviours, for this man the street was a space where he could not be criticised. What Dorothy and Juliet regarded as communal, a place that the corporate body of Kaloleni residents had obligations to maintain, was not apparent to this man (or many others like him). He was burning his cables there precisely *because* the patch of ground was open to all, and, as he saw it, therefore free from restrictions.

In colonial Calcutta, similar tensions arose around divergent ideas about the cleanliness of open spaces. Europeans often critiqued what they saw as Indians' appalling standards of hygiene when refuse was dumped in the streets, squares and rivers. Kaviraj argues that what these commentators failed to realise was that 'when garbage is dumped, it is not placed at a point where it cannot causally affect the realm of the household and its hygienic wellbeing. It is thrown over a conceptual boundary' (1997: 98). He distinguishes between *ghare* and *baire*, Bengali terms that respectively translate to the inside of the house and the 'not-inside' or outside (1997: 93). These cannot, Kaviraj stresses, be neatly mapped on to European distinctions between private and public/civic. Whereas a Habermasian perspective describes that which is outside of the home as a public sphere of civic concern, and conceives of privacy and publicity as reciprocally produced, this is by no means a universal. Kaviraj argues that in Calcutta the street was not a place to which values were attached or which one had obligations towards, it was understood as a negative of the inside, simply not one's own. Therefore, particularly in Brahminical conceptions of cleanliness and purity, discarding detritus there did not constitute pollution in the way that a dirty house was regarded as contaminated. As such, dumping rubbish on a mound immediately in front of the house was not down to ignorance about matters of hygiene, as colonial authorities often assumed, but founded in cosmological differences about the way concepts of cleanliness and purity were mapped on to the material world (Kaviraj 1997: 98; see also Douglas 1966).

In Kaloleni, such conceptual differences are not so explicitly delineated, but nevertheless there are clear parallels. Interestingly, Kaviraj notes that among Calcutta's educated middle classes, many became sympathetic to European distinctions about privacy and publicity, expressing an 'emulative enthusiasm' for orderly public spaces in which conformity to certain behavioural and civic codes was expected (1998: 97). The same could be said for many of Kaloleni's older residents, as manifested for example, in Pamela's enthusiastic recycling of pre-independence 'keep off the grass' signage. The apparent refusal of poorer residents, especially in the extensions, to conform to such codes is a cause of considerable tension, as Juliet's complaints about 'dirty' people imply.

Accumulation

Whether or not tensions over rubbish can be located in cosmological differences, the substance of garbage remains an affective presence in Kaloleni. Rather than sweeping rubbish under the cosmological carpet, as it were, by focusing on deliberations *about* rubbish, it is this materiality – the *stuff* of accumulated dirt and detritus – to which I want to attend. This is not exactly a new approach: studying the refuse of human societies is a mainstay of archaeology, whether the middens of Viking settlements or discarded ceramics in Mesopotamia. More recently, waste has been the empirical basis for archaeologies of contemporary societies, perhaps most famously in the case of William Rathje's Garbage Project, which he has been running since the 1970s (Rathje 1974). Through painstaking investigations of household rubbish bins and landfill sites, his 'garbology' team have shown how important household waste is to fully understanding human relationships to commodities and food; behavioural patterns which they demonstrate are not adequately revealed through surveys, interviews or observation (Rathje 2002). Such studies of discarded materials have predominantly focused on consumption: what people's rubbish can tell us about patterns of acquisition, nutrition, mobility and wealth. This has highlighted a considerable behavioural disjuncture between what people say they do and what their material refuse reveals that they do (Rathje 2002). But here, I am less interested in consumer behaviours than in the cumulative material presence of an environment of dirt and decay, its affects and atmospheres, and the way it structures and constrains people's relationship with a material world.

The build-up of household rubbish is an important characteristic of the material substance of Kaloleni, but it is only one aspect of the estate's accumulated dirt. As we have seen, this encompasses infrastructural failure, mud, crumbling architecture and a pervasive sense of official neglect. How can we adequately account for these multiple substances and processes of decay? In one sense, we could simply say that this is what happens when formality is replaced with informality. With structural adjustment policies in the 1980s and the shrinking of the state, so the informal sector has proliferated; the informal economy in Kenya now employs approximately three out of four workers, according to a recent United Nations report (UN 2015). In Kaloleni this in part accounts for the proliferation of *jua kali* (informal small businesses, literally 'fierce sun') activity, overcrowding in the extensions, and the need to 'hustle'. Similarly, the high rates of institutional corruption and lack of government accountability in Kenya have led to poor infrastructural investment (Adams et al. 2013). What this means for public estates such as Kaloleni is abandonment by the state, and an end of the council's maintenance of and investment in their social housing. For residents, this leads to a 'making-do' culture, in which citizens make the best of what remains, coming up with ingenious fixes and creative solutions to issues such as lack of piped water, unreliable electricity provision and poor sanitation.

At a certain level, all of this may be true. But as far as I am concerned, it doesn't really address the social and material implications of such neglect. As I followed the materiality of decay in Kaloleni, tracing what was disintegrating and what was not, and questioning how people felt about this apparent decay, I began to see decay not as something associated with loss and oblivion, but to see it as accumulation. What I was observing was a build-up of material traces, an accretion of the remains of lives lived. If rubbish is not collected, broken objects are not removed, houses are not repainted, what we are left with is not less, but rather more – what we might term an excess. There is no ruined enchantment to these residues, they are not often beautiful or aesthetically pleasing, but they reveal the way in which a landscape can be inscribed with multiple ordinary histories as they accumulate in the estate.

Residents of Kaloleni live literally with the remains of the past as they appear in the present, reflecting what Laurent Olivier has described as the co-presence of multi-temporalities: 'the time of material culture is in fact a multi-temporal time, formed from accumulating durations, superimposed one upon the other' (2002: 140). From this point of view, decay is historicised matter, in which the past disrupts, but is also generative of, the present (see also Masquelier 2002). Rather than staying neatly in a previous temporal frame, these accretions materialise the past in the present moment; they intrude on daily life, refusing linear temporalities and ensuring that the past remains unforeclosed. Going beyond dirt as analytic category or metaphorical device, dirt-as-history is an intimate, visceral confrontation.

Geoarchitecture

This nascent impression was affirmed by one particular encounter. A large *mtaaro* – open drainage ditch – forms the eastern boundary of Kaloleni. An original feature of the estate's construction, such conduits were a mainstay of colonial infrastructure in Nairobi: relatively cheap to build, easier to maintain than pipes below ground, and useful for forming clear boundaries. Kaloleni is built on low-lying land prone to flooding, and the *mitaaro* were intended to drain the area, channelling waste water out of the estate. After years of neglect, however, the structure has begun to disintegrate, and City Council workers no longer come to clear out the rubbish that blocks it. In some sense, the *mtaaro* is a ruin, a remainder of a colonial project of modernisation. But it cannot be said to constitute an object of contemplation – this is no site of romantic ruination. Despite its breakdown, it is not an object fixed in time; it still exerts a dynamic agency in the landscape of Kaloleni. This mundane drainage ditch brought into focus some of the capacities and temporalities of dirt and decay.

The banks of the *mtaaro* have gradually been occupied by *mabati* (corrugated iron) structures, some used as housing and others as kiosks, bars and other *jua kali* activity. With no alternative, residents are forced to dump their waste where they can, including into the *mtaaro*, which quickly becomes choked. When it rains, this is one of the areas of Kaloleni that regularly become flooded, in part due to a shallow dip in the land and partly because of the larger population and lack of proper drainage. Struggling across this area one day during the rainy season, trying to avoid getting my feet wet, I noticed that I was moving across a series of small hillocks that rose out of the muddy ground. In one of the *jua kali* businesses on the edge of the *mtaaro*, young men shred huge heaps of old textiles into strips, a common and cheap way of recycling old clothes to provide stuffing for mattresses, pillows and sofas. Looking down, I could see that many of these strips had become embedded in the ground, providing a new structural integrity to the soil and making it firmer and easier to walk on.

These strips are a material trace, an excess, of the history of the informal economy in this part of Nairobi; an excess that is operative in novel ways. Over time this detritus has gradually solidified to build up a new micro-topography of *vilima,* or small hills. A new landscape is emerging; one produced by accumulation. A blocked drainage ditch, mud and accumulated waste from an activity that itself is based on recycling discarded clothing come together in an additive process. Together, they constitute an example of what Lindsay Bremner has called 'geoarchitecture': the excavation, mobilisation and reconstitution of earth's materials by humans, the effects of which make architecture – and the social, political, economic nexus in which it is embedded – a geological actor (2012). The role of shredded fabric in creating novel topographies suggests that such remains are not inert. The objects and materials – the matter – of human activity do not stop being efficacious once human interest in them is finished; even as waste they remain vibrant (Bennett 2009). This vital materiality draws attention to how waste and decay are implicated in the future as well as the past. Rather than seeing rubbish or waste as a fixed materiality, recognition of animated processes of decay in the *longue durée* allows us to perceive the production of urban landscapes along a different temporal frame.

This rather visceral encounter with the topography of Kaloleni highlighted how the oblivion and loss usually associated with ruination may emanate not so much from decay as from its elimination. The relationship between people and place is generative; the accumulated traces of decades of habitation have left their mark. They provoke not only practices of relating to the past but also open up unpredictable futures. Though sometimes unpleasant, even revolting, there is a richness and texture to such temporalities; they are literally grounded in the substance of the estate. While dirt and detritus may not be welcomed by many in Kaloleni, as this chapter has demonstrated their affective presence is potent. Which begs the question of what might happen if such decaying deposits are wiped away? Urban regeneration schemes promise to clean up the estate, replacing grimy decay with shiny, smooth surfaces. This cleansing is a process of removal, a clearing out of the excess materiality (and, potentially, humanity) of Kaloleni. Here then is where loss is located: not in decay but in its annihilation. Seen from this perspective, urban renewal can be regarded as a form of erasure. The classification of urban decay censures communities, and it also censors: redacting slowly amassed material and corporeal micro-histories.

By starting to see decay as a process of accumulation rather than loss, new possibilities begin to emerge. Instead of a descent into oblivion, decay remains unforeclosed, an ongoing process of accretion. This vibrant matter, awoken by residents through their engagements with the estate's dirty histories, is opening up ways to dispute the government's potent but ambiguous label of urban decay and to assert different narratives of urban belonging. Instead of an abandoned, dead-end estate, residents' daily negotiations with the materiality of decay have produced a landscape that indexes a particular history of people and place. Government schemes to deal with urban decay in Kaloleni threaten to cleanse not only the waste and dirt of decades, but also the community it constitutes. But urban renewal will also generate its own remains. Its geoarchitecture is likely to be much more vigorous and disruptive than anything that has come before, churning different substances and presencing new pasts even as it redacts others. Such futures are at the moment speculative: the finalised regeneration schemes for Eastlands are still not known, or at least have not been publicly revealed. But perhaps the new topographies of Kaloleni prefigure in some way the unforeclosed work of remains and decay, and their implication in new materialities in the making.

3

Performing Property, Making History

'Kenya grew from here'

In December 2013, I took a walk around Kaloleni with the chairman of KERA, the Kaloleni Estate Residents' Association. We made our way through Kaloleni's warren of paths and curving lines of houses, with the chairman remarking on the disintegration of the route as we walked. Pointing at the crumbling asphalt beneath our feet, he commented, 'You see how it is no longer carpeted?' When we reached the front of the social hall, the chairman stopped and looked up. The building is the tallest of the colonial structures and quite forbidding: high arched windows, whitewashed walls and topped with a steep red-tiled roof (see Figure 12). Gazing up at the many broken panes of glass in the windows, the crumbling tiles and rusting drainpipes, he sighed and said, 'You know, Kenya grew from here'.

The chairman's words placed Kaloleni at the heart of the Kenyan nation, a seed from which its history germinated, of central importance to understanding the development of the country. His remark stayed with me, the horticultural association of the word 'grew' evoking the generativity of place. From this perspective, the flourishing of incremental additions and extensions seemed organic and fecund, a reminder of the shared forward momentum of both making and growing (Ingold 2013). It also evokes the mutually constitutive relationship between people and the places they inhabit. 'The place acts dialectically so as to create the people who are of that place', a process through which feelings of belonging and rootedness in a landscape can emerge (Tilley 1994: 26).

More straightforwardly, the chairman was also referring to the significance of the social hall – and Kaloleni more broadly – in the re-imagination of Kenya and the determination for independence. As explored in Chapter 1, the social hall became a key site where the intentions imbued in the estate's architecture were most obviously undermined. Far from producing servile subjects, the hall – or the 'Houses of Parliament' as it became known – was a place where alternative visions

Figure 12 Kaloleni Social Hall, known as 'the Houses of Parliament' in the independence era, October 2013
(Photo: Author)

of Kenya's future were imagined and the methods by which they would be brought into being were debated. Some of those who participated in these debates visited from other neighbourhoods, and many were residents of Kaloleni. Many went on to be significant figures after independence in 1963. They included Charles Rubia, the first African mayor of Nairobi; Argwings Khodek, a lawyer, politician and head of the Luo Union; and Tom Mboya, charismatic trade unionist leader and member of Kenya's first independent Cabinet, who was assassinated in 1969. Implicit in the words 'Kenya grew from here' is the notion that it was Kaloleni itself that helped to nurture such politics and activism: the reconfiguration of the hall, and the estate more broadly, from a place of conformity to a place of critique indicating its vital significance in the emergence of an independent nation.

The tangible changes residents have made to the architecture of Kaloleni in recent years are thus part of a much longer history of creatively reworking colonial spaces. This has created a powerful sense of place, a history that is embedded in the fabric of the estate, but which has gone unacknowledged: a formal history of Kaloleni has never been written, and the received story of *Uhuru* (independence) does not feature this little-known corner of Nairobi. For residents today, the proposed schemes of Vision 2030 are a further marginalisation of Kaloleni's significance, threatening to obliterate the estate completely. This narrative of Kaloleni as a site of history has come to occupy a central place in the imaginations of many of today's residents and has become implicated in their material engagements with the estate's architecture. As they have taken on responsibilities of home maintenance in the absence of formal management by the City Council, and in contravention of the old colonial tenancy agreements which forbade internal and external modifications, so residents have come to feel that the houses belong to them – and that they belong to Kaloleni.

This chapter takes up such notions of belonging to consider how the making of history in Kaloleni is entangled with the making of property and ownership. Residents increasingly perform the obligations of ownership within Kaloleni, and these investments of time, energy and resources have begun to generate a feeling of proprietorship over the estate. This sense of property goes beyond straightforward legal categories or financial transactions where ownership is based on purchase power. Instead, what surfaces is a notion of property as something contingent and emergent; incrementally produced over time through investments of labour and acts of making – whether material, imaginative or discursive (see Strang and Busse 2011). The repetition of these acts, over several decades and across several generations of Kalolenians, has a performative quality, in which the assertion and appropriation of ownership is performed in acts of fence building, home maintenance and narrative-making. Reflecting on his own experiences of maintaining a garden fence in suburban Vancouver, Nicholas Blomley has argued that it is through such acts that property claims are made and remade, in unpredictable and contingent ways (2013). As such, he proposes, 'performances of property – like fence building – are both citational, referencing numerous other performances, and reiterative, entailing sustained forms of re-performance' (2013: 25). Over time, these performances, which encompass people and things, ideas and actions, the official and the everyday, have developed into an identity (or claim to an identity) of 'owner'. This is akin to what Judith Butler, in reference to gender, has described as 'a performative accomplishment' (Butler 1988: 520). This accomplishment counters official and conventional narratives of Kaloleni's past, its position as a publicly owned estate and the legal status of residents. In this sense, as residents increasingly perform claims to ownership, so they are also actively engaging with the urban history of Nairobi and forging it anew.

By considering the performative entanglement of property-making and historymaking, this chapter takes up ideas about the production of historical knowledge and the politics of representation. It explores how such acts seek to remake Kaloleni, constituting it as a significant site of urban history in ways that assert not only the contribution of Kaloleni to the making of Kenya, but seek to undermine official categories of 'tenant'. Such revisionist urban histories are uppermost in the minds of residents not just for their own sake, but because of their salience with regards to the future. In the shadow of Vision 2030, the contested history of Kaloleni – and the position of its residents – have been thrown into stark relief. Many Kalolenians perceive authority over the past to be key to the renegotiation of official visions of the future. Performances of, and claims to, ownership underlie this renegotiation, a material and corporeal as well as discursive nexus which enables a different mode of historical production. This sheds new light on the continuing afterlives of architecture, showing how such sites not only animate engagements with the past but generate ways of living towards the future.

Temporal property

In April 2014, I was sitting with Izmani, a young man in his late twenties, at his 'base' in Kaloleni's central shopping centre. Izmani has lived in Kaloleni all his life, and now resides in an extension behind his parents' main house. He works hard but struggles to make ends meet. He is a member of a self-help group, a loose collective of men around the same age who have set up some informal income generation projects, such as car washing, delivering water, and renting out plastic chairs and tents for funerals. We were discussing the future of Kaloleni and whether or not Izmani would continue living there. He told me, 'We are just waiting to see if council will demolish or not. We don't know the future'. He is not opposed to a regeneration scheme in principle, he told me, and he thought new houses could be good, 'but we must be sure new ones are affordable' for current residents. He was clear that the people of Kaloleni had to be involved, to be at the centre of whatever came next. 'Now they are like the owners of this land', he said firmly. The relationship between the estate residents and state authorities has been fundamentally altered, he explained: 'You [i.e. the council] are meant to tell [me] what to do on this land, but you are not, so I do it for myself. This place has become like it is owned by the residents and so they need to benefit from whatever comes next.' Izmani expressed a sense of ownership as something generated through labour, longevity and management. With the decline in intervention and maintenance from the council, so people have shouldered responsibility for themselves, and this, in his mind as well as in the minds of many other residents, should entitle them to inclusion in the future.

Izmani's words resonate with scholarly perspectives on the contested nature of land, ownership and property in Kenya. Historians and social scientists of Kenya have consistently tracked the volatile politics that can emerge in relation to land, especially when categories of possession, tenure and title are unsettled by alternative narratives and claims (Berman and Lonsdale 1992; Berry 1993; Lesorogol 2008; Boone 2012; Manji 2015b). But such perspectives are by no means limited to Kenya or Africa. Drawing on diverse ethnographic contexts around the globe, anthropological conceptions increasingly understand property as a relational process of appropriation and claim-making, rather than a fixed legal category (Rose 1994; Hann 1998; Verdery and Humphrey 2004; Strang and Busse 2011). This work reveals how property is always contextual, worked out in relations between people, and between people and the environments that they inhabit. From the workings of intellectual property in Europe to the sociality of Maori land claims and the privatisation of radio frequencies in Nepal, acts of property-making stretch, dispute or unsettle classifications of private property, collective ownership and the gaps between property law and lived practices (Strathern 1996; Durie 2011; Wilmore and Upreti 2011). It takes work to accomplish and to maintain the appropriation and possession that makes property possible, as well as for such acts and claims to be legitimately recognised. As far back as seventeenth-century England, John Locke acknowledged the power of acts of making to the establishment of property when he proposed that the owner of a thing is one who uses their labour to modify a previously unowned thing (Locke 1980 [1690]). More recently, Carol Rose has suggested that the labour involved in making property is always ongoing: what she terms the 'clear-act principle' means that to possess something requires both a declaration of an intention to appropriate, and an ongoing assertion of ownership (1994: 13).

Collectively, such work helps us to take a view on property not as a discrete entity but as an assemblage made up of people and ideas, but also things such as fences, paint, documents, maps, symbols, landscapes and actions. Property is made through the enrolment and arrangement of these entities – human and nonhuman – that acquire particular attributes through their relation with each other. As Blomley describes it, 'property is performed when such entities stabilize and work together' in a particular assemblage (2013: 39). This assemblage is not fixed but constantly being made, crafted and renegotiated. In this sense, rather than conferred through a single, legally recognised transaction, property is temporally produced: it is performed into and towards the future, through the attempts made to sustain the assemblage and keep its composite form together. As Strathern has argued, in this way we can conceive of property as 'potentiality, as the capacity for development as yet unrealised' (1996: 17).

This concept of property as future-oriented suggests that certain powers and potentials may be brought forth in the future if ownership can be assured in the present. This is what Izmani understands by the future benefits that Kaloleni residents can access, if only their ownership can be acknowledged. Izmani seems to recognise the inherent precarity of property assemblages; that though they may appear stable, their alignments can be unsettled and reconfigured in ways that might redistribute their perceived benefits (Blomley 2013: 39). This processual dynamism is what Elliott has explored in her work on 'propertying as anticipatory action' in northern Kenya (2017: 26). As she argues, turning 'property' into a verb captures its sense of 'something that is made, worked, claimed, done and practiced'; a performative process that enables 'a means of acting upon an uncertain future and rendering it more secure and knowable' (2017: 25). In Kaloleni, property is performed in ways that seek to undo official categories of tenure and belonging in order for residents to make certain claims about their own future in Nairobi. What Strathern calls 'the capacity for development as yet unrealised' is thus in Kaloleni not just about the development of the land but also of the self. Property negotiations can hence be seen as part of self-making, as attempts to realise certain future selves.

But the temporality of this performative propertying is not straightforwardly linear. Property is not simply worked from the present towards the future but calls upon and reconfigures the past. Residents seek to align their long history of labour and maintenance with Kaloleni's rich material landscape as a generative site from which Kenya has taken shape. In some ways, this turn to a historicised sense of rightful property is not unusual in Africa, where leveraging the past in the present is a common way of claiming citizenship, authority or belonging. In reference to control over land, Lund has shown how 'Conflicts over land and chieftaincy are characterized by an intense reference to the past as the source of unadulterated legitimacy of claims to the future' (2013: 15, see also 2008). This is particularly the case with land tenure reform, and cases from across the continent demonstrate the contested terrain of rightful belonging, property and citizenship (Berry 1993; James 2007; Lund and Boone 2013; Manji 2013). However, much of this literature focuses on rural land and agrarian change, where the place of the past tends to revolve around autochthonous claims to origin or ancestry (see for example Lesorogol 2008; Berry 2009; Fontein 2011). Given the relatively short history of Nairobi, claims to urban property call upon the past in rather different ways. In Kaloleni, as we will see, the past is indeed understood to hold evidence backing up contemporary residents' claims to housing, as well as demonstrating the historical significance of Kaloleni. But residents' negotiations around property are not so much originary in nature as they are embedded in the labour of making place. This is understood as an incomplete, ongoing process that extends into the future. Anticipating the uncertainty of Vision 2030, yet living with the remains of the colonial past, Kalolenians' sense of urban belonging remixes the past, reconfiguring its salience anew in an active process of historymaking that helps to inform their attempts craft a future of urban presence.

Residents' relationship with their pasts, with memory and with history, is thus crucial to their practices of propertying. Both deliberately and unconsciously, residents turn to the material and social histories of their estate to find purchase on a political present and negotiate an uncertain future. This mode of engaging with the past from the present is a way of making history in everyday life, following what Hirsch and Stewart term 'historicity'; where versions of the past assume present form (2005: 262). Ethnographic consideration of the huge variety of historymaking practices at work in Africa has highlighted the workings of the 'past in the present' and how the production of history, as well as the politics of the present, relies on the dialectical relationship between the two (Peel 1984; see also Makris 1996; Lambek 2002; Argenti 2008). The salience of such temporal and historical encounters do not presume the chronological or linear unfurling of past, present and future (Ginzburg 1980; Hirsch and Moretti 2010). These modes of engaging with the past can differ drastically from the cerebral reasoning of academic historical production, relying more on 'appropriateness of meaning and feeling' (Taussig 1984: 87).

Much of this literature emphasises how aspects of the past can form correspondences with hopes and tribulations in the present, a dialectical engagement where, as Walter Benjamin put it, the past 'flashes up in a moment of danger' (2007: 255). This observation emphasises the way in which the past is not immune from present-day anxieties, but enters, and disrupts, the present in a recursive process (Masquelier 2002). Of course, this can play out in diverse ways; there is no singular past to be called upon, and historical engagements may emerge simultaneously in intersecting or competing claims (Lund 2013: 16). But what I want to emphasise is the active, creative process of such engagements. Here Benjamin's notion of historical materialism is particularly useful, underscoring the way in which our relationship with the past is always dialectical: it materialises in the present, making itself felt, and as we come to know it and see its relevance, so we amend that past, making it anew each time (2007: 253–4). The point is not only that the past never stays neatly in the past, but that historical materialism enables an encounter *with* the past, as it 'flits by'; an image to be seized in the now of its recognisability (2007: 255). To this moment of illumination, neither constant nor predictable, Benjamin gave the character of the lightning flash. This flash is an encounter that 'affects both the content of the tradition and its receivers' (2007: 255). Benjamin noted the urgency of grasping this flash as a moment for understanding, or even revolution, that might not come again. It is a chance to be seized with both hands, offering the possibility of awakening both the past and the future. If this sounds somewhat mystical, then this chapter seeks to show how the political and creative possibilities of history-making are being seized by residents in Kaloleni. They seek to influence the construction of their futures by grasping hold of the past as it flashes up at politically salient moments.

Material memories

The felted texture of Kaloleni is a key part of these practices of engaging with the past. The histories under discussion are not simply discursive but embedded in the materiality of the estate. This became apparent during an early conversation with one resident who went on to become a significant participant in my research. David was born in Kaloleni and still lives in the house he grew up in, now with his elder brother and sister-in-law. He has no regular employment but is widely called upon in the estate for electrical and plumbing jobs – often hooking up informal connections and fixing aging colonial piping – which have earned him the nickname Plumber. I met him late in 2013, and he invited me to his house and agreed to be interviewed about his life in Kaloleni. On the appointed day, I found myself sitting on a threadbare sofa in a sparsely furnished living room, the walls stained and grubby from decades of habitation. David sat opposite me, looking awkward. I tried to get the discussion going, but he was very reticent, answering my questions with just a few words. After several long silences, I began to despair. Finally, I suggested that he could show me around his house and explain to me how his family home had changed over the years. What happened next was a kind of blossoming.

David opened up and spoke at length in a way I would never have imagined possible just a few minutes before. The stories seemed to flow from the fabric of the building, and he touched the wall or traced his fingers across a surface while telling me stories about his past. We were standing outside, and David leant against the wall of his house. He started tracing the outline of the bricks, his fingers running back and forth across a section where the mortar was wobbly and crumbling. Suddenly he began to describe how when he was a small boy, he had nearly been killed by a lorry careering off the road into the house. 'It was in the night, I was sleeping', he said. He showed me the repaired brick and mortar and continued to finger the mortar as he spoke. 'It broke the wall right here. I was almost to die'. He went on to recount how the City Council had come and repaired the wall, and this led to his describing the differences between home maintenance in the past and now. The same side of the house had also been damaged in 2013, when heavy rains and wind brought down a large branch from an old tree nearby. It crashed into the roof and smashed a lot of tiles down one side, the remnants of which we were standing on as we talked. This time the council did not come, and he was left to make the best of things for himself. He reached up and touched the tiles, showing me how he had replaced the broken ones with other original tiles.

What struck me about our discussion was the way that the physicality of the house helped to tell a story that would otherwise go unsaid. David's relationship with his home's material structure helped generate the way he related aspects of the past to me. And it continued with other elements in the house, such as the water meter, which prompted a long explanation of Kaloleni's water problems. Traces of the event remain marked on the building as well as in his memory, but the house was not acting simply as a mnemonic device or 'container' for memory (Hoskins 1998). The materiality of the building was itself implicated in the way David formed and articulated his remembering. He was unwilling or unable to recall these stories, or did not see their significance, when he was not engaging with the house itself.

In his work on architecture and memory in northern Botswana, Morton has observed how, in his interviews with local residents, the house itself acted as 'a generative model for practices of remembering' (2007: 157). The house, he argues, is not just a backdrop to social activity, but an active process within it. Processes of maintaining and building houses across generations interweave temporal elements into the fabric of the house; materials, but also memories, are laid down over time. Morton observed that discussing houses with his informants not only prompted stories about the history of the house or the changing circumstances of the household, but that 'social processes of remembering and the materiality of the house are intimately interconnected over time' (2007: 177). The relationship between the house and remembrance processes is in this sense dynamic; house construction and maintenance practices consolidate and remember aspects of social relatedness over time, underlining genealogical connectedness: 'homestead and family biographies ... are bound together as part of a mutually interpretive relationship' (2007: 176).

But while Morton's work resonates with what I observed at David's house, Morton's account is almost entirely retrospective, and does not explore how remembering may be imbricated in concerns about the future. Neither are linear temporalities problematised. He speaks of the 'layering' of memories in the fabric of houses, and of the house as 'a series of layers which materially reveal experiences' (2007: 157, 168). This is more akin to archaeological time: sedimented into neat strata that can be excavated, rather than a temporal churning in which the past is brought forth into the present in messy and unpredictable ways. In Kaloleni, David's remembering was not an idle recalling of past events or family histories. These moments of the house's history had more the character of Benjamin's lightning flash. The stories of the lorry and the fallen tree illuminated Kaloleni's decreasing capacity to receive services from the council, revealing how house maintenance is a political issue for residents. In this sense David's relationship with the past is a productive one, he is not recalling a sedimented history, but awakening the material traces of a past moment to shed light on a political present.

David was not alone in turning to the materiality of Kaloleni, and the memories imbued within it, to tell his story. Throughout my field-work, I noted how physical features of the estate were called upon to reveal and substantiate particular accounts, as though awoken from within the texture of the landscape. Saleh, whose recollections about the Estate Officer we encountered in Chapter 1, was eager to share his boyhood memories of meeting Queen Elizabeth II some sixty years ago. In 1957, on an official visit to Kenya, the Queen was taken to visit Kaloleni as an example of a model African neighbourhood in colonial Nairobi. There are not many residents remaining who recall this event first-hand, but one who does is Saleh. He insisted on taking me on a walk to retrace the footsteps of the Queen on that day, from the entrance of Kaloleni to the social hall, the clinic and into one of the houses. He took me to the spot where he had waited to see her, a young boy waving a Union Jack flag he had been given by the Estate Officer. 'You see? Here it is, this is the one', he said, pointing to a barely visible kerbstone in the dust at the side of the path. Bending down to touch the stone, his recollection was vivid:

> I was with Odeng, Odeng was my closest friend. This pavement [the kerb] was white, painted white, everything white and then the Queen had white gloves. So we lined up, the children, we lined up and then … she had an opportunity of shaking hands with the children. Even me, I shook her hand! That was 1957.

Saleh's confidence in the stone, that it could validate his narrative in a way that words alone could not, may relate to much older ways of establishing knowledge, of telling histories through recourse to material things. In his fieldwork with Luo in southern Nyanza province in the late 1960s, Ben Blount observed a meeting of several elders who were engaged in a long discursive reconstruction of their clan genealogy. Blount emphasises how the resulting genealogy was produced interactively through negotiation, speech competition and corroboration, via recourse to Luo histories and folklore, that created 'genealogies as history' (1975: 118). Importantly however, this process also appealed to physical objects for further verification, and Blount recounts how the presence of a grinding stone that had belonged to a now-deceased woman was used to confirm her historical existence. This process of historymaking, he observes, relies on 'reference to an object or entity whose physical existence serves to establish the validity of the point made in reference to it. Phenomena outside the realm of descent and filiation can be used to establish the validity of the genealogical claim' (1975: 125).

According to Blount, to make claims about clan and lineage in the present necessitates calling on traces from the past; physical objects that have outlived the lifespan of those with whom they were associated. Something similar seemed to be at work with Saleh's kerbstone and David's hand on the cracked wall. The stone and the damaged house were appealed to for their material presence, and the possibilities of stability this could offer. These were in some sense material validations – physical evidence that that these things actually happened, providing the capacity to make authoritative claims about the past. But they were also more than this. They were dynamic rather than passive, helping to generate histories that might otherwise be left unsaid. Seemingly insignificant traces in the terrain of Kaloleni were revealed to be, for residents, redolent with past actions and experiences. They helped the speakers to constitute certain narratives and claims – in the case of David, he seemed unable to speak without the materiality of his house to support him.

Remembering the future

As residents face the looming uncertainty of Vision 2030 and its ambiguous promises of renewal, such authority over Kaloleni's past is becoming more important, flashing up as a crucial tool for preventing residents' exclusion or displacement from the future. The notion of property as incrementally performative, as generated through longevity, labour and acts of making, has enabled residents to see the history of their neighbourhood differently. This performance of ownership has come to seem full of potential. By invoking alternative histories of ownership, property and rights to housing, residents are reaching back into the past as they attempt to negotiate an uncertain future.

How this manifests within the day-to-day life of Kaloleni is highly varied. Sometimes it is enacted consciously and strategically, at other times this history is assumed as common knowledge. But one recurring narrative is based around a fundamental questioning of the land that Kaloleni is built on, its ownership and the legitimacy of the council's claims over the houses. One resident, Peter, carefully explained to me that the land on which Kaloleni stands is not public at all. According to his narrative, City Hall have never in fact owned the land or the houses, and the money residents pay in rent to the council 'should not be called rent but maintenance fee. The council were meant to be managers only'. In his understanding, the council's 'management' role was meant to include overseeing the enactment of a particular clause in the original colonial tenancy agreements. This clause apparently stated that after a number of years of paying rent/maintenance fees the ownership of each house would pass to its resident. In effect, Peter was arguing that the collected rents were in fact payments in a kind of mortgage scheme. Subsequently, over the course of my fieldwork, I heard many versions of this narrative from other residents. One very elderly lady named Edina recalled that it had been written on her original tenancy card, but that later the City Council had replaced this card with a different one. Discussing the matter in Kiswahili, she said:

> *Ile card ilikuwa ya green. Imeandikwa hiyo maneno yote. Halafu sasa wakati watu walikuwa wanapeleka card, kama inazeeka, hao wanaba-dilisha wanaandika mambo yao. Lakini hizi nyumba zilitengwa file yao kitambo.*

> *Ya pili, haikujengwa na City Council. Hazikujengwa na City Council kulingana na vile nilisikia. City Council ilipatiwa bure ... Walipatiwa bure wakaambiwa mpatie wapangaji. Wakikaa miaka ishirini mwapatie tena bure. ... Sasa hatuna mtu wa kututetea. Tunatakiwa tupatiwe hizo nyumba bure. Wanataka kubomoa.*

> That card was green. It was written with all those words. Now when people went with that card, if it was getting old, they [i.e. the council] changed it and they wrote their [other] affairs. But these houses were allocated in their files long ago.

> Secondly, it was not built by City Council. They [i.e. the houses] were not built by City Council according to what I've heard. City Council was given them free ... they were given them free and they were told to give them to the tenants. If they stay twenty years they are to be given [the house] for free. Now we don't have anyone to defend us. We want to be given these houses free. But they want to demolish.

In Edina's narrative, various intersecting claims come into play. She does not recognise continuity between the colonial and independence era municipal authorities, instead suggesting that Kaloleni's colonial origins throw its postcolonial status into doubt. That the City Council received these houses for 'free' shows that they are seeking to benefit from a gift, taking advantage of the current residents. For Edina, this is reinforced by the council's lack of transparency over the tenancy cards; as the old cards became worn and 'old' they were replaced by new cards that listed a different set of protocols. Edina also invokes the materiality of paper, the green tenancy card, as vindication of her argu-ment. Without this, and given the smokescreens at City Hall, they are left vulnerable, without 'anyone to defend us'. Significantly, she also suggests that it is the act of building which confers ownership, empha-sising that construction was not done by the current City Council but by the previous regime. This is also what Peter implied when he said the council 'were managers only'. This emphasis on labour and prac-tices of making, as well as the investments of energy they imply, resonates with more contemporary claims to performative ownership as described by Izmani.

I heard versions of Edina's narrative from many different residents, with some discrepancy over how many years residency was meant to elapse before ownership was assigned: some say twenty years, others fifty. But the key point remained the same: how can the council redevelop this estate when they themselves do not have a rightful claim to the property? Strikingly, other residents stress that that the City Council do not even hold the title deed to the land that Kaloleni is built on. This narrative came out strongly in conversation with Eddy, whose longstanding presence in Kaloleni was described in Chapter 1. He told me:

> This estate, it does not belong to City Council. It was built by the British. The City Council were the caretakers of the estate ... The council assumed the role of management after independence ... Of course, the 99 years are not over yet. It was built in 1944. According to the law the lease should be 99 years. So, what happens? So it should remain British property.

Like Edina, Eddy went on to make reference to the authority of paper documentation, explaining to me that 'the title deed is still with the British', and thus the Kaloleni houses in fact 'still belong to the Queen'. It was not the case, he continued, that at independence land and title deeds were automatically transferred to the new dispensation: 'different areas were separately negotiated'. Adopting a slightly different tack to other residents, he argued 'The British Government can still claim it ... it is up to the British whether they continue, they can renew the lease, and they themselves [can] develop it to what they want ... they should involve us ... [but] it is not really up to the City Council'.

The possible endurance of British claims to property in Nairobi goes against any academic history of Kenya's independence that I have read. But with regards to the allocation of property to residents, Eddy speaks partly from family experience: the little circle of shops at the centre of Kaloleni, once also owned by the City Council, have long been privately owned and managed. When Eddy was young, his father was one of the shopkeepers there, running a small butchery that he rented from the colonial City Council. Then in the 1950s, Eddy explained, there was a programme to 'Africanise' the City Council shops in the housing estates – including those in Kaloleni – and transfer ownership to the occupants. This scheme was led by Ambrose Ofafa, a prominent Luo figure and one of the first Africans to sit on the City Council.[1] 'So what happened, the

---

[1] Ambrose Ofafa was one of the earliest elected African politicians in colonial Kenya. Though he advocated for the recognition of Africans' contribution to the city, including various rights to housing and property, he did so from within colonial power structures, sitting on the Nairobi City Council. Shortly

shops were sold to people like my father. We have got the title deeds of the shops. The shops now are private', Eddy explained. His father became the owner of his butchery, the deeds to which Eddy has since inherited.

From Eddy's perspective, it does not seem improbable that a similar process could, or should have been, set in motion for Kaloleni's houses. He and fellow residents have gone to great lengths attempting to uncover the evidence to support their claims. In his book *The Method of Hope* (2004), Miyazaki writes of a disconcerting moment in his fieldwork when he encountered his subjects in Fiji's national archive, looking at the very historical files he wished to use. What quickly became apparent during my fieldwork was that residents in Kaloleni had already beaten me to it. Eddy and several other residents had been making enquiries at the National Archives long before I arrived, spending days trawling through files looking for relevant informa-tion on Kenya's transition to independence and title deeds of estate. They had also written letters to the British High Commission and the British Government, as well as visited the offices of a Nairobi law firm who they say were made the 'trustees' of Kaloleni when the colonial authorities departed. They seek to uncover an alternative history of land rights and title deeds in Eastlands, a narrative that was buried during the chaotic years of the Mau Mau uprising, the Emergency and then the upheavals of independence.

So far, even though they legitimise their arguments by reference to colonial agreements, residents have not unearthed physical documenta-tion that incontrovertibly proves the ownership of the estate, or details of any mortgage scheme. But, for Eddy, this lack of evidence simply indicates the desire of municipal authorities to cover up the reality of Eastlands land rights, in order to turn the estate over to property devel-opers. He explained that previous attempts by the City Council to rede-velop Kaloleni had never succeeded, something he put down to the fact that at heart they knew they could not claim rights over the estate. One of Eddy's counterparts in this research, a man called Lumumba, reiter-ated this point: 'Crooks in the system are waiting like vultures', he told me, to grab the land as soon as they have found a means of doing so. The very material presence of Kaloleni was witness to his argument; their plans have been frustrated, he said, 'otherwise this place would not be standing'.

---

after implementing the transferal of title deeds to African shopkeepers, he was assassinated as he stood in the road just outside Kaloleni. His death was claimed by Mau Mau activists, who accused him of collaboration (Ochieng' 2002: 186).

Minor histories

As I accumulated these alternative histories, what I found fascinating was the underlying assumption of many residents that the story of the past is not fixed but a narrative that needs securing in order to maintain or undermine endeavours in the present. These Kaloleni residents see the conventional history of their estate, as public housing built on public land, not as factual but as a perspective employed by those in a position of power. This evokes important academic debates about the power of historical knowledge, about voice and agency and the legitimacy of representation. In many ways, the arguments of postcolonial subaltern historians, as well as more recent debates about decolonising knowledge, seemed second nature to residents in Kaloleni (Spivak 1988; Chakrabarty 1998; Nyamnjoh 2016). They perceive that the struggle for the future of Kaloleni relies on an active process of historymaking, in which residents make use of aspects of the past as they 'flash up' in the 'now of recognisability' and seek to use them to gain traction over an uncertain future.

Such practices of historymaking are by no means limited to Kaloleni but are further iterations of a wider discourse that has been circulating in recent years. To take two recent examples from Kenya, in her work on Maasai land claims, Lotte Hughes demonstrates how contemporary disputes over land rights call on historical narratives that sometimes diverge drastically from the archival records, but nevertheless invoke them as legitimising sources: 'Many factions now seek to make political capital out of past events ... where laying claim to memory, heritage and history, and sometimes reinventing it, is a popular pursuit', she argues, and one that often invokes the 'expiry' of certain agreements and land leases made with the British (2005: 215, 220). Likewise, Willis and Gona's research on the character of recent secessionist politics at the Kenyan coast has particularly strong resonances with the forms of claim-making in play in Kaloleni. They describe how members of the Mombasa Republic Council (MRC) have gradually developed alternative narratives of coastal history that claim to be founded in knowledge of colonial treaties. As in Kaloleni, a common assertion relates to the expiry of a particular agreement, in this case one that united the coastal region with the rest of Kenya. The authors quote one speaker at a rally who claimed that 'documents in the [MRC's] possession indicated that by 2013 the Government of Kenya should return the region to its indigenous people after the expiry of a fifty-year 'lease' agreement signed on October 5 1963' (Willis and Gona 2013: 65–66).

In a now-famous article, Appadurai argues that there is – or was – a widespread assumption within anthropology that 'the past is a limitless and plastic symbolic resource, infinitely susceptible to the whims of contemporary interest' (1981: 201). He argues that this line of thinking, which he blames partly on Malinowski's notion of myth as social charter, is false. For Appadurai, the ways and forms in which the past can be called upon are subject to particular sets of norms and thus must also seek legitimation: to have force, historical utterances require credibility. Not only do norms govern the terms of the debate between various pasts and 'the contingencies of the present', but because this normative framework enables societies to 'talk *about* themselves, and not only *within* themselves' he argues that 'concessions to change are built in'; 'such norms permit new forms of action' (Appadurai 1981: 218). In some ways this logic is apparent in Kaloleni, where historical narratives and their legitimation via appeals to material or textual sources are not so much about the 'management of meaning' as they are about the management of doing: the kinds of actions that a particular past allows in the present, and how the past is brought to bear on the present in specific ways (Cohen and Comaroff 1976). Nevertheless, in Appadurai's appraisal we are still left with the sense that the past is somehow separate from the now, as though it is of a different order or quality. He discusses his framework of norms as a system of mediation, as if there were a gap or space between past(s) and present. He seeks to reframe how we think about the past, shrinking it from 'limitless' to 'scarce', but he still couches it as a 'resource' that can be called upon. This is the filing cabinet approach to history, in which aspects of an inert past are made commensurable with present demands (see Trouillot 1995). It doesn't escape the historicist's linearity.

The character of historymaking in Kaloleni might be better approached as what Pinney (in relation to images) describes as 'compressed performances' caught up in 'recursive trajectories of repetition and pastiche whose dense complexity makes them resistant to any particular moment' (2005: 266). While Kalolenians' narratives are linked to other types of historical production, such as that formed through scrutiny of the archives, they cannot be simply explained by it. Even as they are constituting history, these residents are doing so through recursive temporal eddies that are 'not necessarily coterminous with more conventional [historical] temporalities' (Pinney 2005: 266; see also Kracauer 1995). Though they draw upon them, Kaloleni's new histories are incommensurable with 'formal' accounts produced by what Cohen has called the 'guild' of history (1994: 4).

This incommensurability has posed a problem for scholars trying to rationalise 'vernacular' practices of historymaking with those of the academy, preventing the neat closure of their historical accounts. In their analyses, Hughes and Willis and Gona have recounted what they see as the liberties taken with formal histories of Maasailand and Coast Province respectively. Hughes states that current claims that rest on reviving a 1913 treaty are 'mired in historical distortion' and that websites seeking to promote indigenous rights 'print wildly ahistorical claims' (2005: 213, 214). 'The Maasai's reliance on orality causes them myriad problems', she continues, as 'they cannot reflect upon old texts of their own' (2005: 216–7). Willis and Gona meanwhile describe a 'verbose and jumbled evocation of history'; 'numerous misrepresentations' of colonial documentation that have led to 'the MRC's fictions' (2013: 63, 70). Both articles argue that there is a logic to these distortions, that 'they are the consequence of people's exclusion from powerful knowledge' over many years (Willis and Gona 2013: 70). Yet the authors still privilege what, to paraphrase Latour, we might call the purification between history and myth, the past and the present, orality and the written word. While we should be alert to the abuses of history and the politicisation of the past, it is not as straightforward as stating, as Hughes does, 'and thus myth becomes fact' (2005: 214). Rather than characterise these historical narratives as a faulty mirror that inaccurately reflects the 'proper' history that we have learned elsewhere, what if we take them seriously? What if we regard the 'outpouring' of varied and often incoherent histories 'as an experimental zone where new possibilities and new identities are forged'? (Pinney 2005: 265).

In an article on Vision 2030 and local objections to a proposed deep-water port and free economic zone on the Kenyan island of Lamu, Bremner explores the notion of a 'minor global architecture' for understanding the strategies and politics of residents' demands to be heard (2013). She builds on a concept developed by Jill Stoner, who in turn borrows from Deleuze and Guattari's notion of 'minor literatures' that take on a major language in order to destabilise from within (1986). Through an interpretation of Kafka's writing, they propose a minor literature as one that writes from a marginalised or minoritarian position and which is thoroughly political in its outlook. It is also fundamentally collective, even revolutionary, in its objectives:

> what each author says individually already constitutes a common action … [is] necessarily political … and if the writer is in the margins or completely outside his or her fragile community, this situation allows the writer all the more the possibility to express another possible community and to forge the means for another consciousness. (Deleuze and Guattari 1986: 17)

Stoner takes this idea up to outline a subversive architecture of 'opportunistic events' that seek to undo structures of power: they emerge from the bottom of power structures and, while working within the languages of those structures, force cracks and fissures to appear (2012: 7). A minor architecture is not minor in ambition but in audibility: it is 'not one defined by its scale or significance, but rather one occluded by majority accounts, threaded through, on the margins of or emerging in the wake of its flows' (Bremner 2013: 2).

With this in mind, I suggest that at work in Kaloleni is the development of a 'minor history', a way of burrowing inside the formal narratives and official histories of Nairobi and Kaloleni and staking alternative claims. These claims are based on a performative sense of property, developed through the repeated acts of home maintenance and management that residents have undertaken in the absence of state provision. Over time, this has engendered an active process of historymaking, one which is also oriented towards the future. But this is not so much about breaking *out* of structures of power as it is about breaking *in:* cracking open the schemes of Vision 2030, making them more inclusive and ensuring residents' own participation in the city's future. Sometimes these narratives appeared as an explicit goal, in which some residents adopted a highly politicised and tactical outlook, but it also emerged more implicitly and cumulatively, as they took up certain narratives heard from others and elaborated them further.

The paper it is written on

As I sat with Izmani discussing the possibility of Kaloleni being 'upgraded', I asked him why he thought residents had a right to remain in the estate. The residents 'need to benefit from whatever comes next', he told me firmly, because 'we know from our fathers ... there was an agreement'. This was another iteration of the narrative told by Peter, Edina, Eddy and many others: that after years of occupation, the houses would go to the residents, and that this was enshrined in an agreement that the post-independence City Council had failed to fulfil and which it was now trying to conceal. By the time this conversation took place, I had been in Kaloleni for nine months and I had heard this story frequently. I had also spent considerable time in the Kenya National Archives and MacMillan Library archives, going through colonial administrative files of the Municipal Council, Native Affairs department and Native Housing committee, which though rich in all kinds of detail about Kaloleni's inception, construction and management, seemed to carry no reference to any mortgage scheme or promise of eventual ownership. As a former student of African History,[2] which compared to other subfields of History is necessarily less dependent on formal written sources, I have long been interested in oral histories, the relationship of storytelling and narration to official records and postcolonial historiography. So, I was not in the archives looking for 'verification' of what I had been told by residents; I was fully aware of

[2] That is, 'History' in the academic sense of university-oriented scholarship, or what Cohen calls the 'guild' of history (1994). I capitalise it here to distinguish it from historymaking beyond the academy, though of course the two are interlinked.

the pitfalls of looking for the 'true' story of Kaloleni. But I did become fascinated by the truth that this particular narrative seemed to have attained among residents, gaining credence as it circulated and recirculated in various forms; a minor history threading its way like a wormhole through an old book.

The complex relationship between orality and the written word is a well-worn seam of Africanist historiography (see, for example, Guy 1994; Landau 1995; Hofmeyr 2004). In her analysis of the intersection between historical storytelling and literate bureaucracies in a South African chiefdom, Isabel Hofmeyr shows how, in the 1930s, a new Native Commissioner's Office both bolstered and undermined the authority of colonial agents as well as that of local chiefs and elders (1994: 42). She argues that, far from institutions of colonialism revolutionising local systems of rule, 'The communicative strategies of a predominantly oral community transformed the literate procedures of colonialism' (1994: 42). This is an example of what, in relation to her work in southern Sudan, Sharon Hutchinson has described as the 'hidden powers of paper' (1996: 284; see also Willis and Gona 2013). Likewise, Izmani's narrative was not a simple case of oral narrative or 'myth' against written 'source'. He told me that he'd heard it from 'our fathers', that is, the older generation. When I asked if he knew from where they had learned it, he told me, 'It is written'; they'd found it in the original documents from the colonial period. 'In the archives?' I queried. Izmani nodded yes, but uncertainly. 'They found it written', he repeated; the fact that it was written down, committed to paper, was the salient point, not where that piece of paper was stored. Izmani's comments suggest that one of the 'hidden powers of paper' is its potentially subversive quality, even at a distance. The document itself need not be physically present, but the idea of it holds a certain allure – a promise of stability and fixity even as it is being reappropriated.

In Hofmeyr's account, she shows how in particular moments – such as in the act of writing a letter or reading out loud from a colonial document – creative misreadings and claims to official power could occur. Important here is the materiality of such an encounter: legacies of colonial rule 'not as a disembodied text or ideology, but as incarnations that have complex histories, *surfaces* and appearances' (Pinney 2008: 389). In a context of partial literacy, the power of the 'colonial word' lay partly in its materiality, in its concrete form as page and book. The 'hidden powers of paper' – and other similar creative appropriations of the materials of governance – could be a way in which oral African communities under colonial rule made sense of text-based modernity, to find new ways of constituting knowledge and staking certain privileges in the world.

Urban Nairobi in 2014 is not rural South Africa in the 1930s, but Hofmeyr's account still resonates. The appeal of documentation, and the perceived authority of its materiality, is demonstrated in Izmani's comment, 'It is written'. It also resonates with David and Saleh's appeal to physical objects to substantiate their own accounts. But as we have seen, it is through oral circulation that the narrative regarding Kaloleni's ownership has gradually accrued declarative weight. Spoken word, written text and material form are here mutually imbricated in the emergence of a particular history. This complex interplay resonates with Johannes Fabian's study of the relationship of painting, talking and writing in the painted series *The History of Zaire* by Congolese artist-historian Tshibumba (Fabian 1996). Tshibumba was a street artist producing what have come to be known as 'popular paintings', sold from the side of the road to passers-by. Fabian made his acquaintance and became fascinated by his perspective on Congolese history. Eventually, Fabian commissioned Tshibumba to paint the history of Zaire, as it then was, a project that Tshibumba set about with much enthusiasm. He grew up in the rich storytelling tradition of the Luba region, but also drew stylistic inspiration from newspapers, photographs and comic strips. The history he produced consisted of over 100 works that combined a repertoire of pictorial elements, textual inscriptions and captions, each of which were elucidated through Tshibumba's oral exegesis to Fabian. These different communicative techniques intersect in various ways, making statements that in some paintings reinforce one another, while in others their juxtaposition creates the space for historical perspective or critical comment to emerge (Fabian 1996: 228–36).

Though the different elements can stand alone – not every painting contains text, and Tshibumba sometimes narrated stories that he had not painted – it was in the interrelationship of the different modes that Tshibumba realised the potency of his history (1996: 247). The relationship between orality, literacy and materiality is somewhat dialectical in that these different forms help to constitute each other, as Tshibumba moves back and forth between them. He may take up stories heard orally, produce them pictorially in a style that draws on a photographic snapshot, add a written comment or inscription, and then give the painting a title with a biblical reference that 'gives mythical proportions to a historical incident', so moving again towards a form of storytelling (1996: 255). That Tshibumba's history takes material form is important, as the paintings will continue to generate historical recollection down the years. This characteristic is called *ukumbusho*, a Kiswahili word that translates as 'a quality capable of triggering memories' (1996: 195). As traces or reminders – Tshibumba calls them monuments – they have the capacity to activate critical remembering in a way that words alone cannot. Though not so consciously, we can see a similar interplay between speech, text and material paper at work in Izmani's narrative. It is much more overtly apparent in the activities of the Kaloleni Estate Residents' Association (KERA), which are examined in the next section.

Forensic archiving

The practices of historymaking in Kaloleni and the capacity to make authoritative claims do not just rely on the invocation of old colonial agreements hidden in formal archives such as the Macmillan Library or the Kenya National Archives but have also stimulated alternative forms of recordkeeping. During my fieldwork, it quickly became apparent that KERA are highly meticulous in writing, receiving and archiving correspondence. On my first visit to the house of Enoch, the KERA chairman, I observed that his house was notably austere compared to many others. He lives alone, and his house does not feature the walls of family photographs common to Kaloleni homes, nor the accumulated debris of family life. The layout of his house is still in its original state, and the floor is cold, bare concrete. A large cheap wooden cabinet in the living room is one of the few items of furniture. When he opened it, I began to understand that this is where his attention is focused; he is not concerned with acquiring homely belongings but on assembling, in forensic detail, as much documentation about Kaloleni as he can lay his hands on. He pulled out several large ring binders that revealed an archive of material. There were articles clipped from newspapers, excerpts from history books, official reports and grey literature, as well as letters written to and received from the City Council and other authorities, all of which were neatly rubberstamped with the date of receipt and carefully filed.

The significance of this tangible documentation is not just practical, but strategic as well. The chairman demonstrated to me just how important records are by recounting an event that caused much consternation in Kaloleni. In early December 2013, a new billboard was erected on Jogoo Road, the main road through Eastlands and which borders one edge of the estate. The image on the billboard showed several highrise blocks of exclusive-looking apartments surrounded by landscaped grounds. In the centre, a sign read *Karibu Kaloleni*, Welcome to Kaloleni. This billboard came with no warning and was not accompanied by any public meeting or distribution of information from local or national government.[3] KERA immediately wrote to the council to request more information and to ask why KERA, as an officially registered association, had received no communication on what was apparently the future vision of Kaloleni. The chairman showed me copies of the letters he had sent, along with responses from the housing department. The

[3] See Chapter 6 for more on the billboard and other visions of the future

replies promised further details that had so far not been forthcoming. KERA also held a residents' meeting to discuss the billboard, at which the local County Representative,[4] Peter Imwatok, turned up to speak. Enoch spoke disapprovingly to me about the impassioned speech that Imwatok had made, which he saw as empty political rhetoric. 'He made a lot of comments, a lot of promises, but he's just talking. Politicians only want votes. Will he be around after the next elections?' The chairman doubted Imwatok's capacity or intention to deliver on the promises he made to get to the bottom of what was going on. As he put it, 'there is a big difference between saying something and having written information'.

Enoch's comment is particularly intriguing as it not only asserts the authority of material documentation over verbal assurances but seems to disavow the discursive nature of much Kenyan politics. The loyalties of ethnicity – though not in themselves fixed entities – have tended to generate powerful social networks that underlie the patrimonial character of much Kenyan politics (Smedt 2009). Often marked by clientelist relationships that ensure political loyalty, ethnic political networks are characterised by reciprocal social relations rather than contractual, pen-and-ink correspondence. That such relationships do not always deliver is a recurring theme in the day-to-day politics of the country. Residents of a relatively marginalised neighbourhood such as Kaloleni have little voice in this process, and minimal political clout. The situation was laconically summed up by Dolly, who emphasised the hollowness of politicians' words and the absence of any relationship between promises and action. She told me, 'They do nothing. And when the elections will come, they'll say, "Please just vote for me so that the project I started, I will finish it within those five years." Oh! Again he goes [away] completely.'

KERA too seem to have lost faith in the effectiveness of this discursive politics, and instead are turning to material documentation as they compile an evidenced-based archive of who said what and when. Enoch and his team see this forensic archiving as a crucial way of maintaining residents' participation in the swirling debates about Kaloleni's future, as a way of leveraging power away from the usual political channels – who cannot be trusted not to corrupt the whole process – and keeping it inside Kaloleni. KERA see their archive not as a means to 'misrepresent' the official narratives of the estate's history for their own benefit, but a form of reaching back into the past and constructing it anew. Their material archive seeks to generate a minor history: to open up new

---

[4] Since the new constitution came into effect in 2013, the position of County Representative has replaced that of Councillor. It remains an elected position in local administration, in this case Nairobi County government (formerly Nairobi City Council). There is only one County Rep. per electoral ward.

possibilities and provide legitimacy to claims that a more powerful politics could otherwise easily dismiss. This is a reminder of the dialectical relationship between the past and the present that historical materialism makes possible: it 'affects both the content of the tradition and its receivers' (Benjamin 2007: 255).

Keeping this archive within the estate also contributes to the making of Kaloleni in a different mode. KERA see Kaloleni as constituted not just by the assemblage of humans, houses, remains, infrastructures and belongings but by the archive itself, which seeks to make present the dilemmas, histories and politics in which the estate is embedded, and to constitute it as a – dynamic, living – historical object. Akin to Saleh's cobblestone, or the Luo grinding stone described by Blount, KERA's archive is a manifestation of *ukumbusho*, the quality capable of awakening history, and a part of the materiality of Kaloleni itself. These minor histories echo Pinney's 'experimental zone', a space of transformative practices that seek to fashion new selves through claims to property and ownership. But the audibility of such claims is hard to ensure: the legitimacy of voice and the capacity to represent Kaloleni are subject to larger political currents, in which not only the authority of claims but their material presence is at stake.

Silencing the archive

As the activities of KERA suggest, many in Kaloleni (and elsewhere in Kenya), are cynical of politicians' talk, seeing it all as a lot of hot air without any substance. The very malleability of political narrative has left them feeling vulnerable, feeding the appeal of material documentation. But if the durability of material records is understood as making them more authoritative – and vice versa – then this also foregrounds concerns about control. In a context of political cover-ups and contaminated evidence, for example, while paper might be understood to hold authoritative power it could also be subject to manipulation. This is widely recognised in Kenya, where there have been frequent well-publicised cases demonstrating that official records are far from unimpeachable.

Nicholas Dirks has pointed out that what materials end up in the official archive is the product of governance itself: 'the state literally produces, adjudicates, organizes, and maintains the discourses that become available as the primary texts of history' (2002: 59). In Kenya, this observation is sharpened by people's awareness that the archive may express forms of governmentality not just through the state's ways of seeing and organising knowledge but through the direct manipulation of public records. This is at stake in the recent inquiry into the official secrecy surrounding British colonial actions and abuses during the Mau Mau Insurgency, when records of colonial brutality were suppressed and censored (Anderson 2005). But there are also more routine examples. During my fieldwork, a high-profile battle was played out in the Kenyan press between Charity Ngilu, Cabinet Secretary for Lands, and Mohammed Swazuri, Chairman of the National Land Coalition, a dispute that eventually made its way to the Supreme Court. The dispute was ostensibly over the digitisation of land records but was in reality a power play over the right to control what is seen as Kenya's most potent records office, the Lands Registry (Walubengo 2014).

This saga sputtered on for several years, during which it emerged that millions of land records had gone missing at the Registry, alongside allegations that officers deliberately hide files and then seek bribes for finding them; that title deeds are tampered with and lands reallocated to those willing to pay; that this is facilitating land grabbing at the highest levels in Kenya (Merab 2014; Wainaina 2015). KERA's forensic archiving was thus taking place amid a larger context in which the deliberate mismanagement and obfuscation of public records was understood to enable the kleptocratic distribution of grabbed land.[5] It is not always clear whose hand is at work in such manoeuvres. At the Lands Registry, Charity Ngilu has been quick to say that the fault lies with 'cartels' of officers looking to make a quick buck, while her critics have pointed to Kenya's long history of ministers secretively awarding high-profile figures with land allocations that only came to public knowledge much later.[6] Either way, the significance was not lost on KERA, who perceived that they should make themselves responsible for maintaining accurate records relating to Kaloleni, through which they could represent the interests of the estate.

The affairs of the Land Registry are far from the only example of deliberate or inadvertent tampering with the sorts of records that go on to form the backbone of historical study. In 2004, a huge fire at Nairobi City Hall destroyed three floors of the building, which accommodated the council's housing, engineering and waste disposal sections, among other offices. Thousands of files detailing current and historical municipal works were destroyed in the process – including those pertaining to the management of housing estates such as Kaloleni – as well as urban planning documents outlining the future development of the city. That the fire was

[5] This is far from new – the politicised distribution of land has been a key locus of political debate and conflict in Kenya since the colonial period and probably long before (see, for example, Berman and Lonsdale 1992; Kanyinga 2009; Lynch 2011; Boone 2012).

[6] There have been many examples, but during my fieldwork one notorious case came to light: the illegal allocation of over 500,000 acres of land in Lamu County. Many of the owners of the twenty-two companies to whom titles has been allocated turned out to be senior politicians and public figures (*Capital News* 2014; Shiundu 2014). For historical examples, see (Boone 2014).

a result of arson was generally agreed upon, though who the perpetrators were was unclear (BBC 2004). Many suspected the City Council of an attempted cover up: it was then embroiled in accusations of financial misconduct and conveniently many relevant records went up in smoke. Others saw the fire as a protest, either by disaffected council workers, who at the time were on strike over non-payment of salaries, or by furious residents of the city's informal housing who had been protesting recent demolitions in the slums (Panapress 2004). Official investigations were inconclusive, but public opinion generally regarded the timing and convenient loss of records as sufficient to blame the council.

Wherever responsibility lies, such episodes sweep away any lingering confidence in the sanctity of archives. What Dirks calls the state's adjudication and organisation of discourses are here supplemented by more overt actions of erasure and redaction. Authority over public recordkeeping is contested terrain in Kenya, and one cannot assume that a record that is found today will be there tomorrow. A recent article in the *Nation* newspaper expounded, 'Here's why you should check your land records often', putting the onus on Kenyans themselves to undertake spot-checks on title deeds held at the Lands Registry (Wainaina 2015). If these are the archival documents of the future, it seems all too clear that it is not only the method of their interpretation but their very materiality which is at stake.

Against such a backdrop, KERA's paper-based archive can be seen to acknowledge the authority of the printed word, while aiming to both protect and harness its materiality. By rubberstamping and compiling all their correspondence, and supplementing these files with newspaper and academic articles, KERA seek to develop a mirror archive; one that could potentially still hold officials to account should the council's own records disappear. By locating their archive in Kaloleni, KERA try to ensure it is out of reach from the kinds of manipulations to which more public records have been subjected. Although they are in some respects mimicking the forms of official recordkeeping (that are in turn modelled on British modes of governance), with mimesis comes alterity: the slippage that makes differentiation possible (Taussig 1993). KERA are of course themselves selective in what they choose to preserve and have their own particular agenda: Kaloleni as the site for the development of a minor history. The pronouncement that 'Kenya grew from here' presents Kaloleni as a whole new archive for the future history of the nation.

A place of knowledge

KERA were quite clear about their desire to pull Kaloleni from the periphery into the centre. They argued that recognising and celebrating its historical importance was crucial to overcoming what they perceived as the estate's deliberate marginalisation. Paul, KERA's founder, stressed the vital importance for Kenyans to know their own history. He asserted that residents in Kaloleni 'do not know where they live'; they need to understand the historical significance of the estate to defend their current homes, and their status as residents, from the caprices of state-led regeneration projects. Echoing the sentiments of Tshibumba, he said we should not only rely on what others tell us: 'To know where we are now, we have to know what came before'. It's important here to reiterate that this kind of work cannot be side-lined as 'folk history' or 'memory'. Historymaking does not just occur in the academy – in Cohen's 'guild' of history (1994: 4). Paul and others set out to challenge some of the fundamentals of 'official' history: what they 'know' from the government and City Council, such as their official status as simply tenants. Their methods of relating to the past are creative – and not without their conspiracy theories – but they are also highly politicised. 'If you build a house on top of sand it will fall down', Paul told me; without building strong foundations of historical awareness, any residents' campaign to protect their futures is bound to fail.

KERA seek to generate such awareness not only through their paper-based archive, but through their use of new technologies and modes of communication. KERA has an active online and social media presence, regularly posting Facebook updates about their work, Kaloleni news and interesting titbits. One morning in April 2016, a notification flashed up from KERA's page:

> Kaloleni estate is one of the estate[s] which has produced great minds which has shaped Kenyan history. also many of them are doing great things all over the world
>
>   Those people who respected Kaloleni estate ended up becoming great people … residents and friends of Kaloleni we need to celebrate Kaloleni [*sic*]

What struck me particularly about this post was how the production of place, history and 'great minds' was assumed to go together. The post went on to list some of the distinguished figures who have lived in Kaloleni, from Charles Rubia (first African mayor of Nairobi) to a current professor at an American university. The post suggests that Kaloleni is important as a site of history – not just locally, but as causally related to 'great things all over the world'. This cosmopolitan character is not new: 'wider issues and attentions, rather than narrowly Kaloleni issues, are always afloat in Kaloleni neighbourhoods' (Cohen and Odhiambo 1989: 43). KERA's post didn't mention, though it could have, not only those who have shaped the events of Kenyan history, but also those who have influenced how it is framed and understood.

The majority of Kaloleni's residents identify as members of the Luo ethnic group, and the estate was a centre of urban Luo life in Nairobi from the 1950s to the 1980s. As such, Kaloleni has played an important part in the development of what it means to be Luo in modern Kenya. This relies not only on more recent urban networks of sociality and kinship but to maintaining both imagined and practical ties to a rural homeland near Lake Victoria. Over the decades, Kaloleni has come to constitute what Cohen and Odhiambo describe as a 'Luo landscape in the city' (1989: 43). E. S. Atieno Odhiambo was himself a Luo, originally from Siaya in western Kenya, and he became one of the most prominent – and outspoken – Kenyan scholars of his time. Much of his work explored how the production of historical knowledge was inextricable from wider networks of politics and power (Odhiambo 1991; Cohen and Odhiambo 1992). His experience of teaching, writing and publishing at the University of Nairobi during the 1970s and 1980s underlined the dangers of pursuing this line of thinking in Kenya. During the 'purge-like times' of the 1980s, when President Moi's security forces policed free speech on university campuses, Atieno Odhiambo was forced into hiding (Cohen 2009). He continued to publish and to support other critical figures and for this he was eventually detained and tortured in 1986. Though he never lived in Kaloleni himself, he had family connections there and was a frequent caller, debater and friend to the estate, observing that 'Luo in Nairobi define … their belonging to Kaloleni by the frequency of their activities there rather than by whether they reside in the community' (Cohen and Odhiambo 1989: 43).

Atieno Odhiambo was supervised for his PhD in History by Bethwell Allan Ogot, who is perhaps Kenya's most famous historian. His book *History of the Southern Luo* (1967) broke new ground not just in terms of how to understand the diffuse Luo-speaking peoples around the fringes of Lake Victoria, but how to approach the history of African societies more generally. His search for new bodies of evidence in a landscape not only without documentary sources, but without visible centralised institutions, led him to meticulously study Luo oral narratives of migration and genealogy, arguing that the pre-colonial history of such societies could – and should – be written. Ogot gained his PhD from the University of London in 1965, but in the 1950s he had lived in Kaloleni, staying with his sister and her husband while he attended Nairobi College. I was fortunate to meet him in Kisumu in 2014, now a professor emeritus of Maseno University and approaching ninety years. We chatted about Kaloleni, and he remembered the strict rules of the colonial Estate Officer, but also the complex political climate: 'in those days, you had to know who to drink with', he told me. Luo politics in Kaloleni was by no means uniform or unified, there were schisms between followers of Tom Mboya, Argwings Khodek (Ogot's cousin), the clan affiliations of the Luo Union and Luo Welfare. As nationalist sentiment grew through the late 1950s, Luo politics fragmented; the sands were constantly shifting as different parties and congresses were formed.

But they all felt the need to have a strong foothold in Kaloleni as a heartland of Luo society: 'Odhiambo kept on reminding us, Kaloleni is an outpost of Siaya!' Ogot told me.

In their different ways, Atieno Odhiambo and Ogot sought to re-write knowledge about Kenya, to frame history differently and to use this to particular ends in the present. For Odhiambo, the priority was to open up different narratives, to show how things could have been, and could still be, different in Kenya – a project that was regarded as disturbingly open-ended by Kenya's single-party state. Ogot's target was more the discipline of history itself, and particularly the narrow confines of the academy's idea of satisfactory evidence. He knew that Kenyans them-selves could tell a very different version of the past, and Ogot used their accounts to construct a new type of Kenyan history. But this was a history primarily made for other scholars. His highly technical works are not much read in Kenya today, and even Odhiambo's more acces-sible writing – he and Cohen intended their book *Siaya* (1989) to be 'both about and for the Luo' – is generally forgotten. Their work shows how Kaloleni is enmeshed in histories of knowledge production, of ways of knowing the world, and how networks of Luo affiliation were crucial to making Kaloleni as a site of history. But their work also shows how this knowledge has tended to spiral away from Kaloleni – into central politics, into universities and into printed texts. By contrast, the Kalo-lenians I encountered were, in their fragmentary ways, engaged in how to bring this sort of knowledge back in to Kaloleni, how to build on it, improve it and make it work for current residents.

Histories of possibility

Such struggles have been lent a new urgency by the uncertain future of Kaloleni and the anticipation of what Vision 2030 might set in motion. Like Izmani, many residents were quick to emphasise that they were not against infrastructural development per se; after years of neglect most would welcome some kind of investment in the estate. But they were deeply concerned about the form it might take, how invasive it might be and whether they would be excluded from the process. A discussion with Boniface about the estate's possible regeneration set out many of these intersecting concerns:

> I'm owning this house. It's, like, mine ... the thing is that they don't make it [the plans] inclusive to the residents, like [get] our input ... [Kaloleni] has a very rich history but it's kind of gone under neglect so it's not in the state that it used to be ... But I'd like them not to bring everything down. ... Maybe they won't listen to us because maybe we don't have that financial muscle. They may just move us forcefully ... So that's the fear people have here. It's like they are being excluded

completely, not because they wish for that, it's because they don't have the financial muscle.

One way that residents seek to negotiate these anxieties is by recourse to their deep historical connection to Kaloleni. This means forcing authorities to recognise their presence and take their claims to urban belonging seriously. Throughout this book, I have been careful to avoid using the word 'tenant' except in very specific contexts. This is deliberate; it is a word disliked by most and one that I almost never heard used apart from in discussions about the very early years of the estate. The category of 'tenant' undermines residents' performative accomplishment of a sense of property, of rightful belonging. 'I'm owning this house', as Boniface put it. This sentiment is challenged in official renewal documentation, in which the planners designate residents merely as 'sitting tenants' (NaMSIP 2013: 4). Residents reject this category, refusing the implication that they are passive beneficiaries of a public good, and instead assert their contributions to the making of Kaloleni – and even to the making of Nairobi and Kenya. As Boniface's words above make clear, they want any plans to be inclusive, to involve the input of residents.

In this way, residents do not reject the plans for Vision 2030 outright, but rather seek to become entangled in it. Here we see how the minor history of Kaloleni is part of a larger claim to urban inclusion. By asserting their identity as owners and stakeholders, residents refuse to be side-lined, hoping to fracture planning protocols in such a way that it might enable participation and ensure a future of urban presence. With regards to debates about Vision 2030 on Lamu Island, Bremner noted how residents there staked a position as participants rather than bystanders. One of their banners read 'WE WANT A PORT! ... only after community consultation ... an Environmental Impact Assessment, after land reforms WITH BENEFITS FOR ALL' (2013: 408). As Bremner puts it, Lamu residents

> are not working to break out of the zone, but to break into it, to get inside it, to share its spoils. Protest, engagement, consultation, environmental impact assessment, land reform, biocommunity protocols, etc. are being used as mechanisms to crack fissures in the seemingly impenetrable walls of the zone and to make it more porous and enabling. (2013: 408)

In Kaloleni, a similar attitude was clear. Discussing the uncertainties of regeneration proposals with a group of friends one evening, one man named Besh turned to me and said, 'You know, they can't leave us out. We have come too far', before adding emphatically, 'We are all stakeholders now'.

This chapter has explored how residents' performative sense of property has become the basis for such claims. Their modes of historymaking harness the potentiality of property, asserting the possibility of their recognition and engagement in urban renewal. Besh and many others like him refuse to be just sitting tenants, recipients of whatever the government will dole out. Residents are again taking up the terms of formal documentation, this time not colonial agreements but the language of planning and consultation. By turning these terms on their head, residents assert their right to participate, to be involved in developing alternative visions of the future. As with the powers of paper-based claim-making and the existence of Saleh's kerbstone, this desire to break in to the process also relies on material substantiation. Casting themselves as 'stakeholders' or 'owners', residents take up the minor histories of Kaloleni to reaffirm the intimate attachments of people and place, awakening the material traces of the past to act on an uncertain future. This evokes the significance of property to the making of selves, and how material histories might help a community to ensure future belonging.

This was evocatively illuminated by a man named Lumumba. Born and raised in the estate and now aged around fifty, Lumumba no longer lives in Kaloleni, but he spends his afternoons there, sitting with friends at the back of the social hall. He is very thoughtful and, in some ways, quite nostalgic, but he also spoke eloquently on the power of encountering the past in the present. As we talked one day, he remarked, 'Let them not demolish', he said, 'We are attached. For many of these young people you see, this is the only home they know'. This emotional attachment is powerful, he suggested, and crucial for community: 'this is the compound of the people', he observed. Echoing the KERA chairman's comment that 'Kenya grew from here', Lumumba explained how Kaloleni is important for Kenya as a whole: demolition 'would affect the history of this country'. He added, 'Without the buildings you cannot remember, you have no memories'. Just as David could not find his words without engaging with the fabric of his house, for Lumumba, the materiality of the estate substantiates its historical existence.

This presence – of memory and materiality – is vital to negotiating the future. Lumumba compared Kaloleni to the new Thika Superhighway, one of the Kenyan government's flagship infrastructural projects in recent years (see Manji 2015a). He commented how the area bisected by the massive road has now changed so much that it is unrecognisable to him: 'It has been cleared', he said. 'Nothing is left'. All traces of what was once there have been obliterated, and despite the presence of a huge new infrastructure, it seems futureless: 'That place is empty now'. He told me that these days he struggled to remember what was there before the highway, adding 'You know, I even can't remember what I used to *do* there'. Not only has his visual memory of the scene faded, but he has lost his embodied knowledge, its location in his lived experience. He went on, 'If the buildings come down, Kaloleni will be gone … we are attached ... we have no future without this place.' Through their labours of maintenance, repair and propertying, they have made Kaloleni as much as the place has made them. This generative attachment forges possibilities of belonging to the future as well as to the past. Lumumba's apprehension that this might be broken in part stems from the neighbouring estate of Murthurwa, which has already undergone a series of demolitions. There, the social hall was preserved but now stands, as he evocatively described it, like 'a lonely old man with nothing to say'. It remains as a relic from a previous era, to which no one listens or pays any attention. It stands out of time, unused and no longer relevant to the changes that have sprung up around it. In a Benjaminian sense, its revolutionary potential has gone untapped: there is no lightning flash of recognition between that hollowed-out structure and the Muthurwa of today.

The practices described in this chapter are deeply concerned with power's distribution, and, in their various ways, seek the capacity to make authoritative claims. In doing so, residents open up an experimental – if disjunctive – zone of possibility. The minor historymaking at work in Kaloleni shows residents' deep awareness of Nairobi as a site co-constituted by people and place. For residents, not only their longevity of dwelling but their decades of performing the obligations of ownership have sculpted Kaloleni's rich social and material textures. As property, it is also imbued with Strathernian potentiality, offering a 'capacity for development as yet unrealised' (Strathern 1996: 17). If this latent potentiality is to come to fruition, then residents argue they need not only to protect Kaloleni's buildings, but to nurture its generativity as a site of history. Their recursive interactions with the past of Kaloleni, and Kenya more broadly, help them not only to craft new property assemblages that challenge official narratives of their estate, but to make a minor history that might offer the possibility of belonging to the future.

Part Two
MAKING NEW HORIZONS

4

Land, Home and Funerals

In the middle of May 2014, I borrowed a car from a friend in Nairobi and set off with Tom – my close friend, research assistant and host in Kaloleni – and Kevin, Tom's friend and our regular company on explorations around Eastlands. Our plan was to trace various ex-Kaloleni residents back to their rural upcountry homes, to see how they were living, what kinds of houses they had built and how they remembered Kaloleni. The majority of Kalolenians, including Tom, are from the Luo ethnic group, who hail from the lands around Lake Victoria in western Kenya. In the preceding weeks, we made dozens of calls, spoke with relatives, friends and neighbours in Kaloleni and elsewhere, to track down the locations of homesteads that we could visit. For the three-week trip, we would base ourselves at the home of Tom's parents, Dominic and Judith Nyanya, who themselves had been Kaloleni residents, bringing up their family in house A20 until they retired and returned to their homestead in Busia district.

As intimated in Chapter 1, questions of mobility and flow, as much as dwelling and place, frame life in Kaloleni, influencing how people plan ahead and how they try to turn aspirations into reality. This includes movement between rural and urban Kenya; maintaining a relationship with a rural landscape that is also understood as vital to projects of self-making. The persistence of urban-rural connections has been a longstanding theme in the scholarship of urbanisation in Africa, and researchers have long argued that the making of African cities cannot be understood without reference to the social, political and economic import of rural ties (see, for example, Heisler and Marwick 1974; Geschiere and Gugler 1998; Burton 2001). In Kenya, the relationship between town life and village is one of the enduring themes of the country's history, with important implications for labour, livelihoods and national politics (Collier and Lal 1986; White 1990; Robertson 1997; Carotenuto and Luongo 2009). Rural to urban migration continues to account for a considerable proportion of Nairobi's growth, and exerts a powerful enough hold on the imagination to preoccupy many writers, singers and filmmakers as well as academics.[1]

Much of the literature on rural-urban connectivity has focused on first-generation urban migrants, the importance of remittances to rural homes and home connections to making life in town sustainable (Robertson 1997; Frederiksen 2001; Lonsdale 2001). Yet it is clear that in Nairobi, and probably in many African cities, the consequence of this connection persists over multiple generations of urban life, though it may go through significant recalibrations. The changing character of urban life reshapes Nairobians' relationship with rural landscapes not only in terms of ethnic politics or forms of exchange, but in the way the relationship is maintained across a range of social, material and moral flows. The dynamics of belonging in contemporary Kaloleni, with its decayed infrastructure and future uncertainty, help to understand this shifting urban-rural nexus. While other scholars have noted the significance of rural-urban ties in Kenya for political belonging and allegiance (Carotenuto and Luongo 2009; Lynch 2011), here I focus on the ways that gender, generation and dying refract ideas of home and achievement. For Kaloleni men, achieving urban masculinity is intimately tied to a building a rural home – a process that continues even after death.

Luos return to western Kenya, to the land that most call 'home', for all kinds of reasons, both permanent and transitory: to visit family, to build houses, to maintain farms, but above all to attend funerals. This was brought home to me as I reviewed my notebooks from fieldwork, which are sprinkled throughout with remarks about absences: 'Tried to visit X today, but was told he had gone "home"'; 'Went for my interview with Y as arranged, but he had travelled for a funeral'; 'Today I saw Z, his uncle has died and he is going home for the burial'. Negotiations around funerals and burials have long been central to the mediation of the 'rural-urban nexus' in Africa, leading to what Rebekah Lee has called a condition of 'death on the move' that can both reconfigure and reaffirm attachments to a specific landscape of home (2011: 227). In my fieldwork, the strong association for Kaloleni Luo of 'home' with 'burial' remained persistent. I was frequently told that burial on ancestral land was essential, that 'you cannot be buried in Nairobi'. As will be discussed below, Luo have long insisted on upcountry burials for their kin, but in terms of sheer numbers this mobility has become particularly pronounced in recent years. This is due to a combination of urbanisation, demographic trends and high mortality rates, which are linked partly to HIV/AIDS but also to unaffordable general healthcare and increasingly high rates of accidental death, particularly from road accidents (Lamont 2012; Lee 2012).

---

[1] For example, see Marjorie Oludhe Macgoye's 1986 novel *Coming to Birth*, or for a more recent portrayal, the Oscar-nominated film *Nairobi Half Life* (2012).

My desire to visit these rural homes was therefore not just sparked by an interest in what people who had once lived in Kaloleni had done next or how their life in Kaloleni might have been influential, but to try to understand more clearly this triangulation between home, place and burial. Along with Nairobi-based research involving conversations, interviews, participation in *matanga* (week-long vigils and organisational meetings for the funeral and burial of the deceased) and attendance at funeral services, at which rural homes were invoked discursively and metaphorically, this chapter draws on the materiality and landscape of Luoland, the *dala* (homestead), and the burial sites within them.

This material revealed that for many Luo, death is far from being a full-stop or an end to motion. Rather, it sets in train new types of mobility, from the transportation of bodies across half the width of Kenya to the streams of relatives flowing back from the diaspora to attend the funerals. This seemed to slot in neatly with a deep association in Luo culture between movement and generativity: the cyclical flow of generations and homesteads across a landscape, processes of decay and regeneration as houses and bodies go back in to the ground (see Geissler and Prince 2010). Scholars working across Africa have observed how graves can be vital in generating an attachment to a particular place, anchoring notions of autochthony and belonging (Geschiere 2005; Jua 2005; Whyte 2005; Fontein 2011; Lee and Vaughan 2012). For Luo, burials are no less crucial to the production of landscape. In Luo communities, the 'burial of the dead – male and female – within homesteads provides crucial fixed points on the landscape for the reckoning of personal, familial and political identities and allegiances' (Shipton 2009: 14).

Yet it also became apparent that working against this generative potentiality of death were more ambiguous knots of blockage and stasis – both intentional and involuntary. This chapter also highlights some of the ways that the idealised return does not always come about: people may 'get stuck' in Nairobi or further afield and be unable to return home. This can induce further blockages: for example, an older brother's failure to come home and build on his father's land can leave his younger brothers immobilised, unable to build their own houses and thus flow forward through the sanctioned ways of achieving full manhood.

In material terms, other forms of stasis are also apparent. If the processes of decay observed in Chapter 2 were about accumulation – rotting infrastructures that generate certain ways of being and belonging despite their dirtiness – my research on land and burials shows how the productivity of decay can be arrested. The embalming of bodies to allow for transportation preserves the corpse and curtails decay. Bodies are buried in erosion-resistant cemented graves, and new construction materials mean that the homes of the deceased endure in the landscape. While the durability of new methods and modern materials is what makes them desirable, their permanence can invite problematic side-effects. In the past, the disintegration of houses, graves and bodies enabled the rolling forward of new generations. Today, this is sometimes impeded by decay-resistant materials which fix a death in the landscape, obstructing the next generation's ability to dwell in the same terrain.

Going home

The return 'home' to western Kenya is a journey deeply ingrained in the outlook of Luos in Nairobi, even those born in the city. It features heavily in literature, song and poetry, and is enacted by thousands of Nairobians every Friday evening, as *matatus*, buses and private vehicles do battle with the well-worn, and often hazardous, road that leads across the Kenyan highlands to the shores of Lake Victoria. However, for many in Kaloleni it is a journey that is taken less and less frequently. Tom, for example, recounted making the journey by train as child, when his father would squeeze him, his siblings and their luggage into a third-class carriage where they would often have to stand for hours as all seating and floorspace was occupied. On reaching Kisumu, the end of the railroad, they would continue their journey by bus – Tom recalled the stiff pink cardboard tickets issued by the conductor – taking the road for Uganda but alighting at Bumala, a small market some thirty miles short of the border. From there, they walked the remaining three miles to Tom's grandfather's *dala* (homestead) among the scattered homesteads that made up the village of Boro Kisumo.

But in recent years Tom has made this trip infrequently, and even more rarely taken his children with him. His narrative is a fairly common one in Kaloleni. His retrenchment from employment with Kenya Railways in 2002 has meant that money is tight, and travelling home is expensive. There are the travel costs – these days around 1,500 KSh (about GB £12 or US $15) each way by bus – and the requirement to bring gifts for the family, but there are also certain expectations. Family, extended kin and villagers all assume that a Nairobi visitor equals a wealthy visitor, and there are obligations for him to fulfil a wide range of requests from contributing to school fees, helping supply materials for house building, or simply buying rounds of alcohol in the local drinking den. This was not a trip to be undertaken lightly, then. An upcountry visit is peppered with various commitments and expenses; a network of obligations that don't exert quite the same pull in Nairobi.

For many Luo, this journey has become one associated not only with the maintenance and renewal of kinship bonds, social networks and family homesteads but with funerals and burial (which are, of course, in themselves important sites for renewal and regeneration (see Bloch and Parry 1983)). These days, people move far afield and make their lives not just in Nairobi but across Africa, Europe and the USA, and thus may rarely get to 'go home'. Nevertheless, most Luo will go to great lengths to ensure they are buried there, and to ensure that they attend the burial of others. To be Luo is to have an attachment to a particular place, to a landscape near Lake Victoria and bordering Uganda, where the draw of *dala* (home) remains powerful. This 'ideology of attachment' connects Luos to the land, but also to each other – both the living and the dead (Shipton 2009: 7). Such attachment is substantial enough for Geissler and Prince to make it clear on the very first page of their ethnography of a Luo village: 'Many of them travel widely, but home is never forgotten ... few of them are buried away from the home where they belong by birth or marriage, death being – at least in these days of uncertainty – the definite return home' (2010: 1).[2]

This pattern of rural-urban interconnectivity in part has its roots in colonial labour policy, which for much of the period of British rule tried to prevent the urbanisation of Africans. Africans' presence in colonial Nairobi was tolerated primarily as migrant labour. Even by the time of Kenya's independence in 1963, only three per cent of Nairobi's inhabitants had been born there (Van Zwanenberg and King 1975: 269) The colonial view was that Africans should be sustained by their rural households, giving rise to what Lonsdale has termed 'straddling', where savings accrued from urban labour were invested in rural households (2001: 208). But it was not only colonial officials who were wary of Africans' residence in the city. Many Africans – and particularly African men – were suspicious of town life, and Lonsdale cautions that we should not attribute the impetus behind straddling to colonial policy alone. With its looser kin constraints and opportunities for new types of prestige, urban life could undermine forms of status founded in rural sociality (2001: 218). Over time, this anxiety was ameliorated as straddling grew into a pattern of 'one family, two households'. In this set up, wives and young children tended to remain at home with responsibilities for managing farmland and maintaining rural ties, while older (especially male) children stayed in town with their fathers, seeking waged labour. This allowed for the combination of rural status with urban opportunity, particularly among better-off Africans resident in places like Kaloleni (Hake 1977: Chapter 4; Parkin 1978: Chapter 1).

[2] This now even extends to Barack Obama, whose father – and thus also himself – was Luo, and in fact lived in Kaloleni before departing for the USA in the 1960s. Obama is hugely popular among Luo and Kenyans more widely. His father's birthplace in Kogelo village is often mentioned as the place to which Obama will ultimately 'come home' for burial.

Despite these intentions, balancing interests in two distant locations was not straightforward. In the 1950s, the *Jopango* (a Luo moniker for male urban workers, literally 'outsiders') were regarded by rural Luo as having unsatisfactory houses and were teased that their *simba* (bachelor's hut) could fall down at any time (Cohen and Odhiambo 1989: 57). As this generation of urban workers entered the 1960s, so pressure grew on them from clansmen back home to ensure they maintained their rural homes: a place for vacations, for retirement, but above all a ground to be buried in.

Rural-urban interconnections

Though the reality may be different, the aspiration is usually to die *after* returning home: that is, to retire to an upcountry home, funded by one's savings from urban labour. Even for the second and third generations of Kalolenians, born and brought up in the estate, this remains a marker of prestige and attainment. It was perhaps most succinctly described by Senje, my next-door neighbour in Kaloleni, who said, 'Nairobi is where we come to get some money, send our children to school, then we retire and go home'. This is the process by which children usually 'inherit' their parents' house in Kaloleni. During an interview with Dolly, a divorced woman in her 60s who was born in Kaloleni, I asked whether her daughter would take on the tenancy for her Kaloleni house. 'Oh yes,' she replied. 'I go home, she comes and stays here because she's the one still coming up. Me, I'm growing old now'. There is a clear sense of having had one's time, that the city is a place of youth. Dolly explained it like this:

> You leave room for the young people. You go and look after your chickens, cows and whatever. You are nearing the grave now! [*Laughs*] You don't want to give them a lot of expenses, carrying your body up to *ushago* [upcountry] and all that. You'd rather die there and you are buried there. Let them come and visit you there!

Consequently, elderly folk still resident in Kaloleni were sometimes deemed to be suspect, to have abandoned their roots and 'got lost' in the city, refusing to make way for the next generation. As I chatted with my friend Bilal about one old man in his 80s who was still resident in Kaloleni, I was told:

> According to our culture, he should be at home looking after cows, relaxing. What is he still doing here? ... he's acting like a young man. His sons are not free here, they don't come. How can they drink when their father is sitting there? They are of different generations, they cannot be together like that.

Bilal's comment 'according to our culture' shows just how rooted the old idea of 'straddling' has become. The continuing positive and aspirational associations of a rural home serve as a reminder that this connection cannot be traced simply to a repressive colonial law to which Africans were forced to submit but was a relationship that quickly became meaningful to many African townspeople and which they have both sustained and reconstituted in the decades since independence.

These days, the longest-standing families of Kaloleni are now into their third and even fourth generations and thus one might expect them to hold a more distinctively 'urban' outlook. Yet this attachment to Luo ancestral lands – and to the desire to be buried there – remains surprisingly powerful. This is in contrast to observations from scholars of Nairobi's contemporary middle classes. Rachel Spronk has charted how the outlook of young professionals born and brought up in Nairobi is shifting. Holders of what they see as global careers in ICT, finance, management and development, they no longer maintain the same rural ties as their parents, often do not speak their parents' language and orientate their social and aspirational worlds within Nairobi – or to cities further afield (Spronk 2012). This was the case among some younger people in Kaloleni, notably Stephen's son Calvin, whose ambitions to buy land near to Nairobi were mentioned in Chapter 1. Several others told me they are not interested in rural life, that they don't care for farming. These new ambitions are explored further in Chapter 6. But it is certainly not the case for all young people.

James, a Kaloleni man in his early thirties, lives in the house that was once his father's. James is married with a young baby and works as a hairdresser at an upmarket salon in a large mall. In many ways, he is very cosmopolitan. He has many expat clients and mixes with all kinds of Nairobi society. He has made considerable investments to his house in Kaloleni, tiling the floors, installing a new sofa set and stylish silver refrigerator, painting the walls and even the roof to make his home feel 'fresh' (see Figure 13). He has a car and an iPhone and is proud of his house, saying, 'These days a house is not just for sleeping'. Yet he is also oriented towards a rural home in Siaya, where he intends to eventually return. There he has already built a smart brick *simba* in his father's *dala*, and one day will begin his own *dala*. He told me that those young people who want to acquire land near Nairobi are usually those without land upcountry. That they have reoriented their aspirations towards the city is not so much a choice as an imperative: their connection to Luoland has been cut, perhaps due to their parents' incapacity to maintain the necessary ties.

For Kaloleni Luo then, as for many people, an attachment to place is far from an intrinsic or innate connection, but is produced through the labour of kinship, and through the politics, disputes, economies and socialities of everyday life. Indeed, as Lee has pointed out in reference to townships in Cape Town,

Figure 13 Inside James's house, May 2014
(Photo: Author)

'modernisation' or 'urbanisation' have not collapsed the intricate connectedness Africans continue to feel between rural and urban areas, but are in fact providing new techniques and pathways through which ordinary Africans may interrogate their own histories of migration and participation in the urbanisation process. (2011: 229)

This is clearly apparent in Kaloleni. When I met Stephen and Jemimah, the parents of Calvin, they were preparing to move back 'home' (see Chapter 1). They had already built a rural homestead near Maseno, a couple of hours west of the lakeside city of Kisumu. This *dala* (homestead) is founded on land granted to Stephen by his father, and neighbours the *dala* where Stephen was born and where he grew up until he came to Nairobi as a young man. When Jemimah married Stephen, she also married into this landscape, joining his home and clan. Their planned departure from Nairobi seemed quite momentous to me, and I asked them if they would miss Nairobi – they had after all spent almost a lifetime in the city. Instead, Stephen's answer revealed the entanglement of rural and urban networks that play out over a lifetime: 'I don't think I'll miss Nairobi. I'm known actually more at home than here, because here I'm not very social ... I'm not a guy who can stay for a year without going home. In fact, I used to go at least every month'. Rather than a life-changing event, he saw their move as an extension of his current relationship with western Kenya. The persistent attachment to 'straddling', and the effort to manage urban and rural lives and maintain a foot in both, mean that the relation of the 'rural' to the 'urban' is not a binary relationship but rather a dense web of interconnection in which each helps to constitute the other. Forms of urban belonging and achievement shape the kinds of rural relations that are possible, just as rural homesteads help to mediate life in Nairobi. This attachment between distant landscapes is today regarded as a major trope of Luo culture, but it is a bond constantly under reconfiguration. It requires maintenance and is often threatened by the misfortunes of everyday life.

Dying in town

Although the dream might be to return home earlier, dying in town has always been common enough. Across colonial Africa, the management of death in urban areas was never straightforward. Funerals were sites of contestation, of the working out of ideas of status, resistance and even nationalism (see for example, Ferguson 1999; Lee and Vaughan 2008, 2012; Jindra and Noret 2011; Kalusa and Vaughan 2013). In some areas, burial in town was regarded as socially important. In colonial Zambia, Walima Kalusa has argued, burials in urban cemeteries became signs of modernity, and a means of establishing an African elite in the Copperbelt towns of the north (2013). In contemporary Kinshasa, meanwhile, De Boeck has shown that urban burial rites have become a way of contesting official politics and dominant religious discourses, as well as assertions of new forms of self-making (2008).

Elsewhere on the continent, urban burials were to be avoided if at all possible. In South Africa, an urban death has long demanded – at least ideally – the transportation of the body back to the rural 'reserve' for burial, marking a final return 'home' from an urban lifetime (Lee 2011). Municipal burial grounds were looked down on as a place only for those without name or ancestry, lost souls with nowhere else to go. As a consequence, funeral societies were common, and urban residents made weekly or monthly contributions to ethnic- or clan-based savings organisations that would arrange funerals and burials. In colonial East Africa, Luo funeral associations were common in Nairobi, Mombasa and Kampala, organised around *piny*, the territorial affiliation of the clan. *Piny* simultaneously implies both kin and territory, which also served to reinforce identities based on both birth and death in a specific location or landscape (Cohen and Odhiambo 1989: 32). In Kaloleni, the social hall was a centre for the Nairobi Luo Union meetings. It was here, my elderly informants recalled, that a *harambee* (fundraiser, literally 'pull together') would be held to prepare for the expensive business of a funeral. The Luo Union would call upon kin, clan and *piny* to 'pull together' and contribute towards transporting the body home.

By the time I undertook this research in 2013–14, there was no longer any sign of the Luo Union in Kaloleni. Its clout had long since faded, along with its role in adjudicating funerals. Though many residents still contribute to a collective savings group, known as a *chama*, these tend to be informal gatherings of family and friends. On the occasion of a death in the family, savings from the *chama* may well be retrieved, but a family will also host a *mtanga* to raise the funds for an upcountry burial. A combination of pre-funeral rite and planning meeting, *matanga* (pl., sing. *mtanga*) are a regular feature of everyday affairs within Kaloleni. Whenever a death occurs, family, friends and neighbours will gather each evening for a week or more outside the house of the deceased to reminisce, plan, give support and – crucially – contribute towards the funeral and burial costs. Over the course of my fieldwork I attended many *matanga*, and their atmosphere became somewhat familiar: a mixture of nostalgia, companionship and boredom.

The *mtanga* of Julius, a forty-year-old bachelor, was fairly characteristic. Plastic chairs were arranged in rows under the *hema* [a small marquee], and just outside, a big fire smouldered and sputtered in the rain. It was smoky and cold. People were wrapped in blankets, some already sleeping. There was a small sound system, and later in the night the music started. Even at midnight, people were still arriving. There are so many deaths that there always seems to be at least one *mtanga* going on in Kaloleni, and so these tents have become an ever-present, if mobile, feature of the landscape. They cause temporary alterations to the flow of movement within the estate. The tents fill the whole path, with no way through except through the tent. This makes it almost impossible to pass by without engaging in the affairs of the *mtanga*. With maybe ten days of nightly fires, this means there is also a lot of ash and remains left on the path that stay long after the body has been buried.

In Kaloleni the declaration of death not only sets in motion certain economic transactions but has its own material presence: everyone knows when a member of a certain household has died, the tent going up becomes a kind of public proclamation. People see the tent and stop and ask what has happened. Chairs, ash and other detritus accumulate, marking the duration of the *mtanga*. The grass is trodden down and withers, a muddy, ashy square remaining after the tent is finally removed. This could be occurring outside three or four houses in Kaloleni simultaneously. On the last night of a *mtanga*, the body is retrieved from the morgue and brought into the *mtanga* tent for viewing. Mourners line up to peer through a viewing window in the coffin, revealing the deceased dressed in smart clothes and with a serene expression. Following an all-night vigil, the *mtanga* is concluded, though the procedures surrounding death roll on. The body begins its hazardous journey upcountry and the owner of the tent hires it out to the next bereaved family.

Body conflicts

Bodies do not always make such smooth progress, however, and hiatuses in the flow of mortuary, funeral and burial matters are common. Death in town can catalyse all kinds of competing claims over the body of the deceased, during which the body remains in the refrigerated morgue while knotty disputes invoking belonging, identity and ethnicity are teased apart. One of the most famous such cases followed the death of renowned Nairobi lawyer SM Otieno in 1986. That Luos make a profound connection of home with death and burial is nowhere highlighted more clearly than in the controversy surrounding his death (an event much analysed; see, for example, Ojwang and Mugambi 1989; Cohen and Odhiambo 1992). The dispute that erupted between SM's widow and his Luo clansmen revolved around the two parties' claims on their capacity to bury his body. Kaloleni, the heartland of Luo Nairobi in the 1980s, avidly followed events, and the hall became the meeting place for SM's Umira Kager clan as they developed their case. A 154-day High Court battle ensued, in which SM's widow, Wambui Otieno – crucially, from a different ethnic group, the Kikuyu – claimed to be fulfilling wishes of the deceased by seeking to bury his body at Kiserian, to the west of Nairobi, on farmland the couple had bought, and where they had built a house. Her lawyer, John Khaminwa, argued that SM Otieno lived all his working life in Nairobi and saw himself as a Kenyan first, stating, 'It was never his intention to be subject to African customs' (quoted in Cohen and Odhiambo 1989: 136). He sought to affirm the status of the modern family in Kenya, and the rights of households to make claims outside the control of clan and tradition.

This was intolerable to SM's brothers and Luo clan members, for whom SM was and always would be a son of Umira Kager soil. They sought to prove the primacy of the Luo attachment to homeland, as well as the rights of the lineage above those of marriage. Richard Kwach, the lawyer representing the Umira Kager clan, in presenting his case submitted that the claims of Mrs Otieno 'are not consistent with Luo customary law and burial traditions ... there is no written or general law in Kenya which gives the widow the right to claim the body for burial ... My Lord, in Luoland certain people do certain things. In burial matters, this is an issue for elders only' (quoted in Cohen and Odhiambo 1989: 137). For those elders, lineage, home and land were explicitly gendered. Since Luo women marry in to lineages, and forgo the lineage of their father, their status was more transitory, and their loyalty to ancestral kin, not being bound by blood, could therefore be suspect (see Evans-Pritchard 1950). The status of Wambui Otieno, as a Kikuyu, was even more ambiguous. The clan's lawyer asserted that when Wambui married SM 'she walked out of her tribe and became a Luo. And those are the customs that govern her ... she did not acquire any burial rites which anyone wants to remove from her' (Cohen and Odhiambo 1989: 137). Ultimately, it was the clan who prevailed, convincing the court that, for Luo men, burial at home was an inalienable right/rite. For these men, being buried was an act of dwelling, the final act of making the homestead that is the lifelong project of Luo men, and by which their manhood is measured.

Among the many deaths that sadly occurred during this project, one was notable for a similar – though much less high profile – contest over the body of the deceased and the place it should be buried. This was the death of Derrick, a young twenty-seven-year-old man from Kaloleni. The dispute ended with the opposite outcome to that of SM Otieno: Derrick was ultimately buried in Lang'ata, Nairobi's municipal cemetery. In the introduction to their volume on funerals on Africa, Jindra and Noret note that classic anthropological studies of funerals were inclined to focus on elite burials, which tended to have richer symbolic and political implications (2011: 7). Similarly, such accounts tended to favour 'traditional' death rites, and urban funerals generally received little attention. As a consequence, in the literature on dying in Africa, the deaths of the young, the poor and the ignominious have often been silent (see also Vaughan 2008). The struggles surrounding Derrick's death, funeral and burial, while not as politically explosive as those of SM Otieno, nevertheless brought into focus important dynamics of family and kin, mobility and obstruction, ambition and disappointment circulating around deaths in Kaloleni.

Derrick died suddenly, 'in his sleep', in February 2014. The cause of death remained uncertain, though there was much speculation. As far as anyone knew, he had not been sick and his death was a shock to Kaloleni; he was popular and well-liked. The funeral rites that followed were far from melancholy: the *mtanga*, funeral and burial were all notable for their colour, vivacity and loud 'celebration of life'. But underlying this was a palpable sense of unfulfilled potential, of obstacles and blockages that had thwarted Derrick, abruptly cutting his life short, and which obstructed his family after his death. His burial in the municipal Lang'ata cemetery embodied these ambivalent sentiments: though it was attended by more than a thousand people, there was nevertheless an air of failure and dissatisfaction, a general sentiment that affairs had not been attended to properly, that this had not been a 'good death' (Lamont 2011: 104).

Derrick's funeral was held close to Kaloleni, at St Stephen's, a vast Anglican church on Jogoo Road. The pallbearers, wearing sunglasses and sharp black suits, carried in a coffin topped with elaborate floral bouquets and a framed photo of Derrick. It was a full Anglican service, including hymns in English, Swahili and Luo, interspersed with more informal tributes from family, friends and neighbours. The service was notable for a profusion of screens: personal phones and tablets, on which people photographed and videoed the service, those of the official cameraman, and also TV screens on the pillars, across which scrolled the words of the hymns, karaoke-style. The effect – reinforced by the fashionable clothes of the guests – was glossy: contemporary and slick. This was the funeral of a popular urban guy, a regular figure at club nights and parties, known for his love of hip-hop. It seemed a far cry from the types of death rites favoured in classic anthropological studies – there was little 'traditional' symbolism nor apparently any political import to the death of this Luo man.

After the ceremony, we filed out of the church to view the body, positioned in its shiny wood-effect casket on a plinth in the middle of the car park. Peering in through the viewing pane, we saw the inside of the coffin was of quilted white satin, and the body formally dressed in a white shirt with a red bowtie – presumably not something Derrick would ever have worn in life, judging by the photos of him in the funeral programme. His skin was smooth and pale, with a waxy look that seemed barely human. This, I would come to know after viewing many other bodies, is a common appearance after embalming. The fluids of the body are drained out and replaced with a cocktail of substances, including formaldehyde, glycerine and methanol, which preserve the body for storage, viewing and transportation to the funeral (see also Lee 2011: 236–8).

Derrick's family were seated next to the coffin, but only his father and his paternal aunts were present. His mother, it turned out, was not able to attend the funeral. Separated from Derrick's father (they had never married), she had gone to work in the UK along with her younger daughter, leaving Derrick behind in the house in Kaloleni where he was born. The reason for her absence was unclear. Some said she was sick, others said she could not get a visa, or was not herself legal in the UK. Following the funeral ceremony, we trooped to the house in Kaloleni to begin the overnight vigil. The casket was placed outside, under a window, so that light from inside the house could fall on the casket. But there was a power cut, so we sat in the dark; the deep dark of Nairobi in the midst of a blackout. Not even a streetlight shone. People sang and clapped, grasping each other's hands and arms through the darkness. Then some started to pray, concurrently and out loud, the rise and fall of their citations echoing in the night.

It was at the vigil that I became aware of the dispute over Derrick's body, and the reasons he would be buried at Lang'ata the following day. Despite the fashionable urban gloss of his funeral, the implications of his ambiguous, but nonetheless significant, Luo heritage came back to the fore. To bury one's dead in Lang'ata is considered far from ideal for Luos, a marker of failure on the part of the deceased – or in the case of young people, their family. It was clear from what I knew of the family that they had limited connections to any family upcountry; I was told that Derrick had hardly ever been there. He had been brought up almost entirely by his mother; his parents never married and separated when he was young. In consequence, his mother's link to his father's kin was tenuous (and perhaps difficult) and she had no claim to any rights or land.

It was unclear if Derrick's father had his own *dala*, though people seemed doubtful that he did. Nevertheless, he had wanted to claim Derrick and take his body back upcountry to bury on family land, presumably that of Derrick's grandfather. But Derrick's maternal uncles refused: 'They want to keep him for themselves', I was told. They allowed Derrick's paternal relatives to mourn at the funeral and did not attend themselves. But afterwards, they claimed the body and carried it back to Kaloleni, and from there to Lang'ata the next day. In so doing, they refused to recognise Derrick's paternal ancestry as mean-ingful, and would not allow Derrick to be buried as part of the clan that, in life, had practically disowned him. The maternal uncles represented a formidable force despite the absence of their sister, blocking Derrick's father and shutting down that branch of the lineage. In so doing, they also attempted to turn Derrick's urban immobility – the fact that he had 'got stuck' in Nairobi – into a triumph.

To an extent, they were successful – on the surface at least. The next morning the whole of Kaloleni, it seemed, turned out. Red ribbons were tied to the wing mirrors of the vehicles to show they were being used for a funeral. There was a carnival atmosphere as, in convoy, we drove around Kaloleni, horns blaring and people shouting from car windows. Derrick's friends wore t-shirts personalised with a photo of Derrick and a caption underneath that read 'Sunrise: 21 Sept 1987. Sunset: 6 Feb 2014' (see Figure 14). At Lang'ata there was a further ceremony at which I estimated attendance to be around one thousand, all standing in the glare of the midday sun. Finally, we processed to the grave site, where people crowded six or seven rows deep to see the body interred. Three young men mixed a huge pyramid of cement next to the grave site. Grave robberies have become an increasing problem in Nairobi and now families take the precaution of cementing the grave closed. First a layer of corrugated iron was laid over the casket, and then a piece of metal grille. A small pouring form was made out of planks pushed up against the sides of the grave and the concrete was poured in to form a plinth.

We waited in the hot sun, still carrying the yellow roses we had bought to lay on the grave. But the preparation of the concrete and the

Figure 14 Friends of Derrick sporting custom t-shirts at his funeral, February 2014 (Photo: Author)

construction of an impenetrable grave took so long that many eventually turned to leave. It was at this point that the darker undercurrents of Derrick's death resurfaced. My friends insisted we should depart, pointing out that the family had left almost immediately. This was not a good death, they said. There had been too much arguing and too much uncertainty. Who knew why Derrick had suddenly died? To remain at the graveside was to invite this trouble upon ourselves. 'Why should we be the ones to stay and carry that shadow back?' Doro said. The last people at a grave site can fall into the shadow of the deceased, and only the 'stupid ones' would stay.

The *dala*

If the circumstances around Derrick's passing represented an undesirable death, then planning for a 'good death' has become an important part of self-making in Kaloleni. The ideal – I was frequently told – is to die old and at home, buried in the land to which one belongs either by birth or by marriage. Achieving such a death relies on the establishment of a *dala*, or homestead, a project which preoccupies the aspirations and strategies of many Kaloleni men. The *dala* has long been an important physical manifestation of Luo kinship, with each adult son building a *dala* neighbouring that of their father, on land granted to them by him. In this way, the *dala* marked generations of a family on to the landscape, signifying the achievement of male adulthood.

In 1936, Evans-Pritchard made a brief survey of the Luo areas of western Kenya and described the formation of Luo homesteads:

> The parts of Luoland which lie back from the lake, e.g. Alego and Ugenya tribal areas, are undulating country in which the homesteads are built along the slopes (*thuce*, sing. *thur*, also meaning home) of the successive ridges ... The homestead, the residence of an elementary family or a joint family, is generally called *dala* ... It is usually surrounded by a thick hedge of euphorbia, a narrow gap in which is the entrance to the kraal, round which are the huts and granaries. (1965: 206)

During this fieldtrip, he took a series of photographs of *dala* to illustrate this description, showing circular hedged compounds sparsely dispersed across a hillside with uncultivated, open land between them.[3]

On our trip west, Tom, Kevin and I finally arrived at Tom's father's *dala* ten hours after leaving Nairobi. We turned off the increasingly minimal dirt track and entered the homestead through a narrow gateway in a dense hedge. In front of us was a kraal (*duol*) made of roughly hewn wood, in which three cows were tethered. The houses were arranged in an upside-down horseshoe shape around the *duol*, with the main house at the top facing the gateway. If the correspondence between this description and Evans-Pritchard's is evident, there were also discrepancies. The house of Tom's parents is a large multi-roomed bungalow made from whitewashed bricks and mortar. It has a corrugated iron roof, a water tank and a large cemented veranda. A solar panel has been installed on the roof. The cattle kept in the kraal are imported 'grade' cows rather than the indigenous 'zebu' type. Ornamental trees and shrubs have been planted around the compound and the whole area is seemingly under cultivation, with homesteads and fields of crops snugly up against each other.

The next morning, Tom's cousin Meja explained the layout of the *dala*. The main house (*ot madung* in Luo, or sometimes referred to in Kiswahili as *nyumba kubwa*) should always be uphill, he said, at the top of the *dala* facing down the hill towards the main gateway (*rangach*). We stood on the veranda looking out on the rest of the compound. The

---

[3] Although unpublished in his lifetime, these photographs were gifted to the Pitt Rivers Museum in Oxford and were the subject of a recent exhibition titled *Paro Manene (Paro Ndalo Machon): Rethinking Luo History Through Photograph Collections at the Pitt Rivers Museum*, University of Oxford 2007. The exhibition was part of a larger research project by Christopher Morton and Gilbert Oteyo on the museum's photography holdings from the Luo region. The photographs can be seen at http://photos.prm.ox.ac.uk/luo/page/home

first-born son – in this case Tom's older brother Pawa – always builds to the right-hand side, followed by the second-born son (Tom) to the left-hand side, but slightly further downhill. This alternating pattern continues with each of the sons: first-, third-, fifth-born sons building to the right as one looks out from the door of the *ot madung*, with their even-numbered brothers diagonally opposite them. In the centre of the *dala* is the *duol*, or cattle pen, which is the sanctuary of the man of the homestead. In the Nyanya compound, there is also a separate sleeping house for the daughters when they come home to visit, and behind the main house is a small square mud structure with a *mabati* (iron sheet) roof, used as the kitchen.

On reaching maturity, Luo young men build their own small 'bachelor' house – *simba* – within their father's *dala*, where they live until they are married. In the past, after marriage a son would demolish the *simba* and build a new house for his wife (apart from the *simba*, Luo houses are considered to belong to women) where they would live until after the birth of their first child, at which point the man would found his own *dala* on land granted to him by his father. With the increasing migration of many sons, these days this pattern has altered somewhat. Now men tend to build one *simba*, and then much later – usually as they approach retirement – they will, if they have the resources, begin their own *dala*. In the case of the Nyanya family, there are four sons but only three, Pawa, Tom and Ben, have built their *simba*. Gavin, the youngest, 'got lost' in Nairobi. As their mother Judith put it, 'he never comes'. The *simba* in the Nyanya *dala* index the various economic capacities of the sons. Pawa has a house and family in Nairobi, but lives for much of the time in China, where he is an English teacher. He has recently begun to replace his old *simba* with a sizeable, modern brick construction. Though not-yet completed, it will have paned windows and a *mabati* roof. Tom's original *simba* remains, built in what he called 'style *ya kitambu*', or the style of the old days: a round mud structure with a central pole supporting a pointed thatched grass roof, although it does also have a small paned glass window. Ben, a mechanical engineer in the Kenya Army, has built a small square brick *simba* with a *mabati* roof.

As we walked around, the importance of directionality and movement across the landscape quickly became apparent. Meja pointed out how the younger kin should always build 'below' or downhill from their elders. This is common practice for Luos and is described by Geissler and Prince: 'homes go forward (*dhi nyime*) across the land with the family's developmental cycle ... the home leaves the ancestral old homes (*gundni*, sing. *gunda*) behind it' (2010: 64). A son builds his *dala* on lineage land below/down (*mwalo*) from his father's home. As explained by Meja, this is to prevent contamination: 'dirty water from my bath cannot wash from my home to my father's, no', he said. This would be to reverse the forward direction of generations, where all things must flow from elders to youth. 'As rainwater forms rivulets that flow down the slope, bringing growth and fertility to the land below, life flows from one generation to the next across the land' (Geissler and Prince 2010: 121).

From the Nyanya family *dala,* we left by the side gate and walked a little way up the hill. Following a narrow path, to our right was a thickly overgrown hedge. Entering via a gap in the hedge, we emerged into the old *dala* of Tom's paternal grandfather, Ohito. Standing in the gateway (*rangach*), in front of us at the top of the slope were the remains of two houses standing side by side. Ohito had had two wives, and each had their own *ot* (house). The *simba* of their sons would once have been arrayed before them. This *dala* is now uninhabited; it has become a *gunda,* the ancestral home, or source, of those still living. Ohito and his wives have all passed away and their sons (now senior men themselves) have moved out. Tom's father and his half-brother moved on to lineal land immediately in front/downhill, though the two other brothers have founded their homes elsewhere, on purchased land closer to town.[4]

A small grove of trees at the top of the *dala* behind the main houses revealed the graves of Ohito and his wives. When the man of the *dala* and his wives die, they are buried within the compound and the cycle is complete. The sons will all have left; the homestead is abandoned by the living. Ohito's once-vibrant homestead was now in the process of disintegrating. This is what marked a good death; the houses and the bodies gradually decay together: mud, thatch, flesh, going back into the ground. This land should not be farmed or recycled as a new *dala* by the surviving family members. It remains the dwelling place of the man who made it, with body, land and home intimately bound together. Moving around Ohito's *dala,* I found raised ridges just visible in the long grass, showing the outline where mud *simba* had once stood. But several more-modern structures were more intact. The co-wives' houses were roofed in *mabati* and the mud walls had at some time been plastered. This plaster was now cracked and crumbling, but the sturdy shelter provided by the *mabati* meant that the houses were more-or-less still standing.

Ohito had been a prominent local man, and his *dala* grew accordingly. Filled with many *simba* and later enhanced with more permanent building materials, it would have been vibrant and imposing. Standing amid the remains of this vitality, it was clear that the *dala,* while regarded as the major achievement for Luo men, is – at least ideally – far from being a fixed, stable unit. It is part of a more generative process, of movement across land but also across time, from one generation to

---

[4] The purchase of land for *dala* is becoming increasingly common, partly because the continual subdivision of family lands means the land parcels have become too small to be viable.

the next. There is an ebb and flow as new *dala* emerge on the landscape and older ones recede into it. Death is an important part of this process, and one which itself opens up new pathways for the next generation. In burial, the partible aspects of house, body and land are finally brought together, bringing the unfolding process of making the *dala* – the work of a lifetime – to a conclusion. This reunification helps to answer why burial at home is so important to Luo: it is not just about an attachment to a place, but also about making a landscape.

The changing *simba*

The place of the *dala* in the lives of urban Luo has not been static. The rather idealised process of its formation described above has shifted over time in response to changing social, economic and material concerns. Cohen and Odhiambo note that in the 1940s and 1950s, the poor quality of the rural homes of the *Jopango* (urban workers) was well-known (1989: 57). They were teased by rural kin not only for not founding a *dala* of their own, but for failing even to care for their *simba* within their father's *dala*. In such circumstances, when a body was returned to the countryside for burial, the state of the rural home was a topic of much comment. 'In funeral after funeral, observations were made about the poor, decrepit situation in the countryside compared with the fairly substantial housing that the deceased had occupied in the city' (Cohen and Odhiambo 1989: 57–8).

By the late 1950s and 1960s, this situation began to alter. With Africanisation policies and then independence presenting new opportunities, this was a period of significant upward mobility for many urban Luo. There was increasing pressure on such men to demonstrate their achievements to rural Luo and investing in a rural home became one measure of success. While the ultimate aim remained the foundation of a *dala*, this was postponed to later and later in life and became more closely associated with retirement. Instead, the significance of the *simba* was heightened. In the postcolonial period, it became an increasing focus, and site of some apprehension, for urban Luos, its condition materialising the success or otherwise of its owner. 'The investment in the enhanced *simba* became a new and primary symbol of "making it" in the swirl of politics, business, society, and of course, funerals' (Cohen and Odhiambo 1989: 58).

The *simba* remains a powerful marker of achievement for senior Luo men. Among men in Kaloleni, building an elaborate upcountry *simba* has become a form of conspicuous consumption, an important place to invest savings or disposable income. During 2014, Samuel was in the process of planning a new *simba* and we spent many hours poring over the plans and designs. Though he was born in and has always lived in Kaloleni, Samuel has recently achieved considerable business success and intends to move out of the estate. He is in his late 40s and has two sons, both in high school. He and his wife, Eva, are both from Kaloleni and several of their siblings also still live there. Using his new-found income, Samuel was simultaneously planning for his rural *simba* as well as for a new Nairobi residence on a plot of land he has purchased in Syokimau, a new suburb near Nairobi's main airport. For his *simba*, Samuel has bought a set of off-the-peg architectural plans for an elaborate bungalow. These designs are readily available on the streets of Nairobi, selling on informal roadside stalls for around £10 ($13). Samuel worked with a young architecture student to modify the plans to his needs, extending the veranda and altering the proportions. For Samuel, his *simba* is not just about continuity and tradition but a more contemporary appreciation of leisure. He says it will be 'a place for relaxing, where I will take my family for vacation. We'll relax. It's important to be home.' But ultimately, he also recognises that, as a Luo man, this is where he will end up: 'You know, for us we are Luo. We cannot be buried in Nairobi. After I pass on, they must take me home.'

New materialities

As well as its changing social significance, the substance of the *simba* is also much altered. Unlike Tom's mud and thatch *simba ya kitambu*, Samuel's *simba* will be constructed from brick and mortar on a strong concrete foundation. He is keen to use special reflective glass for the window panes, the veranda will be tiled, and there will be a large plastic water tank supported on the corrugated plastic roof. The introduction of these more durable construction materials has had a pronounced impact on buildings' longevity. Concrete, iron sheet, tiles and paint decay extremely slowly, often far outlasting the lifetimes of those who built them. This can be problematic since these days land is at a premium. Meja explained that, in the old days, abandoning a *dala* was not a problem as the mud houses went 'back to the ground'. Although one was meant to never return to that land, in practice after a long time (perhaps several generations) people often used the land again. But these days the structures within the *dala* endure – they do not decay, which also means that 'you cannot forget', he said.

This new durability applies not only to the *simba* but also to the graves. Until the early twentieth century, most Luo were buried in a sitting position directly in the ground outside their house (Cohen 1994: 150). Conversion to Christianity encouraged the use of coffins, and today a successful life is indexed after death by a suitably monumental gravesite. In many of the compounds I visited, graves were topped with raised cemented plinths and adorned with plaques and headstones. Entombed within these graves are embalmed bodies, themselves encased in synthetic, plasticised coffins. Such forms of burial will endure in the landscape as never before. *Dala*, and the graves within them, have long been symbolic as well as material 'anchors' in the Luo landscape, indicating past and present occupations and locating a sense of belonging (Shipton 2009: 14; see also Fontein 2011). But though their location remained identifiable and their significance retained in memory, processes of decay meant they were not static. The new substances of building and burial have created a more permanent materiality, the ramifications of which are not yet fully clear.

Meja's comment that 'you cannot forget' is an ambivalent one. New construction and burial practices are markers of distinction and modern aspiration, but they can also prove intractable. Their permanence interrupts cycles of growth and renewal, of the waxing and waning of *dala*. Instead of a generative flow of life proceeding down the hillside, things become stuck, blocked, fixed in place. This is further complicated by prohibitions (*kweche*, sing. *kwer*) around the reuse of materials from a 'dead' *dala*. Contemporary building materials are significant investments, and disputes often arise about the possibilities of recycling them. While this can be pragmatically attractive, as Geissler and Prince point out, it can also invite haunting (*chien*) from the dead person whose house has been despoiled, and who can seriously block the way for future generations (2010: 121–3). The result is a landscape increasingly saturated with recalcitrant structures that refuse to disappear. The lack of decay turns a death into a permanent memorial while putting whole tracts of land out of circulation. While in the case of a 'good' death such commemoration may well be embraced, in instances of misfortune or 'bad' deaths it can be problematic.

Death in a landscape

When things are not properly done, flows are obstructed. The issue of blockages or obstacles is common in disputes over the proper iteration of practices (Geissler and Prince 2010: 121–3). For example, a man who builds uphill from his father may become 'blocked', his potential for 'growth' and success impeded. In the worst cases, this can result in *chiraa*, a mysterious illness inflicted on those who bypass sanctioned methods or try to take shortcuts, which can result even in death. The possible magnitude of such obstructions became apparent during a visit to Victor, a middle-aged man born in Kaloleni who moved back to western Kenya in the early 2000s.

Victor's *dala* and large *shamba* (cultivated gardens) occupy a beautiful spot on the shores of Lake Victoria, not far from the small town of Sio Port. Down here by the lake, the land is fertile, saturated with colour. The lush greens of pumpkin, maize and beans contrast with the rich red soil. Victor's grandfather made his *dala* here, and the many *dala* of his male descendants stretch across an area of perhaps thirty acres. Victor's father was born here but left in the 1950s to look for work in Nairobi. After establishing himself as a carpenter, he sent for his wife and they moved to Kaloleni, where they lived in house A16. Victor and his siblings were born there, and it remains the house of the first-born son, John. Victor himself began to relocate to his father's place in 2000, when he was transferred from his job in Nairobi to a position in the town of Kapsabet, a few hours away. Slowly he started to get to know people, mostly through drinking in the *busaa* house.[5] According to Victor, these men eventually said 'Ok, you come and build'. This marked his acceptance by the local community, and he began to build his new *dala*, finishing the construction on the main house in 2002. Though a permanent house, none of the finishing has been completed: the walls are bare brick and the floors have not been cemented. He has been unable to finish it as his funds have dried up: the company he worked for collapsed in 2005 and he lost his job.

Victor's need to explain his acceptance by the community, even though this was his ancestral home, indicates how a family's connection to a particular terrain is not intrinsic but endlessly renegotiated – and can be subject to violent contestation. Their family has experienced a series of tragedies and deaths that have, in a variety of ways, left their marks on the landscape. By the 1980s, Victor's father, Ounda, was a relatively well-established artisan in Nairobi and had used his savings to found his own *dala* on this land by the lake, granted to him by his father. By investing in this place – financially, emotionally and through investments of labour – Ounda was literally preparing the ground for a more permanent return to the land of his birth. But before he could realise such dreams, this idealised narrative of return was brutally cut short.

One day in 1987, Ounda was resting in his *shamba* when he was ambushed by a gang armed with *panga*s (machetes). They attacked him from behind and he was killed. This, according not only to Victor but to several others who recounted the tale, was the upshot of an ongoing land dispute with a local politician. For an artisan, Ounda had a lot of land. The politician, rising in power and eager to shore up his authority by procuring more land, began to encroach on Ounda's, asserting his right to a claim on it. Instead of acquiescing to a 'bigger' man with considerable weight behind him, Ounda resisted and eventually made a formal complaint. The ambush soon followed, and, although the attack

[5] *Busaa* is a locally made beer brewed from millet or maize. It is usually unfiltered, so is thick and retains quite a lot of nutrition from the grains.

was never officially linked to the politician, there seems to be no doubt in people's minds who lay behind Ounda's murder. Following his death, the homestead went into decline for several years. Ounda's widow went to stay with one of her daughters; the sons no longer returned to the land and the wider family felt uneasy and insecure.

In the 1990s, Victor's younger brother also died in what Tom described as 'mysterious circumstances'. A promising young geologist, he was about to go abroad for his masters and had attained a much sought-after scholarship. He died suddenly before he could travel, and there was speculation that his unexplained death was murder: a jealousy attack in which he was poisoned. Shortly after this, another brother committed suicide, a family tragedy and a taboo for many Kenyans. Finally, in January 2014, a few months before my visit, the youngest brother Jeff also passed away, from long-term complications after a violent alter-cation in which he was struck with a hammer. This series of tragedies, some of them shrouded in uncertainty, has led to suspicions that the family is suffering from *chiraa*, or even witchcraft.

Later, discussing the sad story of Victor's family, Tom remarked that he could never be comfortable in that place, saying, 'the land is poisoned'. When pressed, he explained that maybe it was linked to the original political dispute, that the politician had resorted to witchcraft in addition to murdering Ounda. But he also said that many older people of Ounda's generation note that the family have not followed the proper order of things: the oldest son John has never built his *simba* and so has also never founded his own *dala*, yet the younger sons have done so. After it became clear that John, who remains in house A16 in Kaloleni, had disconnected himself from 'home' and refused to even visit ('He got lost' says Victor), the younger four brothers all began to build. By ignoring the proper sequence of sons' building practices, which should take place in age order, the family has upset the generative flow of the younger generation *out* of the *dala* of their father, and instead they have invited *chiraa in*.

Victor told me the story of his family as we walked across the remains of several generations of *dala*, indicating what was left of the houses in each of them as we passed. Reaching a scrubby thicket, he stopped and indicated that I should walk in front. In a small clearing lay the graves of all of the deceased, including his grandparents, in a family grove in the grandfather's *dala*. Perhaps a fifteen-minute walk from Victor's own house, there is now not much left of this *gunda berr* (originary *dala*). It is overgrown and bushy; a few ridges in the grass indicate the footprints of old mud houses and there is a bit of broken concrete where Ounda began a permanent structure that was never completed. The graves, by contrast, look unblemished and well-maintained. The grass has been cleared and each grave is topped with a concrete plinth and embedded with an engraved plaque. We stood at the graveside for some time, looking down at the smooth cement edges protruding from the red soil. The melancholy atmosphere was incongruous with the sharp blue skies and glorious views of the lake. After some minutes of silence, Victor murmured, 'There's just me here now'.

The various *dala* had reached various stages of formation before events overtook them. The remains of these aborted *dala* linger in the landscape, markers of arrested ambitions and lives curtailed. The most abject of these, perhaps because it is so fresh, is Jeff's. Jeff was a scientist with Kenya Fisheries, well-educated and relatively well-off. Shortly before his death, Jeff completed the construction of a very smart permanent house near the shore of the lake. It still stands: a modern design with a veranda, reflective windows and fancy paintwork, topped with a bright blue corrugated plastic roof (see Figure 15). The house was connected to a local electricity supply and inside are expensive light fixtures as well as tiled floors, a full modern bathroom and leather sofas, all barely used. It now stands empty. Victor's teenage son sleeps there sometimes, as the house is more luxurious than his own *simba*. But the house is dusty and mostly vacant. Dead flies litter the windowsills; cobwebs stretch between the handles on the fitted kitchen cabinets.

There is nothing to be done with such a house: no one can permanently move into it, and the materials cannot be recycled. Notably, it is not even decaying. Whereas in the past the mud *ot* of a dead man would slowly disintegrate, ground down by storms and wind and termites, these materials are so durable that the house will remain as an enduring marker of absence. Once an index of prestige and attainment, Jeff's house now signifies something more ambiguous: a longstanding monument to a bad death. Victor lives with these manifestations of tragedy all around him: the forward flow of his own *dala* halted by the loss of his job, while beyond the hedge are the material remains of his brothers' and father's lives. Instead of a slow waxing and waning across a hillside, Victor's family have been stopped short, their progress stalled, whether by misfortune, bad choices or *chiraa*. The resilience of cement, glass and brick are a permanent reminder of the failed dream of embedding generations of kin into the terrain, inscribing a whole landscape.

Conclusion

When I embarked on this project, I did not intend to study death, funerals or burials. Yet it became an increasingly large part of my experience of Kaloleni. As a fairly poor neighbourhood where few people have health insurance and the dangers of road accidents and violent attacks are quite high, death is relatively frequent. The more I got to know people, the more frequently I was invited to funerals and memorial services. The longer I stayed in Kaloleni, and the more I was involved in the daily

Figure 15 Jeff's *ot madung* (main house), standing empty, Siyo Port, June 2014 (Photo: Author)

lives of friends and participants, the greater the expectation on me to be present at *matanga* and to contribute to burial costs, and the more my notebooks filled with references to death and dying. This was in many ways profoundly depressing. My notes chart how some of Kaloleni's most intractable problems – gang violence, lack of clean water, unemployment – coalesced in the unfortunate passing of another member of the community.

It was only when I travelled upcountry myself that I began to fully appreciate the regenerative potential of death for many Luo. The strong desire of most of my participants to 'return home' either before or after death had, up until that point, seemed coloured by nostalgia for or fantasy about an idealised land. A place where water is plentiful, land is free and neighbours respect you. But as I visited more and more upcountry homes, I began to understand that burial is really about completing a lifelong project of self-making. A project that for Kalolenians relies on city life but which manifests in the construction of a rural *dala* and is accomplished by the final reunion of body and land. The forms of labour and investment that go into making this happen remain a focal point for many Luo men, and for some women too. In practice, life often gets in the way of the *dala* and its proper iterative flow. Anxieties about getting stuck, whether in town or upcountry, are ever-present. Modern sensibilities, materialities and misfortunes can cause blockages, ambitions can be thwarted by competitors or by obstinate kin, undermining the possibility of achieving a good death. It is this dialectic of movement and stasis, mobility and obstruction, that framed the way Kaloleni Luo expressed ideas about the interconnected pathways of rural and urban life, about their aspirations, and also their anxiety that such capacities for straddling might be jeopardised by a highly uncertain future.

5

Constructing Security Claims

CCTV footage made public showed KDF [Kenya Defence Force] officers entering the Nakumatt store and later walking out each carrying
paper bags. More footage showed KDF officers ransacking safes in
jewellery stores at the mall but [Chief of Defence Forces] General
Karangi said they were undertaking a procedure he termed as 'saniti-
zation to ensure their safety.' [Other footage showed] soldiers taking
boxes of mobile phones from a shop where a body lies on the ground.

L. Wanambisi, report on looting after the Westgate Mall attack
Capital News, 22 October 2013

I made my way slowly along a muddy path between bungalows hidden
by high corrugated iron fences. Shouts and screams started up behind
me, people began to rush by. There's a shooting! The police are there,
they yelled. Reaching the house, Arina unbolted her heavy front door
and welcomed me inside. Neighbours dropped by, we learned more:
'thugs' fleeing a robbery nearby had sought refuge in a little café in the
estate. The police were alerted, a shootout had ensued. Arina lamented
what a place Kaloleni had become, full of gangs and crime. 'They are
just terrorists,' she sighed. 'These days we don't have security'.

Fieldnotes, 28 August 2014

Making a life in Nairobi has long been about managing insecurity.[1]
This has taken many guises. From colonial refusals to allow permanent
dwelling in the city to fears of violent crime and now the chronic uncertainty of Vision 2030, the felted landscape of Nairobi has been shaped
by the upheaval and rupture of various insecurities. The globalised
insecurity of terrorism has also made itself all too present, with the
1998 bombing of the US Embassy and then, in 2013, the Westgate Mall
attack shockingly exposing new urban vulnerabilities. Security has

---

[1] An earlier version of this chapter was first published in *Etnofoor* 27(2) 2015
as '"They are just terrorists": Constructing security claims in Nairobi'. I am
grateful to the editors for permission to include it here.

become a lens through which life in the city is frequently understood and experienced, whether discursively, in debates about failures of urban policing, or materially, in the proliferation of gated communities. It influences architectural design, the vocabulary of politics, the topics of discussion on Twitter. It is difficult then to discuss the making of Nairobi without considering the ways in which (in)security permeates the atmosphere as well as the substance of the city, from small-scale construction activities to conversations about Kenya's place in the world.

But though security in Nairobi is certainly conspicuous, it can also be ambiguous, crossing categories and seeping in to other domains. The two excerpts quoted above evoke some of these frictions. In the city's streets, different forms of anxiety and different types of insecurity intersect in complex ways. The first passage shows how debates around the Westgate Mall attack – a global terror event – quickly became entangled in a local set of concerns about the conduct and accountability of Kenyan security forces. This manner of localising a terrorist attack, of explaining it through a process of scaling down to local affairs, was brought home to me by the incident described in the second epigraph, in which a reverse process seems to be at work. In August 2014, as I made my way to an interview with a woman named Arina, I was peripherally witness to a shootout in Kaloleni between the police and gang members. It lasted for several hours and two young men were killed. Despite this, the event didn't even make the local news. Nevertheless, as Arina's remarks show, residents explained this event using a vocabulary of terror and security. This dynamic movement of security affairs across different scales and registers caught my attention, and I began to trace how for many in Nairobi, such scalar shifts allow them to use security debates as a fruitful resource for making certain claims.

Much of the scholarship on security has tended to be state-centric, observing how its agencies define and impose 'security' and its affiliated powers of risk mitigation and control – appropriately or disproportionately, depending on scholarly perspective. But as a nascent anthropology of (in)security makes clear – and the excerpts above imply – the ways in which global discourses of security are understood and deployed by communities outside of the state and its institutions can broaden our understandings of what security means, how it is produced, and what it provokes in lived social experience (Hansen 2006; Burrell 2010; Goldstein 2010; Holbraad and Pedersen 2013; Kublitz 2013). In Nairobi, notions of security are invoked at different moments and become implicated in a range of concerns, from crime, accountability and achievement to prestige and home design. It is this lived terrain of security – how it is experienced in everyday life – that remains indistinct if we limit our understanding to a category of special measures imposed by the state. The two epigraphs respectively demonstrate what we might term processes of scaling down and scaling up, as people seek to explain instances of insecurity in their lives. What is it about perceptions and experiences of security in Nairobi that mean local police should be partly blamed for a terrorist attack? Why would Arina desire to scale up the character of violence in her neighbourhood to evoke global terror?

As several scholars have noted, anthropology as a discipline is often unsure how to deal with the specificities of and differences between insecurity, uncertainty, danger and anxiety, with the distinction sometimes made on the basis of scale (Goldstein 2010; Holbraad and Pedersen 2013). This chapter in part explores the plasticity of terminology, highlighting the leakiness of such terms by showing how Nairobians move freely between them. Rather than delineating neat linguistic categories, I trace three examples of online debate about different forms of security – the Westgate attack, coverage of Obama's 2015 visit to Kenya, and the shootout in Kaloleni – to show how security discourses become both reconfigured to fit local concerns and scaled up to make incursions into a global debate. In a country where many feel that the state is failing to fulfil its obligations to provide security, the appropriation of vocabularies of global security is not a superficial linguistic mimicry but is a way of making an appeal in the language that gets heard. In this sense, the reframing of violence through a linguistic scaling up or down is also a way of making a political claim, a performative act that sets in motion new forms of identity-making (Goldstein 2010; Das 2011).

These linguistic and discursive deployments intersect with architectures of security and violence in Kaloleni and elsewhere in Nairobi to make and remake the city, both materially and imaginatively. Beginning with the segregated spaces of colonial Nairobi, security and exclusivity in the city have gone together. While African areas were subjected to various systems of colonial control, it was the European neighbourhoods that were the most tightly secured, so as to keep out a dangerous, unpredictable (African) other. Contemporary attempts to manage urban security both explicitly and implicitly draw on these older colonial practices of securing the city through exclusive spaces, and exclusion continues to be built in to the city's architectures, from private malls to gated enclaves. In this way, security is not only about managing urban safety, but also indexes prestige, with the elite vistas of Vision 2030 promising securitised exclusivity on a grand scale.

Residents of places like Kaloleni are regarded as the 'criminal other', to be sealed out of such prestigious developments, yet nonetheless they are themselves building ad hoc versions of sealed, secure architecture. In part, this is because at a time when many feel that 'the government is unable to guarantee their security', neighbourhoods have been increasingly left to manage security for themselves (Olima 2013: 298). But this chapter also explores how constructions of security are not simply utilitarian responses to urban crime, nor only a mani-festation of 'urban fear' (Low 1997, 2001), but are productive ways to make a space and find a voice for oneself in the city. Architectures that incorporate security features are ways of indexing exclusivity; they are regarded as beautiful and desirable, markers of status and pres-tige. The imitation of such architectures in the DIY projects of Kaloleni takes on new significance when understood through this wider frame of reference. Struggles with security offer fertile terrain for forms of claim-making, for finding ways to enable participation in the city and for forcing debates about urban inclusion. Such claims often reproduce, even as they critique, the segregated spaces of the colonial city and the enclaved zones of contemporary Nairobi. But as with the minor history-making discussed in Chapter 3, these appropriations can also be quietly disruptive, opening up ways of living towards the future, and aspiring to make a different kind of life in Nairobi today.

As such, rather than a state-imposed set of measures, security is some-thing to be constructed – claimed, crafted and negotiated in everyday life. Such claims take place discursively, through redeployments as well as rejections of global languages of terror, but they also emerge through architectures of security that become claims of achievement and of belonging to a more globally connected world. Security can in this way be a productive site or point of emergence, proffering opportunity or possibility for new modes of speaking, doing and building, and so of making lives in the city.[2] Rather than narrower, more specific readings of security-as-politics, by charting the discursive and material nego-tiations around security claims, we see how security in Nairobi goes far beyond functional responses to perceived threat. Building on the affordances of the performance of ownership, the landscape of secu-rity allows for the working out of new subject positions, for exploring new ways of being and doing that repurpose global conversations and which, in the process, radically reshape the city.

Security claims

In the aftermath of 9/11 (and some would argue before that – see Gold-stein 2010), we are living in times of insecurity, whether in Kenya or elsewhere in the world. This does not only describe a moment of height-ened fear of external attack, expansive governmental surveillance, pre-emptive military intervention and reduced personal freedoms, though of course it often means some or all of these. This is also a time in which the language of this politics produces political, economic,

[2] See also Goldstone and Obarrio (2017) for a similar argument about the productivity of 'crisis' in Africa

imaginative and material consequences, influencing forms of voice, collectivity and ways of seeking legitimacy (see also Moore 2016).

This quest for legitimacy echoes an argument made by Veena Das about citizenship, which she proposes is better understood as a moral claim rather than simply a status endowed either instrumentally or constitutively through law (2011). She describes how, in an informal squatter community on the outskirts of Delhi, claims of belonging are negotiated in the interstices of the state. In their everyday lives, the squatters make the most of official ambiguities to make incremental gains towards claiming legal protection. Degrees of official recognition are leveraged by residents through the acquisition of electricity meters, utility bills and official ration cards, as well as through the sheer presence of their informally constructed homes. Reminiscent of similar processes at work in Kaloleni, the Delhi squatters hope that these material and bureaucratic traces will gradually accumulate into authoritative claims for certain rights (Das 2011: 327–8). Rather than overarching Hegelian visions of state and citizenship or Habermasian notions of the public sphere, Das argues for attention to be paid to the 'minutiae of everyday life' to 'bring into view the complex agencies at play in the claim to citizenship' (2011: 331). She recounts how the vocabulary of the local leader who negotiated the squatters' precarious legitimacy is shot through with 'words that were like tracks left by his interactions with various state institutions,' a linguistic trail evidencing his reframing and repurposing of the squatters' demands in the language that will be heard (2011: 329). Das thus highlights the leakiness of categories such as formal/informal; govern/governed; legal/illegal, showing not only how everyday life provides the terrain in which citizenship claims can be presented but also how 'law and administrative procedures themselves come to make slow shifts' in response to residents' claims of new subject positions (2011: 325).

While Das does not explicitly address it, it is the multi-scalar character of this process that I wish to draw attention to here. She is not simply arguing for a fine-grained analysis of what citizenship means 'on the ground' – that is, the localising of a state category – but demonstrating how the squatters' appeals absorb and repurpose a macro discourse of 'citizenship', scaling up their immediate needs into the language of the law to find stronger footholds in the process of claiming legitimacy. Holbraad and Pedersen have appealed for greater linguistic precision on what is meant by 'insecurity' as opposed to 'uncertainty' or 'danger' (2013). Noting a 'tendency in recent anthropological writings to view insecurity as a matter of individual subjects' sense of uncertainty' (2013: 11), they argue for a distinction between a personal realm *of (un)certainty*, and *(in)security* as a politicisation of issues dealt with at a collective or social level (2013: 7–12). The ethnographic terrain of Nairobi, however, suggests that singling out security as a discrete category for interrogation does not give sufficient purchase on how ideas of security are entangled in complex networks of uncertainty and anxiety. Instead, following Das, I trace localising and globalising discourses of security as they bleed into ideas of terror, violence, crime and uncertainty. In doing so, I do not intend to collapse 'insecurity' to mean the same thing as 'uncertainty' or 'crime', but rather to approach it as it is understood and experienced in everyday life. This reveals a mismatch between the kinds of insecurity that become the focus of media attention and those which may be more pressing concerns for many yet go unreported. Residents' attempts to define such concerns within a language of terror and security can be seen as a form of moral claim, an attempt to seek wider recognition of the risky situations they face and leverage some kind of response.

Vocabularies of security

Throughout the research for this book, insecurity in Kenya was the stuff of global headlines, with coverage of terrorist attacks on malls, buses and beachside hotels (see for example Kanini 2014; Poulter 2014). Several governments withdrew embassy staff; official security advisories warned against travel to the northern border with Somalia and certain areas of the coast, Mombasa and Nairobi, with subsequent devastating effects on the tourism industry (Morris 2015). On 21 September 2013, unknown gunmen attacked Westgate Mall, the most upmarket retail destination in Nairobi. More than sixty people were killed over the next four days, in an extended 'siege' that was later claimed by Al-Shabaab, a Somali militant group with links to al-Qaeda. The mall had an elaborate, privately operated security apparatus and constituted what Mike Davis has called a 'fortified citadel', which was in part what made it a favourite hangout of Nairobi's expat and local elites (1990: 238). Westgate quickly became a terror event broadcast on a global scale. Live coverage was streamed on multiple platforms across global media outlets including the BBC, Al Jazeera and CNN, showing gunmen, hostages, explosions and attempted rescues. Yet, as the opening passage of this chapter reveals, the live streaming of the siege also provided footage of other forms of criminal damage conducted by the very forces meant to be providing protection. In the investigations and reporting which followed the siege, it became clear that disentangling what counted as 'terrorism' and what damage was caused by theft, negligence, and incompetence was next to impossible (Howden 2013).

The Westgate attack happened a few days before this project commenced. The attack was broadcast in real time, with not only rolling updates on television news channels but a stream of communications over Twitter and Facebook from those hiding inside. This proliferation of screens – including CCTV, smartphone, TV and laptop screens – catapulted Westgate, as well as the figures of the hostages, the gunmen, and the security forces, into observers' intimate lives. Headlines such as 'Terror at the mall', 'Kenyan mall massacre' and 'Shoppers slaughtered in Kenya bloodbath' circulated, along with hundreds of eyewitness accounts and photos on social media, prompting tens of thousands of comments, shares and reposts. In the first hour of the attack alone, between 12pm and 1pm local time, 6,171 original tweets were recorded (Sambuli 2013). While people around the world, including myself, followed as events at Westgate unfolded over four days of confused and confusing reports, Nairobians had a dual positionality as both witnesses to the event and participants in a global conversation. Kenyans are themselves consumers of the media that presents Kenya as a terrorism hotspot; they follow the news on CNN, the BBC and Al Jazeera – online, on satellite TV, via smartphones – as well as via Kenyan outlets. In Kenya, understandings of insecurity may be shaped, therefore, by first- or second-hand experience *and* concurrently filtered through this more global language and imagery of terror and security, which frames their country in certain ways but which also prompts new kinds of interpretations. Personal experiences of terrorism can occur simultaneously with their consumption as mediatised terror spectacles, provoking reconfigured ideas of state and citizen, good people and bad people, violence and insecurity.

This is apparent in the way discourses about national security issues have been taken up and reconfigured in people's everyday lives. When the shootout in Kaloleni occurred, some eleven months after the Westgate attack, there were no reporters present. Despite the violence, the blood, the deaths, nothing appeared in even the Kenyan media. Violent crime in poorer corners of Nairobi, it seems, is too routine for news. Indeed, this was not the first incident of shooting in Kaloleni, and in fact it was only one of several that occurred during my fifteen months of fieldwork. This lack of attention, however, should not lead us to assume that this incident was regarded as routine by those who experienced it. The kinds of insecurity that grab the media's attention do not necessarily match up with the most pressing concerns of everyday life. While the events of Westgate were undoubtedly brutal and rocked the city for several days, nonetheless for many Nairobians, the threat of terrorism – though real enough – remains a somewhat vague and distant danger, something to be feared but often overshadowed by more immediate insecurities.

As preceding chapters have made clear, Kaloleni no longer receives the services from the City Council to which it is meant be entitled. It is now economically poor and there are few employment opportunities, particularly for young men. Violent crime in the area is common. During the course of this project, several of my neighbours' homes were burgled, two of my informants were killed and I heard many accounts of gang violence and muggings. The police shooting of gang members was far from an isolated occurrence. On the day of that shootout, Arina was not the only resident I spoke with who deployed a vocabulary more usually associated with terrorist attacks. In the afternoon, I met up with Nico, a young man in his twenties who lives near the café where the shootout occurred. Recounting the day's events, he said, 'We were held hostage for several hours,' describing how he and many others had been forced to take shelter in their homes, even hiding under the bed as gunfire continued outside. By using the word 'hostage', he located the shootout within a wider narrative of hostage-taking in Kenya, not only the 'hostages' of Westgate[3] but a spate of kidnappings of foreign tourists by Al-Shabaab-related groups, which has received considerable international coverage.[4]

Nico also posted updates on the shooting to the Kaloleni Facebook page as well as to Twitter. 'This is Nico reporting from Kaloleni', he wrote, before posting several photos of bullet casings littering the paths around his home. Given the total lack of formal media interest in the events of that day, and the ambiguous role of state security personnel – though the police can be seen to have responded to a security issue, they were also responsible for the killings – Nico turned to social media to rouse some commentary and concern. His posts did indeed provoke many further comments, especially from the Kaloleni diaspora, now living in many corners of the world. '*Siku hizi hakuna usalama*', read one comment: 'these days there's no security'.

This turn to what we might call citizen journalism and the choice of a specific vocabulary to describe the incident should not be read as just mimicking a global media language, or an inappropriate equation of a small-scale police shooting with the brutality of Westgate, but rather as a creative repurposing of a narrative. Regarding himself as a local source of news and information, Nico had quite clear ideas of providing a public service by informing Kaloleni's online and offline communities about the day's events. He was making a claim for wider recognition of the insecurities faced in a relatively poor, forgotten corner of the city. Using the language of security, then, is in part a political act, an attempt to make one's situation known in the language that gets heard. In this sense, security – like property – can be seen as a performative process, a form of claim-making. Drawing on speech act theory (Austin 1975), Goldstein has observed how

[3] Though there is some doubt whether the gunmen took hostages in the usual sense of the term (see Howden 2013).
[4] The most notorious recent example being the case of the Tebbutts: Judith Tebbutt was kidnapped and her husband, David, shot dead during a stay at a luxury island retreat north of Lamu, on the Kenyan coast close to the border with Somalia (see BBC 2011).

the ability to make a security declaration – to utter the word 'security' in reference to a particular threat or crisis – is an indicator of the political power of the speaker demonstrated by his or her ability to declare something a security threat and to have that declaration recognised publicly as legitimate. (2010: 492)

But, as with the historical claim-making described in Chapter 3, the right or capacity to use the language of security authoritatively is not a foregone conclusion, but subject to negotiation.

In international media, Kenya is frequently depicted in crude terms as a terror incubator as well as a place of primitive, tribal violence (see Moore 2016). But such lazy portrayals do not go uncritiqued. In July 2015, President Obama was in the middle of his first and only official visit to Kenya during his presidency. His father, Barack Obama Senior, was Kenyan, and in fact lived for some time in Kaloleni before he emigrated to the USA in 1964. The President's visit to Kenya has been eagerly anticipated; the elaborate securitisation of the country less so. Kenyan airspace was closed to make way for Airforce One, the airport crawling with CIA operatives, US marines and secret service agents. Most of the city's central streets were closed for the length of his visit, making local transportation next to impossible and forcing the closure of many schools, businesses and shops. Obama first visited Kenya in 1988, and the beaten-up VW Beetle that met him at the airport – the exhaust pipe of which fell off shortly afterwards – had this time been replaced by 'The Beast', a bombproof limousine with 13cm thick glass and a presidential blood bank in the boot (D. Smith 2015). It was announced that due to security concerns, Obama's visit would be limited to Nairobi; he would not travel outside the capital to visit his family in western Kenya.

CNN's coverage of Obama's visit emphasised the apparent enormity of the security risk, counting the number of military and security personnel – over 10,000 – who were deployed to ensure the safety of his visit. With a headline describing Kenya as 'a hotbed of terror', the report implied that it was foolhardy at best for the then President to enter such an uncontrollable country (CNN 2015). In Kenya, the CNN report was met with hoots of derision. Within a few hours, #someonetellCNN was trending on Twitter as Kenyans lambasted the one-dimensional reporting, and especially the 'hotbed' accusation, by posting images of luxury beds going up in flames and other satirical and humorous photos (see Dearden 2015 for a round-up of the memes and for images of CNN's original broadcast). CNN responded by updating to headline to 'Obama visits homeland', as well as by changing the news anchor from a white to a black woman. Eventually the news channel's managing director was forced to fly to Kenya to make a formal apology in person (Mutiga 2015). The #someonetellCNN hashtag was a revival of a meme that first emerged in 2013 during the Kenyan elections, when simplistic reporting by CNN implied it was inevitable that 'tribal' violence would 'erupt' during the elections. This prompted uproar online, with the hashtag and spoof images of scenes of 'violence' – including gnawed chicken bones, chewed mangoes and people sleeping in voting queues – going viral (see Moore 2016).

In these debates, we see how well-worn narratives of Kenya as a land of violence and terror have been opened up to new forms of local critique that play out on a global platform. This complicates our sense of scale. We are no longer following so-called micro processes as they play out within overarching categories of 'security', but rather we move across scales and registers as the 'big' and the 'small' are increasingly enmeshed, the one complicating the other (Das 2011: 325). The capacity to make security claims and deploy certain vocabularies cannot be assumed: just because CNN is a US broadcaster does not mean that people in Kenya are not listening. Their creative utilisations of language reveal that security discourse is powerful: it grants political power to the speaker. As the popularity of #someonetellCNN exposes, contesting the right to deploy this language is about voice: the capacity to speak up and make oneself heard. It is clear, therefore, that fear or perceived threat are not sufficient organising principles for understanding responses to insecurity. Rather, encounters with security, both first-hand and via mediatised representations, can be transformative, opening up novel engagements and opportunities for new ways of staking a claim in the world. To demonstrate this, I now turn to Nairobi's built environment, to how such claims are materialised in specific ways within the city.

Fortress Nairobi

The distance between the old housing estates of Eastlands and the leafy upmarket neighbourhoods of Westlands is only a matter of a few miles. But psychologically and materially, it is a passage into a very different type of urban space. A *matatu* (public minibus) from Nairobi's city centre heads westward up Museum Hill to the breezy suburbs that under British rule were zoned as white residential areas. These wealthy streets are quieter, and the *matatu* passes under jacaranda and flame trees dating back to colonial times. Today, luxury apartment blocks are more common than colonial detached villas, and many have their own pool and gym. The strange combination of airy leafiness and formidable security infrastructure creates an atmosphere of exclusivity. Though the streets are roomy, buildings are often barely visible behind high concrete walls topped with broken glass or razor wire. Juxtaposing this securitisation are the bucolic names – Brookside Drive, Willow Walk, Arcadia Gardens. The sharp lines and blank walls sit awkwardly with attractive planting on the verges: bougainvillea, jasmine, roses, ornamental hedges.

To reach Spring Valley, one of the Westlands neighbourhoods, it is only possible to go so far without a car. At the limit of the *matatu* routes one must continue on foot: many of the roads through Spring Valley are privately operated, their management taken over by residents' associations who carefully cultivate exclusivity. Signs declare, 'No matatus' and intermittent barriers block the way, manned by *askaris* (guards) working for multinational security firms such as G4S. There are no pavements, so pedestrians must hop between the flowerbeds and the road. The high compound walls on either side all have tall gates. Further sentries control access to these privatised safe zones, the gate swinging open only when the guard has ascertained the purpose and identity of the visitor. Plaques declare the level of fortification: 'AAA Protection by Lavington Security' or 'Secured by G4S: UN Approved'.

The fortification of wealthy neighbourhoods has been underway for several decades in many cities across Africa, but this security architecture was foregrounded in new ways by the attack on Westgate Mall. It changed the way perceptions of danger were mapped on to certain urban spaces. The gated residences, fortified malls and road checkpoints of Westlands and Spring Valley – where Westgate is located – were previously regarded by Nairobi's elite as 'safe zones' within a disorderly and dangerous city. The attack rendered them permeable, opening up exclusive spaces to violent spectacle. It also reframed security architecture as target rather than sanctuary. The apparatus of security that protected expats and wealthy Kenyans alike, attempting to seal them off from the spectres of car jackings and armed home invasions, was violated, and intimate spaces of comfort and leisure intruded upon. Since then, anxiety around entering public spaces and fear of further attacks mean that routines and behaviours have been altered. It is now almost impossible to enter any building, whether it's a hospital, church, mall, supermarket, art gallery, bus or restaurant, without first being body-scanned by a (private) security guard. Whether or not these enhanced performances of security are effective is hard to measure. Certainly, more time is dedicated to their enactment, but it often feels routine. What response these guards are qualified to make if they find something suspicious is also uncertain.

On one occasion when visiting Rebecca, a friend living in Spring Valley, we went to buy groceries. Like many other expats, Westgate had been where she did her shopping, ate out for dinner, went to the cinema and had her hair cut. Instead, we went to another nearby mall, the Sarit Centre, previously the slightly downmarket cousin to Westgate but now enjoying the extra custom. Even though it is a ten-minute walk, we drive there; Rebecca no longer feels comfortable walking around these streets. New security procedures mean long queues at the gate. Eventually we reach the front and guards search perfunctorily under the car and in the boot, ignoring the beeping of their hand scanners.

The barrier lifts, we enter and park. Further checks are located at the entrance, where three G4S guards are staffing an airport-style security system. We empty our pockets into plastic trays and put them on the conveyor belt: no one watches the screen. I walk through the scanner. It beeps loudly, but the guard waves me on. Rebecca rolls her eyes at me. 'Waste of time,' she says.

The Westgate attack exposed old security regimes as insufficient but, as Rebecca's response indicates, there is little faith in new systems either. The reports of looting by Kenyan security agents in the aftermath of Westgate garnered a lot of coverage in Kenya, and contributed to burgeoning public mistrust of the government's security operation. This has added to anxieties around entering busy public places. For months after Westgate, at weekends, malls remained empty in the middle of the day, usually their busiest period. The rest of the time people tended to rush in, get what they needed and leave – malls are no longer the same spaces of leisure and relaxation, no longer regarded as refuges in a city with sky-high rates of robbery and mugging. James, the cosmopolitan young Kalolenian described in Chapter 4, works as a hairdresser in an exclusive salon at Yaya, another upscale mall. He generously offered to cut my hair for free, and, as I sat in the chair, we chatted about how behaviours have changed in these spaces. He described to me how these days he has to go in to work two hours earlier than he used to, as most of his clients don't like to be in the mall in the middle of the day and want to make appointments early in the morning. Observing the outer atrium of the mall reflected in the mirror, I asked him if he was afraid, coming to work in a mall every day. In reply, he began to talk me through the escape route he had worked out: jumping out the salon window on to the car park roof below. He no longer leaves his salon during the day if he can avoid it, feeling safer there than in the exposed plazas and balconies of the mall.

But many affluent Nairobians still prefer to drive to malls rather than enter the centre of the city, and in 2016, after a full refurbishment, Westgate reopened. Though the first weeks were quiet and shops and restaurants reported slow trade, business gradually picked up. Saturdays at Westgate were once again crowded with wealthy shoppers. Memories of terror, it seems, are no match for such venues of leisure and consumption. These enclosed malls are privatised spaces, watched over by corporate security personnel and accessible only to a privileged minority. Similar to Mike Davis's observations of 'Fortress LA' in the 1980s, there has been a 'retreat from the street' in Nairobi, an introversion of public space into the insider/outsider partitioning of gated communities and fortified citadels of malls and business districts (1990: 238). In effect, this turns the notion of public architecture inside out. Instead of an enticing street frontage, the outside is a defensible fortress of high walls, with the pleasure and enjoyment sealed within. Nairobi echoes his description of Los Angeles as a city with an 'obsession with physical security systems, and collaterally, with the architectural policing of social boundaries' (1990: 223).

Fear and loathing?

As my forays into Spring Valley highlighted, Nairobi's security architecture is designed to make it clear that an underclass 'other' is not welcome in the pseudo-public space of malls, business zones and privatised streets. Davis argues that whereas architectural critics do not usually pick up on how such spaces contribute to segregation, 'pariah groups ... read the meaning immediately' (1990: 226). Security comes to be less about ensuring anyone's personal safety than with anxiety over, and insulation from, an uncertain and unpredictable 'public'. In this way, codes of segregation are materialised in the built environment, whether via high walls, guarded gates, barbed wire or notices warning of armed response units. Security becomes accessible only to those with the capacity to buy in to protective services or to a residential enclave.

In her work on gated communities in the USA, Setha Low (1997, 2001) focuses primarily on urban fear as a driving force in the development of enclaves of privately secured housing. She describes gated communities as materialisations of fear, inscribing it on the built environment, which in turn entrenches further segregation, avoidance of (racial/cultural/class) difference and surveillance. She focuses on what one of her informants described as 'fear flight' (Low 2001: 55): the desire to protect oneself, family and property from dangers perceived as overwhelming on the 'outside'. Echoing Davis, she says that 'the walls are making visible the systems of exclusion that are already there, now constructed in concrete' (Low 2001: 55). Similarly, Lindsay Bremner's incisive analysis of gated enclaves in Johannesburg notes how the psychology of anxiety and fear fuses with the figure of the criminal 'other' to create new forms of architectural exclusions and segregations in the post-apartheid city (2004: 455). The smooth, closed walls and tightly guarded openings of the enclave materialise the anxieties of a shaken elite about too-far-reaching, too-fundamental shifts that post-apartheid democracy has brought to the city (2004: 464). Significantly, gating not only seals off residents from a feared 'other', but from a 'polis' more fundamentally. Exclusionary enclaves also facilitate forms of private but collective land tenure that are not under the auspices of local government. New forms of private governance ensue, through 'homeowner associations' that take on functions of policing, management and lobbying that both parallel what might be expected of, but are beyond the supervision of, the state (Low 2001: 47).

But who is this faceless, excluded 'other' from whom residents are trying to shield themselves? Neither Davis, nor Low nor Bremner are explicit, beyond a rather vague idea of the urban poor. In Nairobi, residents of areas such as Spring Valley might expect the person on the other side of the wall to come from poor neighbourhoods such as Kaloleni, where – as the opening epigraph suggests – even Kalolenians despair of the prevalence of criminal thugs. But, as we have seen, violent crime is prevalent across all areas of the city, and residents of all sorts have little faith in the government's ability to deliver services or ensure any standards of policing (Olima 2013). Almost all new construction in the city – not just in the wealthy areas around Westgate – is gated in some form: from the detached villa surrounded by high walls and private security guards, to small 'courts' of a few apartment blocks or houses with a single (guarded) entrance/exit. Across the city, in poor, middle class and affluent areas, 'Nairobi residents are increasingly organising themselves at the neighbourhood level to secure and manage their neighbourhoods' (Olima 2013: 296). What we see are many manifestations of fortification and securitisation, from cheap corrugated iron fences to elaborate architectures.

To my mind, the established discourse of urban fear is not on its own substantial enough to account for the escalation of securitised space in the city. It fails to capture the pride and aspiration indexed by the home, and the desirability of these enclaved zones. Indeed, this is indirectly acknowledged by Low, who remarks that in addition to fear of crime and insecurity, her informants also mentioned investment values, status implications, prestige and their desire for more space and privacy as reasons for their move to a gated community, though 'these concerns are not examined in this analysis' (Low 2001: 52). This seems a significant oversight, given that exclusivity and prestige are crucial attractions of these enclaves. To focus on the 'push' reasons for moving to a gated community at the expense of what the 'pull' might be is only to tell half the story.

The desirability of privatised, screened zones is clear in contemporary Nairobi. This is apparent not just in the construction boom currently engulfing the city but also in a semi-virtual visual realm that precedes and surrounds it. As cities around the world strive for world-class status, to appeal to globalised flows of financial and human capital and to be recognised as nodes in a global urban nexus, the appeal of the enclave has been reinvigorated (Lagerkvist 2007; Brosius 2010; Grant 2014). Computer-generated renderings of apartments, neighbourhoods and skylines shape desires for certain modes of living before such spaces even exist; visions of exclusive urban futures to which architectures of security are a crucial component. The 'enclaved gaze' of these spaces surveys the tidy vista of the compound, producing an aesthetic community insulated from a supposedly chaotic public sphere (Brosius

2010: 189). In Nairobi, the public relations imaginary of property developers and architects create websites, billboards and roadside hoardings featuring architectural renderings that produce what they hope will be self-fulfilling vistas of this new global urbanscape, sealed off from a dangerous urban populace immediately surrounding it, yet connected to other 'global cities' elsewhere (Sassen 1991).

In this way, architectures of exclusion are also architectures of exclusivity; markers of having 'made it' in Nairobi. The enclaved gaze of securitised living has become aspirational: a desirable aesthetic, not merely utilitarian. While high-end gated communities remain exclusive – indicators of financial attainment managed by only a handful of Nairobians – they are deemed prestigious by many more. In the next sections I show how the modified domestic architectures of Kaloleni also emulate the characteristics of enclaved living. But simultaneously, by aspiring to gated privacy, these building practices also turn colonial understandings of security on their head.

Surveillance and enclosure

Though Kenya has acquired new prominence in global terrorism discourses of the post-9/11 world, becoming a target of primarily Al-Shabaab-led attacks as well as an ally in the USA's 'war on terror', insecurity is far from a recent anxiety. Security and order have justified architectural interventions since Nairobi's foundation at the turn of the twentieth century: the wide streets of the colonial city centre, the clearances of cramped African villages and later the demolitions of 'illegal' structures were as much to do with urban control as they were overcrowding or disease (Hake 1977; Myers 2003). The British colonial government sought to discipline bodies through the ordering of urban space, a form of governance that was at once material and ideological. In Nairobi, as in many other colonial cities, discourses of vision, public health and security went together (White 1990: Chapter 3; Achola 2001). Overcrowded slums were regarded as dangerous breeding grounds for vice as well as for disease; the closely packed houses with twisting paths and lack of apparent order made surveillance by colonial authorities impossible. Safety and order were to be found in well-planned, well-ventilated, urban architectures with clear sightlines. Central to this transformation were European techniques of visuality: mapping and surveying, regulating flows of people and infrastructure, and methods of surveillance for the maintenance of order and control (see Joyce 2003). In Kaloleni, the open, fenceless design facilitated scrutiny of its residents. Privacy was disregarded in favour of clear sightlines from one side of the estate to another.

This openness of vision was also combined with strict regulation. The notorious *kipande* system restricted the movement of Africans around the city, requiring them to carry passes permitting them access to certain areas (Lonsdale 2001: 212). In Kaloleni, all new tenants had to sign up to the exacting code of conduct described in earlier chapters. The regulations were stringent and the authorities' surveillance reached into many corners of intimate domestic life. But in Kaloleni today, many older residents are surprisingly nostalgic for the colonial management of the estate. They do not remember it as a form of surveillance and control, but a time of order and neatness. The regular house fumigations are vividly recalled, as they required residents to turn out all their private belongings on to the street and in to the public gaze. Yet many speak of this with admiration for the organisation and energy it demanded, rather than seeing it as a slur on their family's hygiene.

In Hutton's original design for Kaloleni, all outdoor areas were communal and were managed by the city, including trees, flowerbeds and lawns. Older residents remember the strict enforcement of the 'keep off the grass' notices, and one resident, Harriet, showed me the circuitous route she had to take from the main road to her front door to ensure she kept to the paths. Today, the estate is notable for its extensive fencing and the enclosure of public space. This process has largely taken two different, though overlapping, forms. Firstly, the creation of backyards filled with extensions as a means of augmenting household income. Secondly, at the front of the house, another type of enclosure of once-public space has emerged. Many families have fenced in their house to create private compounds of varying complexity, ranging from thorn hedges and picket fences to wire-topped corrugated iron. Within these barricades, some families have planted front gardens while others look out directly on to large gates and security fencing.

These assorted materialisations of enclosure intersect with local discourses on security and safety in different, and sometimes conflicting, ways. The fencing of public space has been done in part to keep mud and rubbish at bay, but also out of a desire for privacy and concerns about household security. That cleanliness and security go together is something that the colonial architects would have agreed with, but the way this is materialised in residents' building practices is at odds with the openness of past planning models. This was made clear by Maggie, a resident in line Y. 'It is what made us now plant these fences', she said. 'To prevent people from throwing bad things and whatever. This fence ... we planted the fence because of that and also security'. The need for fencing was stressed to me many times. One old man named Odhiambo explained that, though fencing materials varied, they were all constructed with one intention, for 'security purposes':

This fence, it is us [that built it]. Some will fence with wire, some will fence with *maua* [plants] like this one. Some are making a gate because of security purposes. You know, people have [be]come many ... There are some needing to steal, there are some need to break, there are some need to hit you when you come late, things like that. Yeah. So that one is because of security purposes. That's why we try to bring in – to make fencing for it.

An intriguing aspect of this partitioning is the way it inverts earlier discourses: colonial authorities feared the dirt and disorder of Africans, and so tried to make their private lives as public and visible as possible. Now, abandoned by the state and struggling with rising dilapidation, insecurity and violence, residents' building strategies have privatised their home spaces, reversing the relationship between vision and security. By redirecting the authority of structures designed to control them, they are reclaiming security as something within their control. As the proliferation of gated communities across the city suggests, this privatisation of security is part of a much wider inversion throughout Nairobi. Rather than safety being generated through unimpeded vision, as was implicit in the colonial boulevards of the 1948 Master Plan, new construction practices mean high walls and electric fences: vision is impaired.

In Kaloleni, as recent events attest, the threat of break-ins and of violence is very real. There is almost no formal police presence in the estate, and no one to call in the event of an incident. The streetlights are broken, and many people, especially women, spoke to me of their anxieties about coming home late or walking around the neighbourhood after dark. As such, the desire to secure one's home is unsurprising. Maggie said it could even be dangerous in the daytime:

Security is very bad ... you can even be slaughtered during the day because if you go behind here, the extensions, they are all over and that place is just a *ka*-small place so when you meet somebody there he can do anything, whatever he wants. Especially for ladies it is very risky.

Often, as Maggie did, residents blamed the presence of violent crime in Kaloleni on the proliferation of extensions. These corrugated iron structures occupy an ambiguous position in relation to notions of security within the estate. On the one hand, they provide a source of relatively reliable income in the face of rising inequality and unemployment, contributing to livelihood security. On the other hand, they bring newcomers into Kaloleni, whose relative anonymity is seen as highly suspect by many. 'I hate these tin structures', Harriet told me. She has refused to build any around her own house, despite the possibility for increased income, preferring to leave her house without any enclosures. 'These extensions are clogging the estate. And you cannot control the people who live there. They are unknown'. Almost everyone in the estate seemed to have lurid stories to tell about neighbours who inadvertently rented out their extensions to people who turned out to be hiding from the police, or even murderers or gang leaders.

Yet interestingly, one resident, Anne, partly traced the rise of insecurity in Kaloleni back to the fundamental planning of the estate. Deliberately designed to move away from a rigid grid structure or barrack 'lines' of earlier housing projects, the spider web plan of Kaloleni takes a more organic form, with loosely circular groups of houses rather than rows, and wide-open spaces in between. This openness is what Anne loved about Kaloleni in the past: 'If I stood at my mother's door I'd see the other neighbour; "Hi", and see the one on the other side; "How are you?"' she recalled. Today this would be impossible, as both houses are enclosed behind high, tangled hedges. Many people have made private compounds and added burglar doors across their front porches. In the past if it was raining, 'People coming from work would run into your veranda and stand there and wait for the rain [to stop]. Nowadays you can't. Very few houses are left like that'.

For Anne, the open design was the foundation of neighbourliness and community. But she acknowledged that, when urban crime began to skyrocket in the 1980s during the era of President Moi, the spacious, more organic plan became an issue. She described how a lot of 'criminals' used to cross from the other side of the valley, from the settlements of Pumwani and Majengo, and if the police were chasing them they would run and hide in Kaloleni, preferring it to the barrack-style railway housing of Makongeni next door. Because of the twisting paths, tree coverage and disorienting layout of structures, Anne said, 'Kaloleni was a very good hideout.' In an echo of the shooting incident I experienced during my fieldwork, she described how 'thugs' would hide in Kaloleni, trying to make their way across to the Industrial Area: 'So once they've done something on the other side [of the valley], they'd run across here being chased by the police, shootout, shootout, shootout ... So these shootouts became a big issue'. But according to her, the partitioning of the communal gardens and enclosure of houses in private compounds has had a discouraging effect. Now, 'when they come in, if they are running, if they are being chased, they just have to go through the road because now they don't know [the way]. They can't access behind [the houses]'. Although she told me several tales of residents renting extensions to people they did not know, only to wake up to the sound of gunfire or the police on their doorstep, she also commented that 'the extensions in some way have improved things because now you have nowhere to run to.'

Residents in Kaloleni consistently spoke with admiration of the gated, fenced, 'beautiful' houses they saw elsewhere in the city. When-

ever I enquired about changes they would like to see in their neighbourhood, or what Kaloleni might be lacking, one recurrent response was a
perimeter wall, 'so that it can be made closed off': secure, private, more
exclusive. Anne, however, was in a minority who criticised the fences.
Their security benefits could not make up for her disapproval of the
change in atmosphere of Kaloleni. She observed how, 'These days, Kaloleni is so private'; it doesn't have the openness of the past. Although she
acknowledged that issues of insecurity had led people to start fencing
in their homes, she shrewdly recognised that the new fences were also
aspirational, symbols of a desire to live a secluded, privatised lifestyle
more in keeping with the fortification of domestic space in the exclusive
suburbs across the city. She commented:

> I hate it ... I hate these plants [the planted hedges]. Why can't you
> just see your neighbour across and say hi? If you people want to live
> in seclusion, why don't you go and buy homes? You know I think the
> idea of living in Kaloleni is chatting with your neighbour, seeing your
> neighbour coming, going out. That's the idea of community. I think
> it's beautiful. But when you want to live secluded, just go buy a home
> and live there with your own compound but stop making this place a
> compound. It's not beautiful.

Anne's astute analysis reveals how notions of security get taken
up and reconfigured, not just discursively, but in the material interventions of daily life. For the majority of estate residents, there is an
element of prestige in the proliferation of fences, burglar doors and
private compounds. While they may not have the capital to move to a
gated community, the fenced houses in Kaloleni are regarded by residents as the nicest and most attractive. People go to extraordinary
lengths to manage and maintain neatly trimmed hedges, ornamental
planting and brightly painted fences in the face of diverse challenges,
including water shortages, minimal disposable incomes and marauding
goats. The examples from Kaloleni show how the introversion of public
space, domestic fortification and privatisation of public services are not
just occurring within the sphere of the elite, but across different neighbourhoods, affluent and otherwise. These securitised spaces are not
only driven by fear of intruders, they index aspirations to the secluded
exclusivity seen elsewhere in Nairobi, materialising claims to a certain
outlook on the world.

Conclusion

Rather than trying to pinpoint distinctions between categories of
security, this chapter has traced it across various scales and registers,
following residents as they fuse security with a wider nexus of urban
safety, citizen voice, official accountability and aspirational futures.

Building on Das's work on citizenship as a moral claim, I see the scaling up and the scaling down of debates around security as a type of claim-making, finding ways to participate in debates about urban security and the state of the city. Recent terrorist events mean that various guises of security in Nairobi have been broadcast on a global stage, from the horrors of Westgate to the shutdown of the city for President Obama's visit. The effect of such spectacles and vocabularies on daily life in Nairobi has been potent, but not simply by creating a climate of fear or sense of threat. Rather, they have been co-opted and reconstituted in processes of claim-making in a range of situations, from unacknowledged cases of violent crime to the accountability of official security agents. Global discourses of security have enabled new forms of voice to emerge, including Kenyans' satirical interventions via digital media and Kaloleni residents' scaling up of local crime in the language of terror. In doing so they have revealed how security can be harnessed to make particular claims – a performative act that offers political potential for those with the authority to deploy it.

Such claims do not exist purely on a discursive level but are also materialised in specific ways within the city. Architectures of security, with their associated aura of prestige and exclusivity, are increasingly desirable, even as they have been exposed as fragile and permeable by the 'image trail' of events such as Westgate (RETORT 2004). The aspirational quality of enclaved life suggests that responses to security in Nairobi cannot be simply understood as utilitarian or driven by fear. Instead, a discursive, visual and physical landscape of security is emerging in which claims for new ways of living, speaking and belonging are being constructed.

6

Making the Future in the Shadow of Vision 2030

On 11 December 2013, a new advertisement appeared on a huge bill-board just outside Kaloleni, along the main road running through Eastlands (Figure 16).[1] Erected during the night, the billboard came with no warning, and was not accompanied by any public meeting or distribution of information to explain its meaning or presence. The image it presents is of a digital rendering of highrise apartment blocks arranged around a large multi-lane highway. In the foreground, in the centre of a landscaped roundabout, is a circular grey sign that reads *Karibu Kaloleni*; Welcome to Kaloleni. The text emblazoned across the billboard states *Mabadiliko Yetu*, Our Changes, as though this is the promise of an inclusive future. The thirteen-storey highrises, uniformly coloured cream and rust-brown, are arranged in orderly rows that recede into the distance. In the foreground, tiny pedestrians – dwarfed by the scale of the project – can be seen walking along yellow footpaths under mature trees. Cars move unimpeded along a smooth tarmacked highway, the speed of their movement indicated by digitally rendered blurring. Coinciding with the billboard, the image also appeared online on Jambonewspot, a widely read Kenyan diaspora blog, along with other images of the same project (Jambone-wspot 2013). These were even more fantastical than the billboard. One was a radical reimagining of the infrastructure along Jogoo Road, featuring futuristic geometric glass and steel skyscrapers, palm trees, and a large highway. A sign proclaiming 'New Kaloleni' directs traffic into the reimagined estate.

These digitally rendered visions are in stark contrast to the present decaying reality of the estate, and the experience of Jogoo Road is also drastically different from the vista that appeared online. Jogoo Road is the main artery of Eastlands, but it is usually clotted with a tight mass of barely moving traffic, thick clouds of fumes choking the atmosphere. The edges of the street are a mishmash of dirt paths, broken street-

---

[1] An earlier version of this chapter was first published in *Urban Planning* 2:1 (2017) as '"Our changes?" Visions of the future in Nairobi'.

Figure 16 The billboard featuring designs for 'New Kaloleni', Jogoo Road, December 2013 (Photo: Author)

lights, thickets of informal hawkers, verges clogged with rubbish and more corrugated iron. The disconnect between image and reality is vast. The fanciful panoramas certainly do not seem oriented towards the current life of the area, a place where unemployment is high and those in work are concentrated in a miscellany of jobs in the informal economy. The strategy behind these images was never made clear – there were no related public announcements – but it would seem highly unlikely that they would be available or affordable to current residents, even if subsidised.

And yet, among Kalolenians, the images were generally regarded positively. The billboard and associated images generated intense discussion both within the estate and on social media after photos were uploaded to Facebook. Online, many comments were favourable, from straightforward 'Wow! Great project' and 'This is amazing!!!' to ones flavoured with the language of development and progress, including 'This is what I see in the first world' and – in an echo of colonial master-planning – 'The real City in the Sun'. In comparison to the extant housing, with its rundown infrastructure and piles of rubbish, the clean, orderly vision on the billboard seemed attractive to many. The image was described as 'smart', 'beautiful' and in Kiswahili *'poa sana'*

– very cool. 'These places are very modern. Who wouldn't want a new kitchen?' one man asked rhetorically.

New urban fantasies have been flourishing across Africa in recent years. Rwanda, Ghana, Angola, Tanzania, Nigeria, Democratic Republic of the Congo as well as Kenya have all seen their governments launch urban megaprojects that promise to radically reshape African cities. Typified by spectacular infrastructural projects and new satellite cities, these schemes are also envisioned as gateways for global capital, forming a new node in a network of hub cities that include Singapore, Kuala Lumpur, Dubai and Hyderabad. These visions seek to extend the enclaved gaze beyond the confines of the compound to the city as a whole. Often described as a 'city within a city' or 'self-contained', one of the attractions of such proposed schemes is their insulation from the supposed disorder and chaos of existing urban life (Watson 2013: 229). Depictions of this imagined future circulate around the city but, though pervasive, the actual realisation of such plans has been slow to materialise.

Yet even though little may have materially manifested on the ground, these images are nevertheless also of the present. The visual realm of Vision 2030 has become part of Nairobi's landscape: featured on billboards, advertising hoardings, on websites and in newspapers, it is thrust into people's everyday lives. This chapter examines how such visions of the future are grappled with and made sense of in everyday life. By capturing the imaginations of a whole range of Nairobians, these images set in motion hopes, anxieties and speculations, influencing lived experiences of the city, as well as personal horizons for the future. As with Daniel's DIY extension in the opening to this book, Nairobians do not only discuss and imagine the future of Nairobi, they also seek to make it for themselves, bringing the future into the present even as it can seem impossibly far off.

The world-class city

'Vision 2030' is the Kenyan government's development blueprint for the country's future (see Linehan 2007; Myers 2014; Manji 2015a). Since its launch in 2007 by the then President Mwai Kibaki, its language and imagery, emphasising the aesthetics and logics of neoliberal development, have circulated throughout the country (Bremner 2013; Elliott 2015; Kochore 2016). Plans and brochures emphasise competition, performance and accountability. Within this larger vision is 'Nairobi Metro 2030', a strategy to reinvent Nairobi as a 'world class African metropolis' and 'an iconic and globally attractive city' oriented towards ICT services, global corporations and business investment (Government of Kenya 2008). In 2008, the Kenyan government launched a new ministry, the Ministry of Nairobi Metropolitan Development, tasked with implementing this vision for the city. The flagship projects of Nairobi Metro 2030 are not located in the existing city, but are two satellite cities planned for Nairobi's periphery: Tatu City and Konza Techno City – dubbed 'Silicon Savannah' by the Kenyan and international media. These satellite cities are examples of the way neoliberal development strategy seeks to bring state governments into collaboration with corporate finance; Konza and Tatu are intended to be financed by private capital and developed and managed through private partnerships (Moser 2015).

Vision 2030 presents a hyper-capitalist, exclusive, technologically futuristic vision of Nairobi as a model global city. It does not seek to develop an urban strategy that would enhance the distinctive qualities of Nairobi, but to envisage a city that in 2030 replicates the forms and aesthetics of global cities elsewhere. In a process Bunnell and Das have described as 'urban replication', a small but seductive set of visions, policies and templates have duplicated the same spectacular skylines, neoliberal structuring and corporate management systems in multiple city plans across Asia and Africa (2010: 278). This process has had the effect of producing an aspirational uniformity; a placeless urban morphology that is at once nowhere and everywhere (Moser 2015: 32). Such imitative practices are in part a consequence of the promise of spectacular technological and infrastructural transformation. In the eyes of many regional leaders, the perceived success of early adopters of the 'world-class' approach made them worthy models for emulation. The global reach of cities such as Kuala Lumpur, Dubai and Singapore has validated a set of urban planning approaches rooted in economic liberalisation, corporate-led urban development and management, and gleaming, highrise architecture. This replication is also shaped by a small but influential network of experts and consultants who have worked on the masterplanning of many world-class cities. Kenya's Vision 2030 strategy was developed in conjunction with the international consultancy firm McKinsey and Company, who over the last few decades have been at the heart of this trend (Linehan 2007). Before arriving in Kenya, McKinsey previously worked on 'Vision Mumbai', also framed as a 'world-class city' (McKinsey 2003), on 'Andhra Pradesh 2020' and on the 'Malaysia 2020' strategy, which was deemed highly successful and set the standard for the new world-class city (Bunnell and Das 2010: 278).

In this way, the reimagining of Nairobi as a gleaming hub for global capital is another iteration of a limited range of transnationally circulating urban policies and architectural aesthetics which are restructuring cities in ways that suit the interests of multinational corporations and affluent, global elites (Murray 2015: 92). The masterplan constitutes 'a document of neo-liberal master planning which functions predominantly as a political manifesto for the continued polarisation of wealth and power' that has marked Nairobi since the colonial period (Manji 2015a: 207). The official websites of Konza City and Tatu City present dramatic, glossy visions of skyscrapers, lakes, parkland and shopping malls, with promises of 'exclusive urban living' that will 'redefine the quality and scale of urban development in Kenya' with the 'potential to become a benchmark for Africa' (Tatu City n.d.). Such imaginings bear little relation to the congested, polluted, densely populated city of Nairobi of today; instead they present an idealised 'capsular' city, sealed off from a much messier urban reality (De Cauter 2004). This enclaved existence is regarded as one of the attractions of such a plan (Watson 2013: 229). For those with the economic and social capital to gain access, Konza and Tatu promise insulation from existing Nairobi life. Following a mode Roy has described as 'worlding', this is a typology for a future city that abandons the perceived failures and decay of the extant city, seeking to begin afresh on vacant land, creating new enclaves for a hyper-connected global elite (Roy 2011). Such 'city doubles' are often privately operated: spaces where companies act as proxies for civic administration, managing urban security, infrastructure, waste management and other facilities for urban elites, while ordinary, lower income citizens make do with an increasingly decrepit urban landscape elsewhere (Murray 2015: 99).

In this way, these urban megaprojects reproduce the spatial logics of colonial cities, perpetuating segregated urbanscapes underwritten by the languages of neoliberal capital that privilege world-class status over the spatial and economic justice of local inhabitants (Watson 2013; Myers 2014; Moser 2015). There are a number of continuities in rhetoric and practice between Nairobi's colonial masterplanning and the current discourses of Vision 2030, not least regarding the perceived dangers of the pre-existing urban fabric and the need to plan secure, self-contained neighbourhoods on empty land (see Chapter 5). Colonial concern about public health and morality feared informal settlements as unchecked breeding grounds not only for disease, but also vice and degeneracy (White 1990). Such fears find their echo in current commentary about the rampant growth of slums, overcrowding and urban crime (Moser 2015: 33). More specifically, in an early case of urban replication, the architect of Kaloleni was A. J. S. Hutton: formerly senior colonial architect in the British colony of Malaya (now Malaysia). He was seconded to Nairobi Municipal Council in 1942 to help reconceive the city's form, following his experience of designing new urban neighbourhoods in Malaya – an intriguing historical reverberation of McKinsey's role in the world-class re-visioning of both Kuala Lumpur and Nairobi.

Yet despite its sweeping vision, pervasive imagery and presence in Kenyan public debate, very little of Vision 2030 has tangibly materialised in the ten years since it was launched. Many Kenyans now jokingly refer to it 'Vision 3020' to reflect the rate at which implementation has been proceeding. Konza City is little more than an enormous fenced-off site in the Ukambani plains; the same grass growing on the inside and the outside of the fence. Both Tatu and Konza have been plagued with political infighting, accusations of land grabbing and community tensions (Nzuma 2014; Kamau 2016). As Manji has noted, there are overlapping and sometimes contradictory external and internal factors that shape how infrastructural development proceeds in Kenya (Manji 2015a). Some commentators question whether the political will at the highest levels is even there: these were projects launched by the last president, and current President Uhuru Kenyatta seems to have little taste for them.

In addition to Konza and Tatu, Nairobi Metro 2030 also works as an umbrella for other fragmentary and less high-profile infrastructural plans in the city. These include a new mass transport strategy, the Nairobi Integrated Urban Plan (NIUPLAN) and the Nairobi Metropolitan Improvement Programme (NaMSIP), the plans that encompass Eastlands urban renewal. Far from being streamlined, these projects are often in competition with each other. Often launched under the aegis of different political factions, there is considerable confusion over institutional responsibility. Analysing the mass transport strategy, Klopp has outlined several factors behind its inadequate implementation that also speak to complications in realising Vision 2030 more broadly:

> No single agency or institution deals with all transport matters for the metropolitan region … The current fragmentation and lack of a public focal point works to allow the existing decision-making network a great deal of leeway to operate. It also allows decisions to be made in ways that favor interested parties within networks of politicians and bureaucrats linked to key ministries, while defusing responsibilities. (Klopp 2011: 11)

Indeed, the Kenyan Anti-Corruption Commission has reported 'rampant corruption in the road construction contracts and collusion between contractors and government' (cited in Klopp 2011: 11). In such a fragmented and murky climate – and in the wake of a global financial downturn that has undermined the investment of corporate capital – it's perhaps unsurprising there is little of Vision 2030 to be seen on the ground.

Nevertheless, despite its lack of implementation, delays and issues of corruption, Vision 2030 has still had a significant impact. The utopian vocabularies and visualisations of Nairobi as a world-class city that are currently in circulation are powerfully affective in their own right. In cities elsewhere, these 'technologies of seduction' have been crucial to the development of global urban 'brands' (Bunnell and Das 2010: 281; Jansson and Lagerkvist 2009; Brosius 2010). In Nairobi, glossy digital simulations of brand-new cities, billboards showing desirable homes, elaborate websites promising a 'competitive and prosperous nation' and 'middle income status by 2030' are aspirational and enchanting (Konza Techno City n.d.). They influence not only policies but also everyday lives in the city, exerting a seductive hold over ordinary Nairobians and producing important material and imaginative effects. In this way, the absence of infrastructural transformation on the ground is not indicative of Vision 2030's failure; rather, its visual and linguistic culture is materially and temporally significant in its own right. Moving away from notions of the success or failure of urban plans, and instead exploring their effects and affects, allows for a more speculative, open-ended approach which recognises how digital simulations, consultancy reports, billboards and images of the future city act in the world. They are part of the composite assemblage of matter out of which urban lives are remade and futures are reoriented – technologies of seductive power that become enmeshed in the fabric of urban life.

The not-yet

Nairobi is far from the only place to experience a breach between urban dreams and their materialisation as physical realities. Discussing the reconstruction of central Berlin after the end of the wall, Andreas Huyssen noted the dazzling power exerted by visualisations of architecture in a mediatised cultural economy. He observed that the monumental effect of architecture can be just as easily – possibly better – achieved through a 'totalising *image* of architecture. No need even to build the real thing' (2003: 47). Instead of demonstrating a future that is to be made actual, 'the very image of the city itself becomes central to its success in a globally competitive market' (2003: 60). A similar process can be seen in the restructuring of Shanghai, where spectacular digital imagery, promotional videos, and graphics-heavy websites have turned the city into a 'visual sign', the production of which is increasingly a political project (Jansson and Lagerkvist 2009: 26). Branded, packaged urban panoramas are not simply or even necessarily premonitions of actual built space to come, but achieve monumental seduction in themselves.

In Kinshasa, capital of the Democratic Republic of the Congo, the urban techno-fantasy *Cité du Fleuve* imagines a vast new satellite city, to be built on artificial islands in the middle of the Congo River. An improbably huge leap from Kinshasa's current chaotic reality, *Cité du Fleuve* is more 'spectral' and 'chimerical' than convincing urban morphology (De Boeck 2012). So vast is the gap between disintegrating urban present and futuristic megalopolis that the otherworldly skyline 'escapes from the real order of things', and 'it almost doesn't seem to matter whether the new city is physically built or not' (De Boeck 2012: 323). Whereas for Huyssen and Jansson and Lagerkvist, it is the seductive power of imagery that constructs the future city without the need for actual materials, in Kinshasa, De Boeck argues, it is words: 'the only place where the city is constantly being built is in language, in the architecture of words' (2012: 324). Rather than expecting these fantasies to produce actual built forms, De Boeck argues that we should focus instead on 'the sheer force of the word' and accept that it is words that offer 'one of the most important building blocks with which to conquer, alter, and erect the city over and over again' (2012: 324).

In Nairobi, the words and images of Vision 2030 are indeed erecting the city afresh, without seeming to advance towards tangible materiality. But this is not the only form of urban envisioning at work. The fantasies of Vision 2030 intersect in important ways with ordinary residents' own modes of imagining and constructing the future. Far from remaining in the distant future, the dazzle of these promised scenes is part of the accumulated texture of the present. Though they may live far from the proposed sites of Konza and Tatu, Nairobians are nevertheless caught up in their swirling image trail. These urban fantasies become entangled with the mundane actualities of ordinary life, in a process Jane Bennett has described as 'the marvellous erupting in the everyday' (2001: 8). The gap between the dream of the plan and its realisation is full of action: new ways of being and doing, of grasping the future and trying to make it real.

One of the counterintuitive aspects of Vision 2030 is just how popular the imagined vistas are across all sectors of Nairobi's population. As the appreciation of securitised architectures explored in the previous chapter suggests, world-class visions of capsular, enclaved futures – though they would seem intended to exclude Nairobi's low-income residents – are regarded as desirable, 'beautiful', 'smart'. This is something that scholars of fantastical masterplanning have noted in other cities. In Baku, capital of Azerbaijan, Bruce Grant observed the popularity of exclusive imagery among poorer residents: 'whether there is an actual place for them in these new structures or not, this new spate of building has had a profoundly inclusive effect' (2014: 503). In Kinshasa, De Boeck noted how even those struggling to get by 'revel as much in this dream of the modern city as the ruling elites' (2012: 323). In Georgia, Pelkmans has suggested that it is the prospective nature of plans that makes them attractive; the fact that these scenes remain unbuilt, unpeopled, is significant. Their emptiness and potentiality afford the possibility of a future of fulfilled aspirations, and the *lack* of implementation in fact enables the maintenance of that dream: 'they belonged to the realm of the future and therefore remained potentially accessible to everyone' (Pelkmans 2006: 207).

While this has certain resonances with the popularity of Vision 2030 in Nairobi, I think a slightly different form of engagement is at work. As we have seen, local residents *are* concerned about their potential exclusion from the seductive vision, but they nevertheless agree that the future it imagines is desirable. Even when the promises of Vision 2030 start to appear fragile, their instability exposed by lack of implementation, political wrangling, corruption or abandoned projects, the expectation and seductive weight of Vision 2030 still seems to hold fast. In a different context, Harvey and Knox have argued that it is not despite the disorderly excesses of planning but *because* of them that infrastructural schemes are able to maintain their capacity to enchant: 'It is through an articulation with the lived, material encounters of stasis, rupture and blockage that infrastructural promises become reinvigorated and recast' (Harvey and Knox 2012: 534). This fragility leaves space for residents to enact their own interpretations of promised futures, to reconfigure them and make them anew.

Temporally speaking, residents also hold on to the forms of linear development that Vision 2030 proposes: the unfolding of processual time that is inherent to governmental planning (Abram and Weszkalnys 2013). Even where residents fear their capacity to reach it is being thwarted, they still aspire to the destination of Vision 2030. The question of why people might approve of models that would appear to exclude them is a tricky one. Of course, we should not assume that everything people say need be fundamentally coherent; ideas and opinions are worked out in the process of discussion and encounter. Furthermore, across a whole neighbourhood like Kaloleni – inevitably shot through with factions and conflicts, like any community – many different perspectives will be in circulation. Nevertheless, I suggest, residents' approval of the fantasy of Vision 2030, even as they fear exclusion from it, is based on particular disjunctive temporal experiences in which present and future become entangled in important ways. As residents try to anticipate and live towards the future, they inevitably do so from the present – a present in which fantastical images of the future are in circulation. By embedding the 'not-yet' into the 'now', juxtapositions such as the billboard among Kaloleni's decrepit houses create disconcerting temporal simultaneity. The schemes of Vision 2030 are based on linear developments and project timelines that envisage a future-perfect city as a destination that will be reached within a specific timeframe. But in their anticipation of this destination, the imaging strategies also give the impression of the future having arrived already (see also Lagerkvist 2007: 160).

The gap between the plan and the future it envisages is filled with discrepancies (Abram and Weszkalnys 2013: 21). Multiple temporalities are in play: the idealised orders imagined in the plan are often disrupted, not only by obstinate landscapes or political reappraisals, but by the anticipations, speculations and anxieties it invokes through its potentiality, its status as 'not-yet' (Elliott and C. Smith 2015). Thus planning may compel other types of action in the present, upsetting processual time with recursive eddies of social, material or political consequence, which in turn may initiate new judgements of the plan, as well as recalibrations of aspiration and ambition (Abram and Weszkalnys 2013: 22; see also Kracauer 1995). Instead of a single flow of processual time in which residents are submissively caught up, this flow is countered by currents that, though small, are nonetheless powerful. For residents in Nairobi, this has considerable import for temporal experience. In one of these eddies, the future appears to be receding ever further into the distance, seemingly out of the reach of ordinary citizens, while in another eddy, time is experienced as compressed and the future already at hand.

Dream houses

The temporal as well as the spatial gap between urban planning and its physical manifestation is a space rich with possibility. This speculative space can generate what Elliott has termed 'an economy of anticipation', in which people set in motion all kinds of practices as they start to live towards the future embodied in the plan (2015: 2; see also Cross 2014). The future vistas envisaged by Vision 2030 and its associated projects are not only forged by technical bureaucrats, political elites or foreign capital, but through everyday dreams and practices. Ordinary people's ways of orientating themselves towards and seeking to know the future can metaphorically and materially reshape the order of the plan, sometimes interrupting its supposedly smooth unfolding. This book has explored several of the ways that this has manifested within Kaloleni, in performances of property, forensic archiving and practices of historymaking. But Kaloleni residents are also trying to claim certain futures beyond the confines of the estate, and in fact many are increasingly keen to do so given the possibly precarious future of Kaloleni itself.

As Chapter 4 explored, many men retain an ambition to build a rural upcountry home, or *simba*, as an important aspect of selfhood and masculinity, of becoming fully Luo. But this is no longer the only form of architectural dreaming that occupies the minds of men – and some women – in Kaloleni. In a discussion about the billboard with Calvin, the young man we met in Chapter 1, the conversation quickly turned towards his own domestic aspirations. Born and brought up in a crumbling house in Kaloleni and earning a meagre income working in a small café, Calvin was nevertheless ambitious: 'I want to build my own house', he said. 'Imagine coming home to a house that is yours'. He frequently imagines the kind of place he will build, he told me: a three-bedroom detached house on its own plot. 'There is nothing like the feeling of coming home from work to a house that is yours, that you do not rent', he anticipates. In his mind he fills the rooms with new furniture, making sure everything is organised and colourful. In particular, he longs for a modern bathroom. In Calvin's imagination, all the bedrooms are en suite, the running water is reliable and he can shower any time. 'Just in your house, relaxing, taking a shower, feeling it's yours...' he mused.

This is partly about a shift in priorities and aspirations that predate Vision 2030: young people in Eastlands increasingly do not speak their parents' mother tongue and do not make such frequent visits to the old upcountry homelands, loosening the dense network of relations that have historically knitted Luo people to a place they called home. Building a 'modern life' entails a more urban outlook, in which cities, and especially Nairobi, are seen as holding the richest opportunities. Calvin was quite clear that his dreams of the perfect house are in part shaped by the sleek images of urban panoramas he sees all around him. 'You see all this real estate up there [indicating the billboard]. You know it's expensive, but of course you want', he told me simply. His fantasies of a particular material future are intimately entangled with the visual culture of digital architectural design that enters the marketing machine of property development and circulates throughout Nairobi.

But for many in Nairobi, this shift in horizons has been intensified by the uncertainty of Vision 2030, by the fear that residents will be excluded or even evicted from future schemes and will be left with nothing. In this sense, the types of anticipatory actions provoked by Vision 2030 are not always so positive. Previous urban renewal projects in Nairobi have been far from transparent, and claims of land-grabbing, corporate intrigue, elite capture and removal of sitting tenants have been rife (see Rigon 2014). The changing horizons of the future were described by Hassan, a man in his fifties who has lived in Kaloleni all his life. His own father left Kaloleni after retiring and returned to western Kenya to take up dairy farming. Hassan 'inherited' his father's house, and in turn raised his own sons, now in their twenties, in the estate. He sees that things are changing for them, and fears for their future:

> Like me I can say now I'm growing old, maybe I can follow my father's footsteps. I can go there but let me tell you, look at my son. I don't think whether he'll go there ... They are becoming city people. They don't want ... you know if you go home, you'll have to plan to do many things and hard work ... this generation they do not want to do hard work ... ok, they work but [they do] hard work with brain not physically ... So, they are not thinking about, 'Oh, we can go back to Mumias [western Kenya]', they are thinking about, 'I can buy my house at Kitengela,

Syokimau, Embakasi there, build my home, I stay there' ... That is the
modern life.
[...]
So even our worries are there 'cause when they bring these houses
down, they'll build modern houses ... we won't get, and we cannot
afford. This Vision what-what. So even our children are thinking 'so,
we move. We move now, or we wait, and [then] we cannot afford'. You
know, cost is rampant in this Nairobi. Up, up, up. So we say better [to]
plan now.

In Hassan's plans to move his family from the estate, we see how an
uncertain future inserts itself into the present and compels new types
of actions. Vision 2030 – even if it remains immaterial – creates new
economies of anticipation, desire and apprehension as local people
recalibrate their aspirations and try to predict what horizons will
remain open to them. Dream houses take shape like castles in the sky,
shaped by the glossy prestige of digitally rendered horizons, but also by
the exclusivity of their visions.

'There's nothing we shall get!'

How could residents feel so invested in the 2030 visions while concurrently also deeply suspicious that they will never benefit from its promises? In their work on infrastructural projects in Peru, Harvey and Knox
take up the notion of enchantment to understand how such schemes
retain their lustre and promise 'even in the face of specific circumstances
in which they are acknowledged as having failed to deliver' (2012: 523).
Following Bennett (2001), they take enchantment not as superstition or
belief in the supernatural, but as a 'visceral, affective form of relating to
that which is side-lined or cast out of formalised, rationalised descrip-
tions of material and social phenomena' (Harvey and Knox 2012: 523).
As the positive commentary the billboard prompted on social media
suggests, its imagery was enchanting because the future it seemed
to promise offered the possibility of transcending existing social and
material arrangements. But it was also precisely this promise that
made it dubious in the eyes of many residents.

For several nights after it appeared, the billboard dominated discussions at the 'bases' in Kaloleni. Dotted around the estate, the bases are
outdoor spots where mostly men of different age groups and friendship
circles gather to drink, chew *miraa* and wile away the evenings. In their
animated dissections, different opinions were aired, many echoing
approval of the glossy, 'smart' life the billboard seemed to promise. But all
expressed frustration that there had been no other information provided
to residents; no consultation, no meetings, no leaflets or communication.
One vocal speaker was a man in his forties named Duncan, who had once

looked set to become a lawyer, before personal circumstances forced him to drop out and come back to Kaloleni. He is often turned to for his expert opinion, recently in relation to such matters as Vision 2030 and urban renewal. Duncan stated firmly: 'No one can be for that image', explaining that precisely *because* it was so enticing, *because* the apartments looked so expensive and exclusive, 'definitely they will be out of our league'. This seems to be a future indefinitely out of reach.

In this way, the gap between the material present and the future envisaged in digital renderings can feel impossible to overcome. Many Kalolenians caveated their endorsement of the billboard with doubts about the practicalities: how could such a project be built without displacing residents? Would the apartments be for rent or for sale? For how much? Wasn't it likely that current residents would never benefit? In their discussions about the billboard, residents often simultaneously evoked fantasies about what the vision might bring, and fears about what it might take away. Boniface said, 'I for one would like to get a bigger house. This billboard, yes, it can be good. I would like to get a house that gives me a big living room'. But he also added, 'Let me tell you for a fact, when things become practical, a lot of guys who have money will be the ones benefitting from this'. Juliet was fairly typical when she said, 'I'm on the side of change. If they can take us to a modern system it can be good', and then qualified this with doubts about the implementation:

> if those who are going to do it are genuine people, if they are trans-parent, [if] they are trustworthy is when it will be ok. In Kenya there's a lot of corruption. You can't say it will be good. It might have some problems with maybe those who are going to build houses, the tenders ... those who are going to get tenders and how the tenders will be, you know, will be given. You never know.

Such ambivalence also tinted Maggie's comments as she summed up the shades of local opinion:

> Some of us are happy because we might get these modern houses and it will be good ... some people say we don't know. Even if they are to be built, they have to allocate [properly] ... Some of us are even saying no [to the billboard]. Maybe those houses when they'll be built, maybe it might go to the big people, and we'll be left with nothing. Peasants, there's nothing we shall get!

As Kaloleni residents described their fears of exclusion, that the future would be 'for the big people' and not for the likes of them, they expressed frustration at being left behind, where they felt that time seemed to stand still, or even to go backwards. This was apparent in the views of Dolly, another local resident. Though neat and tidy, Dolly's council house is very worn, the walls engrained with dust and grubby finger marks. The old concrete floor is bare, and no repairs have been undertaken for many years. Dolly expressed her frustration about life in Nairobi, of the failures of its governance and of waiting for things that never come: 'We are left behind. We used to have water, [today] there's no water. The roads – you see how they are. We used to have footpaths, they are no longer there. These houses are just like museum anyway. But people are still living in them!' In her assessment, a museum is not a positive comparison: the implication is that the houses are static, stuck in place and time, while the city moves on around them. 'They say we are going to Vision 2030, but we are going back', she concluded. Even as residents seek to anticipate the future, they simultaneously describe a sense of temporal inertia, of living in an endless present.

Residents' anxieties about being excluded from such visions show how the material conditions of their living and dwelling seem to make the fantasy both more alluring and more out of reach. Their critiques of opaque implementation methods suggest a certain amount of disillusionment with the visions, but this disenchantment only goes so far. In Astana, Laszczkowski has observed that, though people criticised the availability of promised glossy futures, their critiques did not transcend the linear temporality of the development narrative, in which achievement is gauged by progress towards technological or infastructural indicators (2011: 88). Likewise, in Nairobi, the breach between promises and practices seemed not to make the promise less desirable but all the more enchanting. But rather than experiencing the steady progress of developmental time, where one thing comes predictably after another, many Nairobians feel themselves thrust out of this temporal stream and stuck in a recursive loop.

As critics of Vision 2030, they cast themselves in the role of catchers-up on a road where the destination seems to be slipping further and further away. Or, as Dolly tells it, 'we are left behind', living in a museum where time stands still. Tony was another resident who expressed a sense of losing his grip on steady chronological time. Throughout 2014, Tony was campaigning to get Kaloleni's water reconnected – a politically thorny matter. 'The issue of water, it has really made us to lag behind', he told me. Echoing a powerful colonial trope linking public health and modernity, he went on:

> you know, water goes hand in hand with hygiene. If you don't have water, hygienically you won't be, things won't be ok because you want to wash, for example your clothes, your body … We are going to Vision 2030 and still we are using buckets to go to the toilet … We are going to Vision 2030, but we are going back.

Tony, like Dolly, does not disavow the future vision, but observes that in Kaloleni they are not able – or not allowed – to proceed towards that vision at the same rate as others, and are being left behind in a temporal hiatus.

Speculative zone

In their discussions about Vision 2030, residents often seemed to simultaneously evoke fantasies about what the vision might bring, and fears about what it might take away. That they could feel so invested in the concept while concurrently highly critical of it, is a consequence, I have suggested, of a dissonant coexistence of temporalities. Time is on the one hand compressed and the future seems to have already arrived, and on the other hand time feels so stretched out that it almost seems to stand still, or even go backwards. Residents seem to hold on to both feelings at the same time, flitting between the future-now and the ever-present.

There are a few Kalolenians, however, who have been able to turn their dreams of new horizons into something material. Across the generations, the most successful in Kaloleni have tended to move on from the estate, seeking larger, more luxurious homes elsewhere. In the early postcolonial years, they moved to the newly accessible neighbourhoods of western Nairobi such as Lavington, Kileleshwa and Muthaiga, previously the domain of whites only. But more recently the ambition has become, as Hassan mentioned, the new suburbs: places like Syokimau, Kitengela and Athi River on the eastern and southern sides of the city. During my fieldwork I was able to follow the plans of Samuel, a businessman born and brought up in Kaloleni who has recently been highly successful. His project to build his own upcountry *simba* was described in Chapter 4. At the same time, he has been preparing to move his family from Kaloleni to Syokimau, where in 2013 he bought a small plot of land. Out beyond the airport east along the Mombasa Road, Syokimau sits on a wide-open plain. Nairobi is on the edge of the Kenyan highlands, a fertile upland area, but to the east of the city the land rapidly drops away to dry grasslands with minimal vegetation. Here the sky is huge and the land stretches on to the horizon. Although now the setting for incremental peri-urban sprawl, it still feels far from the packed-in, concrete jungle of Nairobi.

Samuel's plot is part of a tract of land about two kilometres off the Mombasa Road that has been parcelled out into a grid and sold as individual plots. Each owner is responsible for the construction of their own house and its utilities. As yet, Syokimau has no services – the roads are mud tracks, there is no piped water, no sewerage facilities and no shops, schools or hospitals. Nevertheless, it has become highly sought-after among upwardly mobile Nairobians like Samuel. By December 2013, my first visit there, most of the plots had already been sold. Though most construction sites were in their early stages, there were several huge mansions hiding behind tall fences and high security gates. Samuel pointed out a couple of them – 'he is a pilot; that one there is a lawyer', he told me proudly. Samuel spread out the architectural plans for his house on the bonnet of his car to show me. Filling almost the whole of the 400 square metre plot, the two-storey house is rather grand, with a balcony, galleried hallway, and pillars in the open-plan living-dining area. There are to be four bedrooms, all of which – just as in Calvin's dream house – are en suite. Samuel confirmed there is no formal sanitation in Syokimau – 'We are just emerging', he said. Instead he is responsible for installing a large underground water tank as well as a septic tank, a situation repeated in each of the plots. Despite the expense and management that will accompany this self-help water system, he is enthusiastic about the bathrooms: 'They will be very modern', he told me, 'Clean, modern showers, everything'.

In April 2014, I returned to the site for the 'groundbreaking', the literal first cut of the ground that marked the start of the construction. In the five months since my last visit, Syokimau was notably more developed – houses had mushroomed and now gleaming windows, red-tiled roofs and high fences were becoming visible on all sides (see Figure 17). But there were still no proper roads, no shops and barely any people visible. That day it was raining hard and the tracks were treacherous. Even in Samuel's SUV we slipped and slid, at one point coming to a complete stop as the traffic backed up behind a car immobilised in the deep mud. Samuel, usually a calm man, roared in frustration. 'Now we are stuck!' he shouted. 'You see? This is what they do. This City Council. *Huku kuna cartel*'; here there is a cartel. According to Samuel, this is the way the city works: the City Council promise to bring services that never come. When the number of residents reaches a critical mass then they start to agitate, making complaints, but nothing happens; council officials are waiting to be paid off in order to even grade the road. 'They say we are going to Vision 2030, but we are going back!' Samuel's words were a remarkable echo of what I heard almost daily in Kaloleni. His angry outburst perhaps reflected his self-awareness of this; even though he was successful, though he was now one of those who had 'made it', in some ways it didn't make a difference. Even in Syokimau, he had not escaped the sense of being stuck in the not-yet.

Peri-urban Nairobi, including Syokimau, forms a speculative zone around the more established city, a place where new ideas of cityness are negotiated. This is not just building the city with words, as De Boeck described in Kinshasa: speculation here has material effects that occur in the foreground of vast state-led visions of the future. In Syokimau, land is cheaper, planning control is not well enforced, the opportunity to self-build reduces costs and promises the accomplishment of a common Kenyan aspiration to build one's own home. New tracts of housing, each with their own below-ground infrastructures, are springing up at an incredible rate. But these houses also index other kinds of speculation and social achievement; the slick, gleaming aesthetics are a far cry from the old *simba*s of Luoland. Instead they reflect relatively recent

Figure 17 Half-built mansions of the future, Syokimau, April 2014
(Photo: Author)

personal and social aspirations of professional success, becoming upwardly mobile and making one's own urban horizons. Places such as Syokimau have become the ground on which new ways of making it in Nairobi are worked out. But as people try to anticipate the digital futures promised by grand schemes such as Vision 2030, a temporal disjuncture emerges, indicated by the incongruity between Samuel's aspirational modern bathrooms and his frustration that 'They say we are going to Vision 2030, but we are going back'. The tempopolitics of Vision 2030 implies progress towards a destination seemingly already visible on the horizon. But while the beautifully rendered vistas can give the impression that the future has arrived already, the muddy, emergent landscapes of Syokimau, as well as the decayed materiality of Kaloleni, reinforce the challenges of making a place for oneself in the shadow of Vision 2030.

Conclusion

The experiences of many ordinary Nairobians do not match up with the panoramas and new beginnings envisaged by Vision 2030 and its promises of a 'better future for all' (Government of Kenya 2007: 3). Many in Eastlands feel themselves enchanted by digital vistas that give the impression that the future is already at hand, even as they remain in a perpetual not-yet. This dissonance is deeply influenced by the seductive power of Vision 2030's visual culture. The image trail that circulates in Nairobi is not immaterial but part of the stuff of the city, an entangled accumulation reconfiguring urban spaces and urban lives. Fantasies of an enclaved 'world city', though seemingly far removed from Nairobi's current disintegrating materialities, nevertheless have become enmeshed in the everyday lives of ordinary citizens.

In the discussions, dreams and building practices of Kalolenians, we see how seductive imagery and utopian language surrounding projects that may never be built can still have tangible effects. Living among the dream images of Vision 2030 has set in motion new types of actions, as people plan alternative futures or take up new construction practices, seeking to remake the city in ways that go beyond De Boeck's 'architecture of words'. The spatial and temporal gap between the dream of Vision 2030 and its implementation has left room for anticipatory actions that try to make the future city more knowable. In so doing, residents in Eastlands seek to upset the exclusivity of a dazzling, capsular future Nairobi. But at the same time this gap can feel vast, even insurmountable, as their own experiences have bitterly revealed. Even as they work to make it present, the seductions of Vision 2030 are entwined with exclusionary forces that keep them at arm's length, the future-perfect city remains an exclusive mirage always just out of reach.

Conclusion:
Belonging to the Future

If you leave Kaloleni and cross the Nairobi River, on the other side of
the valley you reach an area densely packed with decaying *mabati*
structures. This is Majengo, a slum area where many in Kaloleni go
to procure *miraa*. Little stalls line the road, bundles of the leafy plant
neatly arranged ready for purchase by those who like to chew it for its
stimulant properties. Accompanying friends there one day, I noticed
one kiosk in particular, painted bright blue. Pictures of *miraa* were
painted on the blue wall and above it, in neat lettering, 'Small World
Miraa. Digital Vision 2030' (see Figure 18). Majengo's infrastructure is
makeshift, the *mabati* rusted and patched. Ad hoc electricity connections are rigged up, loops of wire drooping dangerously between the
buildings. The wonky angles and leaky roofs indicate the lack of technical expertise of its builders. There seemed to be nothing 'digital'
about this kiosk, certainly nothing to suggest that it was an official
Vision 2030 project. Though the shopkeeper would undoubtedly have
had a mobile phone, there was no sign of any other digital technologies.
The corrugated iron, cash-only shop with bundles of *miraa* left out in
the dusty, polluted Majengo air seemed about as far from the futuristic
imagery of the 'digital age' as it is possible to get, and a long way from
the digital panoramas of Vision 2030.

Yet the Majengo kiosk is just one of many 'digital' shops in Nairobi,
and shop signs have become just one of many iterations in which both
Vision 2030 and ideas about 'the digital' are invoked. In Kenya, 'digital'
has come to indicate a mode of belonging and a desire to participate in
a certain kind of future. The term is not, as one might understand the
words in a British or American context, simply a reference to the age of
the internet, to new technologies or to the speed at which knowledge
can travel, though such capacities are significant. Rather, the 'digital'
has come to signify both a temporal period and a set of attitudes and
aspirations (Moore and C. Smith forthcoming). In the copious fieldnotes
and interview transcriptions generated by this research project, the
word digital appears again and again, dropped in to conversations as

Figure 18 'Digital Vision 2030' kiosk selling *miraa*, Majengo, July 2014
(Photo: Author)

shorthand for all kinds of ways of anticipating and claiming the future. It has a sense of active urgency about it; not waiting for the steady unfolding of processual time, for things to arrive in due course, but actively seeking them now.

During conversations, on the radio, on TV and even in parliament, one frequently hears people remark, '*siku hizi, tuko digital*', 'these days, we are in digital': inside it, a part of it. In Kiswahili -*ko*- is an infix to describe physical placement, but it can also imply a state of being. '*Uko sawa?*' means 'Are you ok?' but its literal meaning is 'Are you in a place of ok-ness?' In this sense then, '*Tuko digital*' implies a place of being digital: it is something lived, something that Kenyans are – or feel they should be. It is both epochal and an indicator of a personal subjectivity. When I asked James, the cosmopolitan young man we met in Chapter 4, why he had expended so much energy and money in making his Kaloleni house comfortable and stylish when he really wanted to move upcountry, he told me, 'We're in digital now: friends come and visit, they see where you stay. A house is not just for sleeping'. His words indicate an epochal break, a shift in outlook about what a house is for and resultant expectations on him to live up to a certain temporal way of being. Whereas his parents' generation were not so invested in the house as a home, for James it is much more than shelter. It is about a certain – digital – way of living. To 'be digital', then, refers to both a desired way of being and belonging to a temporal frame.

As such, the digital is a participatory temporality, a tempopolitical way of working on the future to bring it within reach (J. Smith 2008). This book began with Daniel describing his self-built extension to his Kaloleni home in terms of Vision 2030, that Nairobians like him must do their own 'urban renewal'. Similarly, the Majengo shopkeeper grasps hold of evocative terms like 'digital' and 'Vision 2030' and makes them meaningful in new ways. The digital, like Vision 2030, becomes a form of temporal engagement through which people can stake their participation in a fast-changing world, as they anticipate and live towards both a new kind of self and a new kind of future. The digital future as imagined in schemes like Vision 2030 is not a decade away but understood as available – up for grabs – in the present. The sign declares that the kiosk, and thus its owner, is contemporary and modern. It is at once aspirational and self-realising. By asserting him or herself as part of Kenya's digital epoch, the shopkeeper contributes to Kenyans' sense of 'the digital': an epoch defined by those who dream it, assert their claims over it, and make it real. In this sense, the notion of living 'digitally' becomes a way for ordinary Nairobians to upset exclusive or elite visions of a future Kenya. The digital is speculative space from which to anticipate and influence the form and imagination of the city, and to try and ensure a place for oneself in the city's future.

The emergence of 'digital' life in areas of Nairobi that are usually regarded as far removed from the gleaming panoramas of Vision 2030 shows once again the incapacity of the categories 'formal' and 'informal' to satisfactorily account for difference within Nairobi. Self-build projects such as the kiosk, or Daniel's DIY extension, explicitly engage with official planning by taking up its frameworks, styles and vocabularies and use them to open up a different set of possibilities. Here we see how the building practices of ordinary Nairobians are also forms of imaginative claim-making through which they seek to disrupt urban planning as a linear mode of attaining a predetermined future (see also Nielsen 2014). Official visions of the future are not rejected out of hand, but instead worked upon and remade anew. In this way, the 'digital' also reveals how makeshift interventions and DIY projects in Nairobi are not just about surviving the urban day-to-day – a common assumption in the scholarship on informality – but also seek to intervene in future flows and frictions. As Hecht and Simone have put it, 'the need to survive does not … swallow up the need to imagine' (1994: 13).

This is particularly clear in the way Nairobians have engaged with proliferating regimes of security in the city. Amid Nairobi's securitised architectures, residents of places like Kaloleni tend to be regarded as the 'criminal other', to be sealed out of prestigious developments, the apex of which are the satellite enclaves of Vision 2030. Yet we have seen how Kalolenians are also building their own versions of sealed, secure architecture. This kind of built space has accrued its own aesthetics of status and prestige, showing how the construction of fences, walls and gated compounds cannot be understood simply as ways of surviving crime or other insecurities, but are also aspirational. Such building practices make claims to a future of urban inclusion and presence – claims that echo, even as they critique, the segregated spaces of the colonial city and the enclaved zones of Vision 2030.

It is in this sense that a focus on making can give purchase on the dynamic material, imaginative and political accumulations that come to constitute urban landscapes in a way that the categories of 'formal' and 'informal' cannot. Making, as an art of enquiry, is an intervention in a contingent world, a provisional, future-focused engagement that draws on historical knowledge, skill and materialities (Ingold 2013). As such, tracing processes of making can reveal how the material substance of the city and the transformative labour of urban residents are entangled with larger projects of city-making that play out across multiple scales and temporalities. The practices of historymaking at work in Kaloleni draw on both the architectural fabric of their homes and a rich variety of documents to produce a 'minor history' of Kaloleni and Nairobi that seeks to unmake both official narratives of the city's past and plans for its future. Likewise, efforts to be a part of 'the digital' are interventions in a larger, shifting domain, in which Nairobians refuse to accept the future as a fixed destination but instead seek to influence its emergent shape. The daily life of Nairobi is in this way also about making time and making place; remixing the past and the future from the present and carving a space for themselves within the city's shifting assemblage. This is how the accumulated landscape of the city emerges across the *longue durée*.

* * * * *

This book has argued that, as people make places, they also make themselves, and in the process, they offer new possibilities for urban histories and prospective futures. Instead of following a chronological approach or archaeological excavation, it has highlighted how the remains of the past are encountered from the present. It explores how the relationship between people and architecture is generative; shaping ideas about the past, about ideal selves and about how the future city should be. By tracing forms of dwelling and making amid the material remains of colonialism, it has examined the emergence of a textured, felted place over time. The accumulated pasts of Kaloleni enable residents to engage with their neighbourhood as a powerful site of history and make claims to alternative authoritative knowledge. This sheds new light on the continuing affective influence of material remains, showing how such sites not only animate engagements with the past but generate ways of living towards the future.

Caught up in a 'meantime' between promises of futurity and the remains of empire, we have seen how Kalolenians have taken up a variety of projects in an attempt to belong to the future. The shadow of Vision 2030, while offering tantalising glimpses of glossy skylines, has also animated new anxieties that centre on the possibility of exclusion. In a conversation about the potential redevelopment of Kaloleni estate, Hassan expressed this succinctly when he asked rhetorically, 'Will there be space for us in that future?' The strategies, narratives and practices of people like Daniel and Hassan, I suggest, are a means to realise not-yet identities of spatiotemporal inclusion (see Melly 2017: 75).

The way that people live towards the future, hoping, strategising and making plans, is fundamentally enmeshed in larger debates about what that future should look like. These larger dynamics are often unpredictable, particularly in a city that is envisioning a radically different future of global consequence. Though access to the detail of Vision 2030 may be limited, when viewed from a place of decay and disintegration its gleaming spectacle can seem alluring, setting in motion new aspirations and anticipatory actions. In the process of their reception and interpretation, such visions do not remain entirely at an aesthetic or temporal distance; they are encounters shot through with affect and fantasy (Moore 2013). Rather than accepting their fate as poor 'sitting tenants' who face exclusion, Kalolenians instead attempt to break open the exclusivity of Vision 2030 and assert their right to participate in the future. They do so from a place that is porous to various elsewheres and subject to all kinds of competing allegiances and tensions (Simone 2016).

It is from this perspective that urban belonging emerges as a future-focused possibility. Rather than identitarian assertions rooted in claims to autochthony or ancestry, belonging is about crafting a place for oneself in the future. Contemporary politics and inequalities, as well as historical legacies of unhomeliness, mean that making a life in the city is neither assured nor stable, but nevertheless has a rich potentiality; a promise to live towards that is worth the hustle. This forward momentum makes use of the resources of the present and the remains of the past and seeks to remix them anew. It is in this sense that the past of Kaloleni finds its salience among residents. What Simone (2016: 143) has called the 'excess of past use' – the wear and tear, the makeshift and the cast-off, the vestiges of the past – continues to interpose, its vitality shaping ideas and possibilities, ways of being and making a life in Nairobi. It is in the work of household maintenance, in the accumulation of landscapes, in the desire to be digital, in the cross-cutting lines of connection and friction, that ordinary people's aspirations for a future of belonging are crafted and made.

To think about a city as a landscape of accumulation, as a densely matted, felted place of pathways and plans, obstructions and aspirations, residues and endurances, offers possibilities for understanding urban change beyond Nairobi. As cities everywhere grow larger and seemingly ever taller, so globally urban geoarchitecture is reaching new intensities. Urban accumulations are endlessly churned, not just by processes of demolition and construction, but in the frictions of gentrification, migration and displacement. The way in which we intervene in landscapes that are always in the making, altering incremental urban assemblages, is in this sense a highly politicised way of acting on time, of forming constellations between the vestiges of the past and the uncertainty of the future. This occurs across different scales, from new topographies created by urban expansion or landfill to the disarticulation of longstanding urban communities. People's own yearnings for mobility and change also carve new desire lines through and beyond the fabric of the city, inscribing alternative pathways of connection across imaginative and material worlds. Attending to processes of accumulation, as well as interventions into landscapes of accretion, enables a perspective on city-making in which the distinctive politics of the human and the material are mutually imbricated across time. In seeking to understand how city dwellers are both affected by their material landscapes and also creatively manage and negotiate them as part of a process of self-making, this approach explores the pathways of an environing material world and the forms of transformative encounter it can provoke. Tracing the temporalities and materialities of accumulation, how they are implicated in geologies that are always in the making, it also becomes possible to visualise – or at least speculate on – the place of these socialities and substances in future urban ecologies, in all their decay and rejuvenation.

Recent calls for a more 'global urbanism' argue that we need to find ways of thinking about cities that are not based on indicators or theories set from within the conglomerations of the global north, but which write from the urban realities of the rest of the world (Robinson and Roy 2016). This is what Jennifer Robinson has described as 'thinking with elsewhere', a way of thinking with disparity, contradiction and messiness rather than trying to 'control for difference' (Robinson 2016: 188). This book has tracked the ambiguities and incongruities of life in Nairobi, not in order to control them or explain them away but to show how such contradictions can be generative. Life in Nairobi is full of inconsistencies but Nairobians find possibility and room for manoeuvre in what can seem the most unlikely places. It is from such sites that the city takes shape: impossibility and potentiality, presence and absence are not so much opposites as they are entangled and conditional. But while scholars of global urbanism may categorise Nairobi as an 'elsewhere', for Nairobians themselves it is their here and now. They too seek to draw lines that connect between Nairobi and other places and times, forging linkages to digital futures and world-class opportunities as much as to histories of nationalism and rural landscapes of belonging. To 'think with elsewhere', then, is not only a scholarly challenge but also an ethnographic reality: a way in which both the particular texture of a city and its tangible and imagined connections to global elsewheres are constituted. These frictions and flows are forms of navigating urban life as well as challenges of self-making. They have played out across the history of the city, leaving vestiges and traces that will continue to shape future possibilities.

What the future ultimately promises may be opaque, but nevertheless can generate new constellations of thought and action, from which the landscape of the city will continue to emerge. Yet urban residues, traces and histories remain crucial to what the city can be; awkward endurances that can constrain as well as enable urban futures. In the rush to conceive of a future for urban Africa that radically departs from a supposedly failing and disorderly present, it is these accretions that are often overlooked. In the shifting assemblages of Nairobi, we see how traces of the urban past have powerful afterlives. These are historical landscapes deposited across time; they have been constructed and destroyed, contaminated and cleansed. But in the felted frictions of the city, these residues forge new linkages with contemporary concerns and future anxieties, constraining and enabling forms of mobility, authority and action. Vital and unforeclosed, this landscape of accumulation will continue to churn long into the future.

Bibliography

Primary Sources

Kenya National Archives, Nairobi:
JA/1 – JA/16/83: Files of the Nairobi Municipal Council, annual and
  monthly reports, 1941–1970
JA/4/1 – JA/4/6: Files of the Nairobi Municipal Council Native Affairs
  Committee, including the Housing Committee, 1941–1963

Secondary Sources

Abram, Simone and Gisa Weszkalnys (eds) (2013) *Elusive Promises:
  Planning in the Contemporary World*. New York: Berghahn Books.
Achola, Milcah Amolo (2001) 'Colonial policy and urban health: The
  case of colonial Nairobi.' *Azania: Archaeological Research in Africa*,
  36–37(1) pp. 119–37.
Adams, Arvil V., Sara Johansson da Silva and Setareh Razmara (2013)
  Skills Development in the Informal Sector: Kenya. The World Bank,
  pp. 147–77.
Amis, Philip (1984) 'Squatters or tenants: The commercialization
  of unauthorized housing in Nairobi.' *World Development*, 12(1)
  pp. 87–96.
Andersen, Hans Skifter (2002) 'Excluded places: The interaction
  between segregation, urban decay and deprived neighbourhoods.'
  Housing, Theory and Society, 19(3–4) pp. 153–69.
Anderson, David M. (2001) 'Corruption at City Hall: African housing
  and urban development in colonial Nairobi.' *Azania: Archaeological
  Research in Africa*, 36–37(1) pp. 138–54.
—— (2005) *Histories of the Hanged: Britain's Dirty War in Kenya and the
  End of Empire*. London: Weidenfeld & Nicolson.
Appadurai, Arjun (1981) 'The Past as a Scarce Resource.' *Man*, 16(2) pp.
  201–19.

——(1986) *The Social Life of Things: Commodities in Cultural Perspective.* Cambridge, UK: Cambridge University Press.

Argenti, Nicolas (2008) *The Intestines of the State: Youth, Violence, and Belated Histories in the Cameroon Grassfields.* Chicago; London: University of Chicago Press.

Austin, John Langshaw (1975) *How to Do Things with Words.* Oxford: Clarendon Press.

Basso, Keith H. (1970) '"To give up on words": Silence in Western Apache culture.' *Southwestern Journal of Anthropology*, 26(3) pp. 213–30.

BBC (2004) 'Kenya investigates city hall fire.' *BBC News.* [Accessed on 4th April 2016] http://news.bbc.co.uk/1/hi/world/africa/3524855.stm.

—— (2011) 'British tourist kidnapped in Kenya "held by al-Shabab".' *BBC News.* [Accessed on 27th July 2015] www.bbc.co.uk/news/world-africa-14943300.

Bender, Barbara (2002) 'Time and landscape.' *Current Anthropology*, 43(S4) pp. 103–12.

Benjamin, Walter (2007) *Illuminations: Essays and Reflections.* New York: Schocken Books.

Bennett, Jane (2001) *The Enchantment of Modern Life: Attachments, Crossings, and Ethics.* Princeton, NJ: Princeton University Press.

—— (2005) 'The agency of assemblages and the North American blackout.' *Public Culture*, 17(3) pp. 445–65.

—— (2009) *Vibrant Matter: A Political Ecology of Things.* Durham, NC: Duke University Press.

Berman, Bruce and John Lonsdale (1992) *Unhappy Valley: Conflict in Kenya and Africa.* Oxford: James Currey.

Berry, Sara (1993) *No Condition Is Permanent: The Social Dynamics of Agrarian Change in Sub-Saharan Africa.* Madison, WI: University of Wisconsin Pres.

—— (2009) 'Property, authority and citizenship: Land claims, politics and the dynamics of social division in West Africa.' *Development and Change*, 40(1) pp. 23–45.

Bhabha, Homi (2004) *The Location of Culture*, 2nd ed. New York and Abingdon, UK: Routledge.

Bloch, Maurice and Jonathan Parry (eds) (1983) *Death and the Regeneration of Life.* Cambridge, UK: Cambridge University Press.

Blomley, Nicholas (2013) 'Performing property: Making the world.' *Canadian Journal of Law & Jurisprudence*, 26(1) pp. 23–48.

Blount, Ben G. (1975) 'Agreeing to agree on genealogy: A Luo sociology of knowledge.' In M. Sanches and B. G. Blount (eds) *Sociocultural Dimensions of Language Use.* New York: Academic Press, pp. 117–35.

Boone, Catherine (2012) 'Land conflict and distributive politics in Kenya.' *African Studies Review*, 55(01) pp. 75–103.

—— (2014) *Property and Political Order in Africa: Land Rights and the Structure of Politics.* Cambridge, UK: Cambridge University Press.

Branch, Daniel and Nic Cheeseman (2009) 'Democratization, sequencing, and state failure in Africa: Lessons from Kenya.' *African Affairs,* 108 (430) pp. 1–26.

Branch, Daniel, Nic Cheeseman and Leigh Gardner (eds) (2010) *Our Turn to Eat: Politics in Kenya since 1950.* Münster: LIT Verlag.

Bremner, Lindsay (2004) 'Bounded spaces: Demographic anxieties in post-apartheid Johannesburg.' *Social Identities,* 10(4) pp. 455–68.

—— (2012) 'Geological London lab.' *Geoarchitecture.* 26th October. [Accessed on 25th November 2015] https://geoarchitecture.wordpress.com.

—— (2013) 'Towards a minor global architecture at Lamu, Kenya.' *Social Dynamics,* 39(3) pp. 397–413.

Brenner, Neil and Christian Schmid (2017) 'Elements for a new epistemology of the urban.' In S. Hall and R. Burdett (eds) *The SAGE Handbook of the 21st Century City.* London: SAGE, pp. 47–67.

Brosius, Christiane (2010) *India's Middle Class: New Forms of Urban Leisure, Consumption and Prosperity.* Delhi, India and Abingdon, UK: Routledge.

Buchli, Victor (2013) *An Anthropology of Architecture.* London: Bloomsbury Academic.

Bunn, Stephanie (2011) 'Materials in the making.' In T. Ingold (ed.) *Redrawing Anthropology: Materials, Movements, Lines.* Farnham, Surrey: Ashgate Publishing, Ltd, pp. 21–32.

Bunnell, Tim and Diganta Das (2010) 'Urban pulse – a geography of serial seduction: Urban policy transfer from Kuala Lumpur to Hyderabad.' *Urban Geography,* 31(3) pp. 277–84.

Burrell, Jennifer (2010) 'In and out of rights: Security, migration, and human rights talk in postwar Guatemala.' *The Journal of Latin American and Caribbean Anthropology,* 15(1) pp. 90–115.

Burton, Andrew (2001) 'Urbanisation in Eastern Africa: An historical overview, c.1750–2000.' *Azania: Archaeological Research in Africa,* 36–37(1) pp. 1–28.

Butler, Judith (1988) 'Performative acts and gender constitution: An essay in phenomenology and feminist theory.' *Theatre Journal,* 40(4) pp. 519–31.

Capital News (2014) 'Politicians behind the massive Lamu land grab.' *Capital News.* [Accessed on 7th April 2016] www.capitalfm.co.ke/news/2014/08/politicians-behind-the-massive-lamu-land-grab.

Carotenuto, Matthew and Katherine Luongo (2009) '*Dala* or diaspora? Obama and the Luo community of Kenya.' *African Affairs,* 108(431) pp. 197–219.

de Certeau, Michel (1984) *The Practice of Everyday Life.* Berkeley, CA: University of California Press.

Chakrabarty, Dipesh (1998) 'Minority histories, subaltern pasts.' *Postcolonial Studies*, 1(1) pp. 15–29.

Charton-Bigot, Helene and Deyssi Rodriguez-Torres (2010) *Nairobi Today: The Paradox of a Fragmented City*. African Books Collective.

Clark, Gracia (2005) 'The permanent transition in Africa.' *Voices*, 7(1) pp. 6–9.

CNN (2015) 'Obama's trip raises security concerns.' *CNN Politics*. [Accessed on 8th June 2016] www.cnn.com/2015/07/22/politics/obama-kenya-visit-al-shabaab-threat/index.html.

Cohen, Anthony P. and John L. Comaroff (1976) 'The management of meaning: on the phenomenology of political transactions.' In B. Kapferer (ed.) *Transaction and Meaning: Directions in the Anthropology of Exchange and Symbolic Behavior*. Philadelphia: Institute for the Study of Human Issues, pp. 87–107.

Cohen, David William (1994) *The Combing of History*. Chicago, IL: University of Chicago Press.

—— (2009) 'Remembering Atieno Odhiambo.' *Daily Nation*. Opinion. 4th March.

Cohen, David William and E. S. Atieno Odhiambo (1989) *Siaya: The Historical Anthropology of an African Landscape*. London: James Currey; Nairobi: East African Publishers.

—— (1992) *Burying S.M.: The Politics of Knowledge & the Sociology of Power in Africa*. Nairobi: East African Educational Publishers.

Collier, Paul and Deepak Lal (1986) *Labour and Poverty in Kenya, 1900-1980*. Oxford: Clarendon Press.

Comaroff, Jean and John L. Comaroff (1991) *Of Revelation and Revolution*, Volume 1: *Christianity, Colonialism, and Consciousness in South Africa*. Chicago, IL: University of Chicago Press.

Cooper, Frederick (1983) *Struggle for the City: Migrant Labor, Capital, and the State in Urban Africa*. Beverly Hills and London: SAGE.

Cooper, Frederick and Ann Laura Stoler (1997) *Tensions of Empire: Colonial Cultures in a Bourgeois World*. Los Angeles, CA: University of California Press.

Cormack, Zoe (2016) 'Borders are galaxies: Interpreting contestations over local administrative boundaries in South Sudan.' *Africa*, 86(3) pp. 504–27.

Cross, Jamie (2014) *Dream Zones: Anticipating Capitalism and Development in India*. London: Pluto Press.

Das, Veena (2011) 'State, citizenship, and the urban poor.' *Citizenship Studies*, 15(3–4) pp. 319–333.

Davis, Mike (1990) *City of Quartz: Excavating the Future in Los Angeles*. London: Verso.

—— (2006) *Planet of Slums*. London: Verso.

Dawdy, Shannon Lee (2010) 'Clockpunk anthropology and the ruins of modernity.' *Current Anthropology*, 51(6) pp. 761–93.

De Boeck, Filip (2008) '"Dead society" in a "cemetery city": The trans-formation of burial rites in Kinshasa.' In M. Dehaene and L. de Cauter (eds) *Heterotopia and the City: Public Space in a Postcivil Society.* London: Routledge, pp. 297–308.

—— (2012) 'Spectral Kinshasa: Building the city through an architec-ture of words.' In T. Edensor and M. Jayne (eds) *Urban Theory Beyond the West.* London: Routledge, pp. 311–28.

De Boeck, Filip and Marie-Francoise Plissart (2004) *Kinshasa: Tales of the Invisible City.* Ghent: Ludion.

De Cauter, Lieven (2004) *The Capsular Civilization: On the City in the Age of Fear.* Rotterdam: NAI Publishers.

Dearden, Lizzie (2015) 'Kenyans ridicule US network CNN on Twitter for "hotbed of terror" report.' *Independent,* 23rd July.

Deleuze, Gilles and Félix Guattari (1986) *Kafka: Toward a Minor Litera-ture.* Minneapolis, MN: University of Minnesota Press.

—— (1988) *A Thousand Plateaus: Capitalism and Schizophrenia.* London: Bloomsbury.

DeSilvey, Caitlin (2006) 'Observed decay: Telling stories with mutable things.' *Journal of Material Culture,* 11(3) pp. 318–38.

Dillon, Brian (ed.) (2011) *Ruins.* London: Whitechapel Art Gallery; Cambridge, MA: MIT Press.

Dillon, Brian (2014) *Ruin Lust.* London: Tate Gallery Publishing.

Dirks, Nicholas B. (2002) 'Annals of the archive: Ethnographic notes on the sources of history.' In B. K. Axel (ed.) *From the Margins: Historical Anthropology and Its Futures.* Durham, NC: Duke University Press, pp. 47–65.

Dornan, SS (1927) 'Rainmaking in South Africa.' *Bantu Studies,* 3(1) pp. 185–95.

Douglas, Mary (2003 [1966]) *Purity and Danger: An Analysis of Concepts of Pollution and Taboo.* Abingdon, UK: Routledge.

Durie, Edward Taihakurei (2011) 'Cultural appropriation.' In V. Strang and M. Busse (eds) *Ownership and Appropriation.* London: Berg, pp. 131–48.

Edensor, Tim (2005) 'The ghosts of industrial ruins: Ordering and disordering memory in excessive space.' *Environment and Planning D: Society and Space,* 23(6) pp. 829–49.

Elliott, Hannah (2015) '"Knowing the value of land": Speculative futures at the gateway to Kenya's "new frontier".' University of Copenhagen, Denmark: Unpublished paper.

—— (2016) 'Planning, property and plots at the gateway to Kenya's "new frontier".' *Journal of Eastern African Studies,* 10(3) pp. 511–29.

—— (2017) *Anticipating Plots: (Re)Making Property, Futures and Town at the Gateway to Kenya's 'New Frontier'.* PhD thesis. University of Copenhagen.

Elliott, Hannah and Constance Smith (2015) 'Towards an anthropology of the "not-yet": Development planning, temporality and the future.' University of Exeter: Association of Social Anthropology 2015 Conference panel.

Evans-Pritchard, E. E. (1950) 'Marriage customs of the Luo of Kenya.' *Africa*, 20(02) pp. 132–42.

—— (1965) 'Luo tribes and clans.' In *The Position of Women in Primitive Societies and Other Essays in Social Anthropology*. London: Faber & Faber.

Fabian, Johannes (1996) *Remembering the Present: Painting and Popular History in Zaire*. Berkeley, CA: University of California Press.

—— (2000) *Out of Our Minds: Reason and Madness in the Exploration of Central Africa*. Berkeley CA: University of California Press.

Farías, Ignacio and Thomas Bender (2012) *Urban Assemblages: How Actor-Network Theory Changes Urban Studies*. Abingdon, UK: Routledge.

Ferguson, James (1999) *Expectations of Modernity: Myths and Meanings of Urban Life on the Zambian Copperbelt*. Berkeley, CA: University of California Press.

Fontein, Joost (2011) 'Graves, ruins, and belonging: towards an anthropology of proximity.' *Journal of the Royal Anthropological Institute*, 17(4) pp. 706–27.

—— (2015) *Remaking Mutirikwi: Landscape, Water and Belonging in Southern Zimbabwe*. Woodbridge: James Currey.

Frederiksen, Bodil Folke (1992) 'Making popular culture from above: Leisure in Nairobi, 1940-60.' In L. Gunner (ed.) *Collected Seminar Papers*. London: Institute of Commonwealth Studies, pp. 68–73.

—— (2001) 'African women and their colonisation of Nairobi: Representations and realities.' *Azania: Archaeological Research in Africa*, 36–37(1) pp. 223–34.

Gates, David (2017) 'From "in our houses" to "the tool at hand": Breaching normal procedural conditions in studio furniture making.' In T. H. J. Marchand (ed.) *Craftwork as Problem Solving: Ethnographic Studies of Design and Making*. Abingdon, UK: Routledge, pp. 115–32.

Geissler, Paul Wenzel and Ruth Jane Prince (2010) *The Land Is Dying: Contingency, Creativity and Conflict in Western Kenya*. New York: Berghahn Books.

Gell, Alfred (1998) *Art and Agency: Towards a New Anthropological Theory*. Oxford: Oxford University Press.

Geschiere, Peter (2005) 'Funerals and Belonging: Different Patterns in South Cameroon.' *African Studies Review*, 48(2) pp. 45–64.

Geschiere, Peter and Josef Gugler (1998) 'Introduction – The urban-rural connection: changing issues of belonging and identification.' *Africa: Journal of the International African Institute*, 68(3) pp. 309–19.

Ginzburg, Carlo (1980) 'Morelli, Freud and Sherlock Holmes: Clues and scientific method.' *History Workshop*, 9 pp. 5–36.

Goldstein, Daniel M. (2010) 'Toward a critical anthropology of security.' *Current Anthropology*, 51(4) pp. 487–517.

Goldstone, Brian and Juan Obarrio (eds) (2017) *African Futures: Essays on Crisis, Emergence, and Possibility.* Chicago, IL: University of Chicago Press.

Gordillo, Gastón R. (2014) *Rubble: The Afterlife of Destruction.* Durham, NC: Duke University Press.

Government of Kenya (2007) *Kenya Vision 2030: The Popular Version.* Nairobi: Government of the Republic of Kenya.

—— (2008) *Nairobi Metro 2030: A World Class African Metropolis.* Nairobi: Ministry of Nairobi Metropolitan Development.

——(n.d.) *About Vision2030.* Kenya Vision2030. [Accessed on 21st April 2016] www.vision2030.go.ke/index.php/about-vision-2030.

Grant, Bruce (2014) 'The edifice complex: Architecture and the political life of surplus in the new Baku.' *Public Culture*, 26(3) pp. 501–28.

Guy, Jeff (1994) 'Making words visible: Aspects of orality, literacy, illiteracy and history in Southern Africa.' *South African Historical Journal*, 31(1) pp. 3–27.

Guyer, Jane (2004) *Marginal Gains: Monetary transactions in Atlantic Africa.* Chicago, IL: University of Chicago Press.

Hake, Andrew (1977) *African Metropolis.* Brighton, UK: Sussex University Press.

Hall, Catherine (2002) *Civilising Subjects: Metropole and Colony in the English Imagination 1830–1867.* Chicago, IL: University of Chicago Press.

Hallam, Elizabeth and Tim Ingold (2016) *Making and Growing: Anthropological Studies of Organisms and Artefacts.* New York and Abingdon, UK: Routledge.

Hann, C. M. (1998) *Property Relations: Renewing the Anthropological Tradition.* Cambridge, UK: Cambridge University Press.

Hansen, Thomas Blom (2006) 'Performers of Sovereignty: On the Privatization of Security in Urban South Africa.' *Critique of Anthropology*, 26(3) pp. 279–95.

Harley, J. Brian (1988) 'Maps, knowledge and power.' In D. Cosgrove and S. Daniels (eds) *The Iconography of Landscape.* Cambridge, UK: Cambridge University Press, pp. 277–312.

Harms, Erik (2011) *Saigon's Edge: On the Margins of Ho Chi Minh City.* Minneapolis, MN: University of Minnesota Press.

Harris, Richard (2008) 'From trusteeship to development: How class and gender complicated Kenya's housing policy, 1939–1963.' *Journal of Historical Geography*, 34(2) 311–37.

Harris, Richard and Alison Hay (2007) 'New plans for housing in urban Kenya, 1939–63.' *Planning Perspectives*, 22(2) pp. 195–223.

Hart, Keith (1973) 'Informal income opportunities and urban employment in Ghana.' *The Journal of Modern African Studies*, 11(1) pp. 61–89.

——(2010) 'Informal economy.' In J.-L. Laville, A. D. Cattani and K. Hart (eds) *The Human Economy: A Citizen's Guide*. Cambridge: Polity Press, pp. 142–53.

Harvey, Penny and Hannah Knox (2012) 'The enchantments of infrastructure.' *Mobilities*, 7(4) pp. 521–36.

—— (2015) *Roads: An Anthropology of Infrastructure and Expertise*. Ithaca, NY: Cornell University Press.

Hecht, David and AbdouMaliq Simone (1994) *Invisible Governance: The Art of African Micro-politics*. New York: Autonomedia.

Heisler, Helmuth and Maxwell Gay Marwick (1974) *Urbanisation and the Government of Migration: The Inter-Relation of Urban and Rural Life in Zambia*. London: Hurst.

Hirsch, Eric and Daniele Moretti (2010) 'One past and many pasts: Varieties of historical holism in Melanesia and the West.' In T. Otto and N. Bubandt (eds) *Experiments in Holism: Theory and Practice in Contemporary Anthropology*. Chichester, UK: Wiley-Blackwell, pp. 279–98.

Hirsch, Eric and Charles Stewart (2005) 'Introduction: Ethnographies of Historicity.' *History and Anthropology*, 16(3) pp. 261–74.

Hofmeyr, Isabel (1994) *'We Spend Our Years as a Tale that is Told': Oral Historical Narrative in a South African Chiefdom*. Johannesburg: Witwatersrand University Press.

—— (2004) *The Portable Bunyan: A Transnational History of 'The Pilgrim's Progress.'* Princeton, NJ: Princeton University Press.

Holbraad, Martin and Morten Axel Pedersen (2013) *Times of Security: Ethnographies of Fear, Protest and the Future*. New York and Abingdon, UK: Routledge.

Hoskins, Janet (1998) *Biographical Objects: How Things Tell the Stories of People's Lives*. Abingdon, UK: Routledge.

Howard, Ebenezer (1902) *Garden Cities of Tomorrow*. London: Swan Sonnenschein & Co.

Howden, Daniel (2013) 'Terror in Westgate mall: The full story of the attacks that devastated Kenya.' *The Guardian*. World news, 4th October.

Huchzermeyer, Marie (2008) 'Slum upgrading in Nairobi within the housing and basic services market a housing rights concern.' *Journal of Asian and African Studies*, 43(1) pp. 19–39.

Hughes, Lotte (2005) 'Malice in Maasailand: The historical roots of current political struggles.' *African Affairs*, 104(415) pp. 207–24.

Hunt, Nancy Rose (1990) 'Domesticity and colonialism in Belgian Africa: Usumbura's *Foyer Social*, 1946–1960.' *Signs: Journal of Women in Culture and Society*, 15(3) pp. 447–74.

Hutchinson, Sharon (1996) *Nuer Dilemmas: Coping with War, Money and the State*. Berkeley, CA: University of California Press.

Huyssen, Andreas (2003) *Present Pasts: Urban Palimpsests and the Politics of Memory*. Stanford, CA: Stanford University Press.

IFRA (2012) *Slum Upgrading Programmes in Nairobi: Challenges in Implementation. Contributions from the Conference.* Nairobi: Institut Français de Recherche en Afrique.

ILO (1972) *Employment, Incomes and Equality: A Strategy for Increasing Productive Employment in Kenya.* Geneva: International Labour Office.

Ingold, Tim (2013) *Making: Anthropology, Archaeology, Art and Architecture.* New York and Abingdon, UK: Routledge.

—— (2016) *Lines: A Brief History.* New York and Abingdon, UK: Routledge.

Jambonewspot (2013) 'How the Kibera and Kaloleni areas will look like after ambitious project.' 8th December. [Accessed on 14th May 2018] www.jambonewspot.com/new/photos-how-the-kibera-and-kaloleni-areas-will-look-like-after-ambitious-project.

James, Deborah (2007) *Gaining Ground? Rights and Property in South African Land Reform.* Abingdon, UK: Routledge

—— (2014) *Money from Nothing: Indebtedness and Aspiration in South Africa.* Stanford, CA: Stanford University Press.

Jansen, Stef (2015) *Yearnings in the Meantime: 'Normal Lives' and the State in a Sarajevo Apartment Complex.* New York: Berghahn Books.

Jansson, André and Amanda Lagerkvist (2009) 'The future gaze: City panoramas as politico-emotive geographies.' *Journal of Visual Culture*, 8(1) pp. 25–53.

Jindra, Michael and Joël Noret (2011) *Funerals in Africa: Explorations of a Social Phenomenon.* New York: Berghahn Books.

Joyce, Patrick (2003) *The Rule of Freedom: Liberalism and the Modern City.* London: Verso.

Jua, Nantang (2005) 'The mortuary sphere, privilege and the politics of belonging in contemporary Cameroon.' *Africa*, 75(3) pp. 325–55.

Kalusa, Walima T. (2013) 'Corpses, funerals, imageries of modernity and the making of an African elite on the Zambian Copperbelt 1935–64.' In Walima T. Kalusa and Megan Vaughan, *Death, Belief and Politics in Central African History.* Lusaka, Zambia: The Lembani Trust.

Kalusa, Walima T. and Megan Vaughan (2013) *Death, Belief and Politics in Central African History.* Lusaka, Zambia: The Lembani Trust.

Kamau, John (2016) 'Greed, deceit and a web of underhand deals: The sad story of Tatu City.' *Daily Nation.* 13th March.

Kanini, Margaret (2014) 'Tourism numbers plummet on back of insecurity, VAT Act.' *Standard Digital News.* Business. 26th April.

Kanyinga, Karuti (2009) 'The legacy of the white highlands: Land rights, ethnicity and the post-2007 election violence in Kenya.' *Journal of Contemporary African Studies*, 27(3) pp. 325–44.

Kaviraj, Sudipta (1997) 'Filth and the public sphere: Concepts and practices about space in Calcutta.' *Public Culture*, 10(1) pp. 83–113.

King, Kenneth (1996) *Jua Kali Kenya: Change and Development in an*

Informal Economy, 1970-1995. London: James Currey; Athens, OH: Ohio State University Press.

Klopp, Jacqueline M. (2011) 'Towards a political economy of transportation policy and practice in Nairobi.' *Urban Forum*, 23(1) pp. 1–21.

Knappett, Carl and Lambros Malafouris (2008) *Material Agency: Towards a Non-Anthropocentric Approach*. New York: Springer Science & Business Media.

Koch, Insa (2014) 'Everyday experiences of state betrayal on an English council estate.' *Anthropology of this Century*, 9.

—— (2015) '"The state has replaced the man": Women, family homes, and the benefit system on a council estate in England.' *Focaal*, 2015(73) pp. 84–96.

Kochore, Hassan H. (2016) 'The road to Kenya? Visions, expectations and anxieties around new infrastructure development in Northern Kenya.' *Journal of Eastern African Studies*, 10(3) pp. 494–510.

Konza Techno City (n.d.) 'Konza: The vision.' [Accessed on 3rd January 2017] www.konzacity.go.ke/the-vision.

Kracauer, Siegfried (1995) *History: The Last Things Before the Last*. Princeton, NJ: Markus Wiener Publishing.

Kublitz, Anja (2013) 'Seizing catastrophes: The Temporality of Nakba among Palestinians in Denmark.' In M. Holbraad and M. A. Pedersen *Times of Security: Ethnographies of Fear, Protest and the Future*. Abingdon, UK: Routledge.

Küchler, Susanne (1993) 'Landscape as memory: The mapping of process and its representation in a Melanesian society.' In B. Bender (ed.) *Landscape: Politics and Perspectives*. Oxford: Berg, pp. 85–107.

—— (2002) *Malanggan: Art, Memory and Sacrifice*. Oxford: Berg.

Lagerkvist, Amanda (2007) 'Gazing at Pudong – "with a drink in your hand": Time travel, mediation, and multisensuous immersion in the future city of Shanghai.' *The Senses and Society*, 2(2) pp. 155–72.

Lambek, Michael (2002) *The Weight of the Past: Living with History in Mahajanga, Madagascar*. Basingstoke, UK: Palgrave Macmillan.

Lamont, Mark (2011) 'Decomposing Pollution? Corpses, Burials And Affliction among the Meru of Kenya.' In M. Jindra and J. Noret (eds) *Funerals in Africa: Explorations of a Social Phenomenon*. New York: Berghahn Books, pp. 88–108.

—— (2012) 'Accidents have no cure! Road death as industrial catastrophe in Eastern Africa.' *African Studies*, 71(2) pp. 174–94.

Landau, Paul Stuart (1995) *The Realm of the Word: Language, Gender, and Christianity in a Southern African Kingdom*. Portsmouth, NH: Heinemann.

Larkin, Brian (2008) *Signal and Noise: Media, Infrastructure, and Urban Culture in Nigeria*. Durham, NC: Duke University Press.

Laszczkowski, Mateusz (2011) 'Building the future: Construction, temporality, and politics in Astana.' *Focaal*, 2011(60) pp. 77–92.

Latour, Bruno (1993) *We Have Never Been Modern*. Cambridge, MA: Harvard University Press.

——— (2007) *Reassembling the Social: An Introduction to Actor-Network-Theory*, New Edition. Oxford: Oxford University Press.

Lee, Rebekah (2011) 'Death "on the move": Funerals, entrepreneurs and the rural-urban nexus in South Africa.' *Africa: The Journal of the International African Institute*, 81(2) pp. 226–47.

——— (2012) 'Death in slow motion: Funerals, ritual practice and road danger in South Africa.' *African Studies*, 71(2) pp. 195–211.

Lee, Rebekah and Megan Vaughan (2008) 'Death and dying in the history of Africa since 1800.' *Journal of African History*, 49(3) pp. 341–59.

——— (2012) 'Introduction: Themes in the study of death and loss in Africa.' *African Studies*, 71(2) pp. 163–73.

Lefebvre, Henri (2004) *Rhythmanalysis*. London: Consortium.

Lesorogol, Carolyn K. (2008) *Contesting the Commons: Privatizing Pastoral Lands in Kenya*. Ann Arbor, MI: University of Michigan Press.

Lewis, Joanna (2000) *Empire State-building: War & Welfare in Kenya, 1925–52*. Oxford: James Currey.

Lindsay, Lisa A. (1999) 'Domesticity and difference: Male bread-winners, working women, and colonial citizenship in the 1945 Nigerian general strike.' *The American Historical Review*, 104(3) pp. 783–812.

Linehan, Denis (2007) 'Re-ordering the urban archipelago: Kenya Vision 2030, street trade and the battle for Nairobi city centre.' *Aurora Geography Journal*, 1 pp. 21–37.

Livingstone, I. (1991) 'A reassessment of Kenya's rural and urban informal sector.' *World Development*, 19(6) pp. 651–70.

Locke, John (1980 [1690]) *Second Treatise of Government*. C. Macpherson (ed.). Indianapolis, IN: Hackett.

Lonsdale, John (2001) 'Town life in colonial Kenya.' *Azania: Archaeological Research in Africa*, 36–37(1) pp. 206–22.

Low, Setha M. (1997) 'Urban fear: Building the fortress city.' *City & Society*, 9(1) pp. 53–71.

——— (2001) 'The edge and the center: Gated communities and the discourse of urban fear.' *American Anthropologist*, 103(1) pp. 45–58.

Lund, Christian (2008) *Local Politics and the Dynamics of Property in Africa*. Cambridge, UK: Cambridge University Press.

——— (2013) 'The past and space: On arguments in African land control.' *Africa*, 83(1) pp. 14–35.

Lund, Christian and Catherine Boone (2013) 'Introduction: Land politics in Africa – constituting authority over property and persons.' *Africa*, 83(1) pp. 1–13.

Lynch, Gabrielle (2011) *I Say to You: Ethnic Politics and the Kalenjin in Kenya*. Chicago, IL: University of Chicago Press.

Macaulay, Rose (1953) *Pleasure of Ruins*. London: Walker and Company.

Makachia, Peter A. (2013) 'Design strategy and informal transformations in urban housing.' *Journal of Housing and the Built Environment*, 28(1) pp. 167–86.

Makris, G. P. (1996) 'Slavery, possession and history: The construction of the self among slave descendants in the Sudan.' *Africa*, 66(02) pp. 159–82.

Manji, Ambreena (2013) *The Politics of Land Reform in Africa: From Communal Tenure to Free Markets*. London: Zed Books.

—— (2015a) 'Bulldozers, homes and highways: Nairobi and the right to the city.' *Review of African Political Economy*, 42(1) pp. 1–19.

—— (2015b) *Whose Land Is It Anyway? The Failure of Land Law Reform in Kenya*. London: Africa Research Institute (Counterpoints). [Accessed on 20th March 2019] www.africaresearchinstitute.org/newsite/publications/whose-land-is-it-anyway

Marchand, Trevor H. J. (2001) *Minaret Building and Apprenticeship in Yemen*. Abingdon, UK: Routledge.

—— (2009) *The Masons of Djenné*. Bloomington, IN: Indiana University Press.

—— (2011) *Making Knowledge: Explorations of the Indissoluble Relation between Mind, Body and Environment*. Chichester, UK: Wiley-Blackwell.

Masquelier, Adeline (2002) 'Road mythographies: Space, mobility, and the historical imagination in postcolonial Niger.' *American Ethnologist*, 29(4) pp. 829–56.

Massumi, B. (2009) '"Technical mentality" revisited: Brian Massumi on Gilbert Simondon (with A. de Boever, A. Murray, J. Roffe).' *Parrhesia*, 7 pp. 36–45.

Mbembe, Achille and Sarah Nuttall (2004) 'Writing the world from an African metropolis.' *Public Culture*, 16(3) pp. 347–72.

McKinsey (2003) *Vision Mumbai: Transforming Mumbai into a World-Class City*. Mumbai, India: Bombay First.

Melly, Caroline (2017) *Bottleneck: Moving, Building, and Belonging in an African City*. Chicago, IL: University of Chicago Press.

Merab, Elizabeth (2014) 'Seeking sanity at Ardhi House.' *Daily Nation*. Life and Style. 22nd May.

Miller, Daniel (ed.) (2001) *Home Possessions: Material Culture Behind Closed Doors*. London: Berg.

Miller, Daniel (ed.) (2005) *Materiality*. Durham, NC: Duke University Press.

Miller, Daniel (2010) *Stuff*. Cambridge, UK: Polity Press.

Mitchell, J. Clyde (1987) *Cities, Society and Social Perception: A Central African Perspective*. Oxford: Oxford University Press.

Mitchell, Timothy (1988) *Colonising Egypt*. Cambridge, UK: Cambridge University Press.

Miyazaki, Hirokazu (2004) *The Method of Hope: Anthropology, Philosophy, and Fijian Knowledge.* Stanford, CA: Stanford University Press.

Moore, Henrietta L. (2013) 'Protest politics and the ethical imagination.' *openDemocracy.* 12th August. [Accessed on 27th February 2015] www.opendemocracy.net/transformation/henrietta-l-moore/protest-politics-and-ethical-imagination.

—— (2016) 'Democracy and the ethical imagination.' In J. Cook, N. J. Long and H. L. Moore (eds) *The State We're In: Reflecting on Democracy's Troubles.* New York: Berghahn.

Moore, Henrietta L. and Constance Smith (forthcoming) 'The "dotcom" and the "digital": time and imagination in Kenya.' *Public Culture.*

Morris, Hugh (2015) 'Kenya visitor numbers fall 25 per cent as terrorism hits tourism.' *The Telegraph.* Travel, 12th June.

Morton, Christopher (2007) 'Remembering the house: Memory and materiality in Northern Botswana.' *Journal of Material Culture,* 12(2) pp. 157–79.

Moser, Sarah (2015) 'New cities: Old wine in new bottles?' *Dialogues in Human Geography,* 5(1) pp. 31–5.

Mueller, Susanne D. (2008) 'The political economy of Kenya's crisis.' *Journal of Eastern African Studies,* 2(2) pp. 185–210.

Murray, Martin J. (2015) '"City doubles": Re-urbanism in Africa.' In F. Miraftab, D. Wilson and K. Salo (eds) *Cities and Inequalities in a Global and Neoliberal World.* London and New York: Routledge, pp. 92–109.

Murunga, Godwin R. (2007) 'Governance and the politics of structural adjustment in Kenya.' In G. R. Murunga and S. W. Nasong'o (eds) *Kenya: The Struggle for Democracy.* London: Zed Books.

Mususa, Patience (2012) 'Mining, welfare and urbanisation: The wavering urban character of Zambia's Copperbelt.' *Journal of Contemporary African Studies,* 30(4) pp. 571–87.

Mutiga, Murithi (2015) 'CNN executive flies to Kenya to apologise for "hotbed of terror" claim.' *The Guardian,* 14th August.

Myers, Garth A. (2003) *Verandahs of Power: Colonialism and Space in Urban Africa.* Syracuse, NY: Syracuse University Press.

—— (2014) 'A world-class city-region? Envisioning the Nairobi of 2030.' *American Behavioral Scientist,* September, pp. 1–19.

Nairobi City County (2014) *The Project on Integrated Urban Development Master Plan for the City of Nairobi: Final Report.* Nairobi, Kenya.

NaMSIP (World Bank) (2013) *Terms of Reference: Consulting Services for Development of Eastlands.* World Bank and Nairobi Metropolitan Services Improvement Project, pp. 1–15.

Navaro-Yashin, Yael (2009) 'Affective spaces, melancholic objects: Ruination and the production of anthropological knowledge.' *Journal of the Royal Anthropological Institute,* 15(1) pp. 1–18.

Nielsen, Morten (2014) 'A wedge of time: Futures in the present and presents without futures in Maputo, Mozambique.' *Journal of the*

Royal Anthropological Institute, 20 (April) pp. 166–82.

Nuttall, Sarah and Achille Mbembe (2008) *Johannesburg: The Elusive Metropolis.* Durham, NC: Duke University Press.

Nyamnjoh, Francis B. (2016) *#RhodesMustFall: Nibbling at Resilient Colonialism in South Africa.* Bamenda, Cameroon: Langaa RPCIG.

Nzuma, Victor (2014) 'Ranching society vows to resist bid for Konza City land.' *Standard Digital News,* 7th April.

Ochieng', William R. (2002) 'Thunder from the islands: Mau Mau in western Kenya.' In W. R. Ochieng' (ed.) *Historical Studies and Social Change in Western Kenya: Essays in Memory of Professor Gideon S. Were.* Nairobi: East African Publishers, pp. 181–218.

O'Connor, Erin (2005) 'Embodied knowledge: The experience of meaning and the struggle towards proficiency in glassblowing.' *Ethnography,* 6(2) pp. 183–204.

Odhiambo, E. S. Atieno (1991) 'The production of history in Kenya: The Mau Mau debate.' *Canadian Journal of African Studies,* 25(2) pp. 300–307.

Odhiambo, E. S. Atieno and John Lonsdale (2003) *Mau Mau & Nationhood: Arms, Authority & Narration.* Athens, OH: Ohio State University Press.

Ogilvie, Gordon C. W. (1946) *The Housing of Africans in the Urban Areas of Kenya.* Nairobi: Kenya Information Office.

Ogot, Bethwell A. (1967) *History of the Southern Luo: Migration and Settlement, 1500-1900.* Nairobi, Kenya: East African Publishers.

Ojwang, J. B. and Jesse Ndwiga Kanyua Mugambi (1989) *The S.M. Otieno Case: Death and Burial in Modern Kenya.* Nairobi: Nairobi University Press.

Olima, Washington (2013) 'Residents' participation in neighbourhood management and maintenance: Experiences and lessons from Nairobi, Kenya.' *Housing Symposium,* 3 pp. 293–305.

Olivier, Laurent (2001) 'The archaeology of the contemporary past.' In V. Buchli and G. Lucas (eds) *Archaeologies of the Contemporary Past.* London: Routledge.

——(2002) 'Review feature: A review of *An Archaeology of Socialism,* by Victor Buchli.' *Cambridge Archaeological Journal,* 12(01) pp. 131–50.

Otiso, Kefa M. (2009) 'Colonial urbanization and urban management in Kenya.' *In African Urban Spaces in Historical Perspective.* Rochester, NY: University Rochester Press, pp. 73–97.

Panapress (2004) 'Fire razes down Nairobi City Council hall.' *Panapress.* [Accessed on 4th April 2016] www.panapress.com/Fire-razes-down-Nairobi-City-Council-hall--13-542456-17-lang2-index.html.

Parkin, David J. (1978) *The Cultural Definition of Political Response: Lineal Destiny Among the Luo.* London: Academic Press.

Peel, J. D. Y. (1984) 'Making history: The past in the Ijesho present.' *Man,* 19(1) pp. 111–32.

Pelkmans, Mathijs (2006) *Defending the Border: Identity, Religion, and Modernity in the Republic of Georgia*. Ithaca, NY: Cornell University Press.

Perlman, Janice E. (1979) *The Myth of Marginality: Urban Poverty and Politics in Rio de Janeiro*. Berkeley, CA: University of California Press.

——— (2005) 'The myth of marginality revisited: The case of *favelas* in Rio de Janeiro, 1969–2003.' In L. M. Hanley, B. A. Ruble and J. S. Tulchin (eds) *Becoming Global and the New Poverty of Cities*. Washington, DC: Woodrow Wilson International Center for Scholars, pp. 9–53.

Pinney, Christopher (2005) 'Things happen: Or, from which moment does that object come?' In D. Miller (ed.) *Materiality*. Durham, NC: Duke University Press, pp. 256–72.

——— (2008) 'Colonialism and culture.' In T. Bennett and J. Frow (eds) *The SAGE Handbook of Cultural Analysis*. London: SAGE.

Poulter, Sean (2014) 'Kenya tourist trade wrecked by terror fears: Numbers plummet after extremist groups warn visitors to the country "do so at their own peril".' *Daily Mail*, 18th June.

Rathje, William (1974) 'The Garbage Project: a new way of looking at the problems of archaeology.' *Archaeology*, 27 pp. 236–41.

——— (2002) 'Integrated archaeology: A garbage paradigm.' In V. Buchli and G. Lucas (eds) *Archaeologies of the Contemporary Past*. Abingdon: Routledge, pp. 63–76.

RETORT (2004) 'Afflicted powers: The state, the spectacle and September 11.' *New Left Review*, II(27) June, pp. 5–21.

Rigon, Andrea (2014) 'Building local governance: Participation and elite capture in slum-upgrading in Kenya.' *Development and Change*, 45(2) pp. 257–83.

Robertson, Claire C. (1997) *Trouble Showed the Way: Women, Men, and Trade in the Nairobi Area, 1890–1990*. Bloomington, IN: Indiana University Press.

Robinson, Jennifer (1998) '(Im)mobilizing space – dreaming of change.' In H. Judin and I. Vladislavić (eds) *Blank – Architecture, Apartheid and After*. Rotterdam: NAI Publishers, D7.

——— (2016) 'Comparative urbanism: New geographies and cultures of theorizing the urban.' *International Journal of Urban and Regional Research*, 40(1) pp. 187–99.

Robinson, Jennifer and Ananya Roy (2016) 'Debate on global urbanisms and the nature of urban theory.' *International Journal of Urban and Regional Research*, 40(1) pp. 181–86.

Roitman, Janet (2017) 'Africa otherwise.' In Goldstone and Obarrio *African Futures*.

Rose, Carol M. (1994) *Property and Persuasion: Essays on the History, Theory, and Rhetoric of Ownership*. Westview Press.

Roy, Ananya (2011) 'Urbanisms, worlding practices and the theory of planning.' *Planning Theory*, 10(1) pp. 6–15.

Sambuli, Nanjira (2013) 'How useful is a tweet? A review of the first tweets from the Westgate Mall attack.' *iHub Kenya*. [Accessed on 27th July 2015] www.ihub.co.ke/blogs/16012.

Sanders, Todd (2008) *Beyond Bodies: Rainmaking and Sense Making in Tanzania*. Toronto, Canada: University of Toronto Press.

Sassen, Saskia (1991) *The Global City: New York, London, Tokyo*. Princeton, NJ: Princeton University Press.

Schapera, Isaac (1971) *Rainmaking rites of Tswana tribes*. Cambridge, UK: University of Cambridge African Studies Centre (African Social Research Documents).

Scott, James (1998) *Seeing Like a State: How Certain Schemes to Improve the Human Condition Have Failed*. New Haven, CT: Yale University Press.

Searle, Llerena Guiu (2016) *Landscapes of Accumulation: Real Estate and the Neoliberal Imagination in Contemporary India*. Chicago, IL: University of Chicago Press.

Shipton, Parker (2009) *Mortgaging the Ancestors: Ideologies of Attachment in Africa*. New Haven, CT: Yale University Press.

Shiundu, Alphonce (2014) 'Storm as MPs discuss alleged Lamu land grab.' *Standard Digital News*, 6th August. [Accessed on 7th April 2016] www. standardmedia.co.ke/article/2000130624/storm-as-mps-discuss-alleged-lamu-land-grab.

Simone, AbdouMaliq (2004a) *For the City Yet to Come: Changing African Life in Four Cities*. Durham, NC: Duke University Press.

Simone, AbdouMaliq (2004b) 'People as infrastructure: Intersecting fragments in Johannesburg.' *Public Culture*, 16(3) pp. 407–29.

—— (2016) 'Rough towns: Mobilizing uncertainty in Kinshasa.' In Goldstone and Obarrio *African Futures* pp. 139–50.

Slaughter, Joseph R. (2004) 'Master plans: Designing (national) allegories of urban space and metropolitan subjects for postcolonial Kenya.' *Research in African Literatures*, 35(1) pp. 30–51.

Smedt, Johan de (2009) '"No Raila, no peace!" Big man politics and election violence at the Kibera grassroots.' *African Affairs*, 108(433) pp. 581–98.

Smith, Constance (2015) '"They are just terrorists": Constructing security claims in Nairobi.' *Etnofoor*, 27(2) pp. 133–55.

—— (2017) '"Our changes?" Visions of the future in Nairobi.' *Urban Planning*, 2(1) pp. 31–40.

Smith, David (2015) 'Barack Obama lands in Kenya amid huge security operation.' *The Guardian*, 24th July. [Accessed on 27th July 2015] www.theguardian.com/us-news/2015/jul/24/barack-obama-lands-in-kenya-amid-huge-security-operation.

Smith, James Howard (2008) *Bewitching Development: Witchcraft and the Reinvention of Development in Neoliberal Kenya*. Chicago, IL: University of Chicago Press.

Spivak, Gayatri Chakravorty (1988) 'Can the subaltern speak?' In C. Nelson and L. Grossberg (eds) *Marxism and the Interpretation of Culture*. Basingstoke, UK: Macmillan pp. 271–313.

Spronk, Rachel (2012) *Ambiguous Pleasures: Sexuality and Middle Class Self-definitions in Nairobi*. New York: Berghahn.

Stoler, Ann Laura (2008) 'Imperial debris: Reflections on ruins and ruination.' *Cultural Anthropology*, 23(2) pp. 191–219.

—— (2013) *Imperial Debris: On Ruins and Ruination*. Durham, NC: Duke University Press.

Stoner, Jill (2012) *Toward a Minor Architecture*. Boston, MA: MIT Press.

Strang, Veronica and Mark Busse (eds) (2011) *Ownership and Appropriation*. London: Berg.

Strathern, Marilyn (1988) *The Gender of the Gift: Problems with Women and Problems with Society in Melanesia*. Berkeley CA: University of California Press.

—— (1996) 'Potential property: Intellectual rights and property in persons.' *Social Anthropology*, 4(1) pp. 17–32.

Stren, Richard E. (1978) *Housing the Urban Poor in Africa: Policy, Politics and Bureaucracy in Mombasa*. Berkeley, CA: Institute of International Studies, University of California.

—— (1992) 'African urban research since the late 1980s: Responses to poverty and urban growth.' *Urban Studies*, 29(3–4) pp. 533–55.

Syagga, Paul and J. M. Kiamba (1992) 'Housing the urban poor: A case study of Pumwani, Kibera and Dandora estates in the city of Nairobi, Kenya.' *African Urban Quarterly*, 7(1–2) pp. 79–88.

Tatu City (n.d.) 'Tatu City: Live, work, play.' [Accessed on 3rd January 2017] www.tatucity.com/project-details/plans.

Taussig, Michael (1984) 'History as sorcery.' *Representations*, (7) pp. 87–109.

—— (1993) *Mimesis and Alterity: A Particular History of the Senses*. New York: Routledge.

Thieme, Tatiana Adeline (2017) 'The hustle economy: Informality, uncertainty and the geographies of getting by.' *Progress in Human Geography*, 42(4) pp. 529–48

Thomas, Lynn M. (2003) *Politics of the Womb: Women, Reproduction, and the State in Kenya*. Berkeley, CA: University of California Press.

Thornton White, L. W., Leo Silberman and P. R. Anderson (1948) *Nairobi: Master Plan for a Colonial Capital: A Report Prepared for the Municipal Council of Nairobi*. Nairobi: H.M. Stationery Office.

Tilley, Christopher (1994) *A Phenomenology of Landscape: Places, Paths, and Monuments*. London: Berg.

Tonkin, Elizabeth (1995) *Narrating Our Pasts: The Social Construction of*

Oral History. Cambridge, UK: Cambridge University Press.

Trouillot, Michel-Rolph (1995) *Silencing the Past: Power and the Production of History*. Boston, MA: Beacon Press.

Tsing, Anna Lowenhaupt (2011) *Friction: An Ethnography of Global Connection*. Princeton, NJ: Princeton University Press.

UN (2015) *Economic Report on Africa 2015: Industrializing Through Trade*. Addis Ababa, Ethiopia: United Nations Economic Commission for Africa.

Van Zwanenberg, R. M. A. and Anne King (1975) *An Economic History of Kenya and Uganda 1800-1970*. London and Basingstoke: Macmillan.

Vaughan, Megan (2008) '"Divine kings": Sex, death and anthropology in inter-war East/Central Africa.' *The Journal of African History*, 49(3) pp. 383–401.

Verdery, Katherine and Caroline Humphrey (2004) *Property in Question: Value Transformation in the Global Economy*. London: Bloomsbury Academic.

Wainaina, Eric (2015) 'Here's why you should check your land records often.' *Daily Nation*. Life and Style, 8th October.

Waitatu, Nicholas (2013) 'Nairobi's Eastlands set for facelift with plan to build 80,000 houses.' *Standard Digital News*. Business News, 19th November.

Waithaka, James (2013) 'Nairobi county looks to create new districts.' *The Star*. News, 20th November.

Walubengo, John (2014) 'Why digitising land records is a challenge in Kenya.' *Daily Nation*. Op Ed, 4th November.

Wanambisi, Laban (2013) 'Karangi: My boys were carrying water at Westgate.' *Capital News*, 22nd October. [Accessed on 27th July 2015] www.capitalfm.co.ke/news/2013/10/karangi-my-boys-were-carrying-water-at-westgate.

Ward, Stephen Victor (ed.) (1992) *The Garden City: Past, Present, and Future*. London and New York: Spon Press

Watson, Vanessa (2013) 'African urban fantasies: Dreams or nightmares?' *Environment and Urbanization*, 26(1) pp. 215–31.

Weiss, Brad (2017) 'Getting ahead when we're behind: Time, potential, and value in urban Tanzania.' In Goldstone and Obarrio *African Futures* pp. 199–210.

Were, Graeme (2010) *Lines that Connect: Rethinking Pattern and Mind in the Pacific*. Honolulu, HI: University of Hawai'i Press.

Werlin, Herbert H. (1974) *Governing an African City: A Study of Nairobi*. New York: Africana Publishing Co.

White, Luise (1990) *The Comforts of Home: Prostitution in Colonial Nairobi*. Chicago, IL: University of Chicago Press.

Whyte, Susan Reynolds (2005) 'Going home? Belonging and burial in the era of AIDS.' *Africa*, 75(2) p. 154.

Willis, Justin and George Gona (2013) 'Pwani C Kenya? Memory, documents and secessionist politics in coastal Kenya.' *African Affairs*, 112(446) pp. 48–71.

Wilmore, Michael and Pawan Prakash Upreti (2011) 'Can't find nothing on the radio: Access to the radio frequency spectrum in Nepal.' In Strang and Busse (eds) *Ownership and Appropriation* pp. 217–37.

Wood, Denis and John Fels (1992) *The Power of Maps*. New York: Guilford Press.

Yarrow, Thomas (2017) 'Remains of the future: Rethinking the space and time of ruination through the Volta Resettlement Project, Ghana.' *Cultural Anthropology*, 32(4) pp. 566–91.

Index

Eastern Africa Series

EASTERN AFRICAN STUDIES

These titles published in the United States and Canada by Ohio University Press

Revealing Prophets
Edited by DAVID M. ANDERSON &
DOUGLAS H. JOHNSON

*East African Expressions of
Christianity*
Edited by THOMAS SPEAR
& ISARIA N. KIMAMBO

The Poor Are Not Us
Edited by DAVID M. ANDERSON &
VIGDIS BROCH-DUE

Potent Brews
JUSTIN WILLIS

Swahili Origins
JAMES DE VERE ALLEN

Being Maasai
Edited by THOMAS SPEAR
& RICHARD WALLER

Jua Kali Kenya
KENNETH KING

Control & Crisis in Colonial Kenya
BRUCE BERMAN

Unhappy Valley
Book One: State & Class
Book Two: Violence & Ethnicity
BRUCE BERMAN
& JOHN LONSDALE

Mau Mau from Below
GREET KERSHAW

The Mau Mau War in Perspective
FRANK FUREDI

*Squatters & the Roots of Mau Mau
1905-63*
TABITHA KANOGO

*Economic & Social Origins of Mau
Mau 1945-53*
DAVID W. THROUP

Multi-Party Politics in Kenya
DAVID W. THROUP
& CHARLES HORNSBY

Empire State-Building
JOANNA LEWIS

*Decolonization & Independence in
Kenya 1940-93*
Edited by B.A. OGOT
& WILLIAM R. OCHIENG'

Eroding the Commons
DAVID ANDERSON

Penetration & Protest in Tanzania
ISARIA N. KIMAMBO

Custodians of the Land
Edited by GREGORY MADDOX,
JAMES L. GIBLIN & ISARIA N.
KIMAMBO

*Education in the Development of
Tanzania 1919-1990*
LENE BUCHERT

The Second Economy in Tanzania
T.L. MALIYAMKONO
& M.S.D. BAGACHWA

*Ecology Control & Economic
Development in East African History*
HELGE KJEKSHUS

Siaya
DAVID WILLIAM COHEN
& E.S. ATIENO ODHIAMBO

*Uganda Now • Changing Uganda
Developing Uganda • From Chaos
to Order • Religion & Politics in East
Africa*
Edited by HOLGER BERNT
HANSEN & MICHAEL TWADDLE

*Kakungulu & the Creation of Uganda
1868-1928*
MICHAEL TWADDLE

Controlling Anger
SUZETTE HEALD

Kampala Women Getting By
SANDRA WALLMAN

*Political Power in Pre-Colonial
Buganda*
RICHARD J. REID

Alice Lakwena & the Holy Spirits
HEIKE BEHREND

Slaves, Spices & Ivory in Zanzibar
ABDUL SHERIFF

Zanzibar Under Colonial Rule
Edited by ABDUL SHERIFF
& ED FERGUSON

*The History & Conservation of
Zanzibar Stone Town*
Edited by ABDUL SHERIFF

Pastimes & Politics
LAURA FAIR

*Ethnicity & Conflict in the Horn of
Africa*
Edited by KATSUYOSHI FUKUI &
JOHN MARKAKIS

*Conflict, Age & Power in North East
Africa*
Edited by EISEI KURIMOTO
& SIMON SIMONSE

*Property Rights & Political
Development in Ethiopia & Eritrea*
SANDRA FULLERTON JOIREMAN

Revolution & Religion in Ethiopia
ØYVIND M. EIDE

Brothers at War
TEKESTE NEGASH & KJETIL
TRONVOLL

From Guerrillas to Government
DAVID POOL

Mau Mau & Nationhood
Edited by E.S. ATIENO
ODHIAMBO & JOHN LONSDALE

*A History of Modern Ethiopia,
1855-1991(2nd edn)*
BAHRU ZEWDE

Pioneers of Change in Ethiopia
BAHRU ZEWDE

Remapping Ethiopia
Edited by W. JAMES,
D. DONHAM, E. KURIMOTO
& A. TRIULZI

*Southern Marches of Imperial
Ethiopia*
Edited by DONALD L. DONHAM &
WENDY JAMES

*A Modern History of the Somali
(4th edn)*
I.M. LEWIS

*Islands of Intensive Agriculture in
East Africa*
Edited by MATS WIDGREN
& JOHN E.G. SUTTON

Leaf of Allah
EZEKIEL GEBISSA

*Dhows & the Colonial Economy of
Zanzibar 1860-1970*
ERIK GILBERT

*African Womanhood in Colonial
Kenya*
TABITHA KANOGO

African Underclass
ANDREW BURTON

In Search of a Nation
Edited by GREGORY H. MADDOX &
JAMES L. GIBLIN

A History of the Excluded
JAMES L. GIBLIN

Black Poachers, White Hunters
EDWARD I. STEINHART

Ethnic Federalism
DAVID TURTON

Crisis & Decline in Bunyoro
SHANE DOYLE

*Emancipation without Abolition in
German East Africa*
JAN-GEORG DEUTSCH

*Women, Work & Domestic
Virtue in Uganda 1900-2003*
GRACE BANTEBYA KYOMUHENDO
& MARJORIE KENISTON
McINTOSH

Cultivating Success in Uganda
GRACE CARSWELL

*War in Pre-Colonial
Eastern Africa*
RICHARD REID

*Slavery in the Great Lakes Region of
East Africa*
Edited by HENRI MÉDARD
& SHANE DOYLE

The Benefits of Famine
DAVID KEEN